THE STORY OF MEDITATION

...based on the writings written, more than two thousand years ago and research of sage Patanjali in his Yoga Sutras

THE STORY OF MEDITATION

Sneh Chakraburtty

New Age Books

ISBN: 978-81-7822-321-6 (Indian)
ISBN: 0-9730057-3-4 (Canadian)
First Edition: Delhi, 2009

Published by
New Age Books
A-44 Naraina Industrial Area Phase I
New Delhi-110028 (India)
Email: nab@vsnl.in
Website: www.newagebooksindia.com

Printed in India
at Shri Jainendra Press
A-45 Naraina Phase-I, New Delhi-110028

Dedicated to the Master Swami Chinmayanânda

Appreciation is felt for my husband
Joti Chandra Chakraburtty and my friend Carolyn Gray
for suggestions during its writing

Preface

The Story of Meditation is based on the writings and research of Sage Patanjali in his *Yoga Sutras.* Written more than two thousand years ago, the sources of the 196 sentences that make up the *Yoga Sutras* are believed to be the *Mahabharata,* and the *Bhagavad-Gita.* A study of the *Yoga Sutras* compels a study of *Vedic* philosophy and a comprehensive spiritual journey into meditation. Patanjali's seven disciples, as you will discover during the course of this book, are spiritual hopefuls who change their own particular tendencies and traits to reach the Goal in defeating the individualistic self [ego] and discovering the true Self [Soul]. A spiritual journey should enable us, the seekers, to recognise the statements and observations made in the *Yoga Sutras,* to experience them, and reproduce them in meditation. The most essential contribution to a successful spiritual journey is the seeker's inherent self-discipline to fast, to study, to conceptualise.

The paths to spiritual success, of course, vary. Patanjali examined the many paths to reaching the Goal and found that some seekers are naturally inclined to search and arrive at tranquility and contentment. Some find inspiration in reflection, chanting and devotion. Some respond to a form of integral discipline – which can vary from self-deprivation to altruistic acts of devotion. Some can achieve growth through *samadhi.* Though there are many paths, seekers of spirituality find success when all eight elements of *ashtanga yoga* cooperate.

In-built Programming Governs Us...

Thousands of years ago, Indian sages outlined scientific

theories about the body, the mind and the intellect. These men of learning set down the inner sciences in sacred scriptures. They deduced that these truths formed the basis of human health and spirituality, like codes form the base of any software. These 'truths', embedded in *Vedanta,* outline how every human is governed by rules called *samskaras* and how every human behaves only – and exactly – according to this in-built programming. So, unless a seeker learns to decode these messages, he cannot decipher or hope to understand the larger Truth.

Many sages, including *Patanjali, Shankaracharya, Vyasa* and *Chinmayananda,* created scientific 'programming' designed to heighten and hasten the process of spiritual learning. By mapping the paths of inward processing, they learned how to train the inner operations of their bodies and minds. After that, they devised ways to apply these ideas to the traditional scriptures, or the old way of achieving enlightenment. The purpose was to speed up spiritual evolution, stabilize the intellect and achieve an undisturbed enduring state of spiritual awareness. The descriptions they have left behind, of their individual journeys, have survived time and age ... even rapid and consistent change.

These ideas are the steps to a spiritual life. A seeker has to understand, assimilate and practise these concepts. And, if one wants to embark on the path of spiritual awakening, one can. Throughout these pages, essential truths from Sage *Patanjali's* journey have been deciphered, and the Sanskrit terms explained in a glossary at the end of the book [so the flow of reading is uninterrupted]. 'Man', as used in the text, refers to 'humankind', and to no particular sex.

Sneh Chakraburtty

Acknowledgements

Swami Tejomayananda of the Chinmaya Mission Worldwide, for permission to use material written and commented on by Swami Chinmayananda.

B K S Iyengar, who personally wrote to me and was gracious enough to let me use statements from his writings.

Vivek Pareek for his help in editing the book.

Contents

Patanjali: The Master of Ashtanga Yoga

Most of what we know about Patanjali is through mythology, legend and folklore. Even his birth and life dates see variance of centuries. But this could be because sages traditionally assign their wisdom to their Preceptors, who then earn an unquantifiable longevity. Yet, old records and sages say *Patanjali* lived between 500 BC and 200 AD. *Sutras,* or terse aphorisms, were the chosen form of telling around 400 and 200 BC, and *Patanjali's Yoga Sutras* are considered one of the finest examples of this form. Probably, therefore, he lived between these centuries. But there have been references about *Patanjali* meeting the prolific Chinese traveling saint *Huen Tsang,* who lived between 603 and 664 AD.

Patanjali is considered born in *Ilavrita,* an astral angelic place. This is the home of gods and spiritual beings that have achieved supreme *kaivalya* or emancipation. Word-of-mouth has it he is an incarnation of *Shesha,* the Lord of Serpents. He is also said to be a *Svayambhu,* a soul born of his own Will. He is without past *karma,* and took birth to help human culture. He elected to take the mortal form so he would experience impermanent existence with its temporary joys, sorrows and compulsive tendencies. In ancient art and sculpture, *Patanjali* is depicted as half-human and half-serpent. His human torso emerges from the Serpent Lord's coils. He surfaces from the coils in meditation, with his folded hands showing a blessing for humankind. This is directed to those who seek his help at spirituality. It is also an entreaty to his Master to bless those who crave to discover this passage of evolution. Some sculptures of *Patanjali* feature four hands. One hand holds the *shankha* or clarion of conch shell and the other has a *chakra* or flywheel perched on the tip of the index finger. *Patanjali's* preceptor is *Vishnu* whose *astra* or weapon of preference is the Wheel of Time.

He received the gift of communication as soon as he was born. His intellectual wealth was vast, one that is normally amassed after years of study. *Patanjali* is of the lineage of *Hiranyagarbha* and *Kapila,* for he built on their systems of *yoga* of *Sankhya.* He assembled *ashtanga yoga,* the eightfold path to meditation. His learning was a genuine wealth of his own experiences. Added to this is the wisdom of his earthly mother, *Gonika,* and of her ancestors. Some records also show *Patanjali* as a great dancer. *Ashtanga yoga,* with its dependence on dance-like *asana,* is a sign of this. Records state the purpose of *Shesha's* incarnation on Earth was to learn the Dance of Infinity. The journey among mortals was to please his Master, *Vishnu.*

Patanjali was skillful at *Sanskrit.* Even today, the *Mahabhashya* on *Panini's* grammar that he wrote is considered an accomplishment. It redefined the rules of *Sanskrit* grammar, enlarged its phraseology and made it more flexible. In addition, *Patanjali* was a teacher of *Ayurvedic* medicine, which helped him master diagnosis of disease and develop curative techniques to keep the body fit. Through intense study and practice, *Patanjali* described ways to overcome the fickle mind and dissected the body – layer after layer after layer. He reached the core of Man's being. Though already complete in himself, he chose to experience the obstacles of *sadhana* or spiritual practices.

Dissenters and skeptics may think it impossible for one man to have mastered so many aptitudes, but that is a cynical view. For a *Svayambhu, Patanjali* had heavenly powers which allowed him right of entry to information faster than any mortal. Each of the arts *Patanjali* excelled at finds mention in his enterprise. It was following research of medicine, grammar and *Vedic* literature the *Yoga Sutras* were born.

A *sutra* is a thought and an idea tied together, each word of which is logical, precise and direct. The *Yoga Sutras* consist of 196 aphorisms that cover every aspect of life, beginning with the prescribed codes of conduct. They lead the reader through a process of physical, mental, psychological and intellectual integration. *Patanjali's Yoga Sutras* also bring together ideas and research from many sources, some of which would otherwise have been lost. *Patanjali* reinterpreted and simplified topics in the *Vedas* and *Upanishads,* distilling their knowledge into practical and understandable principles. The *Sutras* also contain ideas extracted from the *Mahabharata* and the *Bhagavad Gita.* The *Sutras,* finally compiled by his seven disciples, are considered among the most comprehensive studies of the human body and mind.

The reason for *Sutras'* longevity is that they handled both academic and practical departments of spirituality. Understanding these *sutras* is the first step to Self-Realization. Putting them into routine daily exercises is to transform you. They lead Man to clarified wisdom and take seekers to their true Self. A spiritual journey is a process of physical and thought development. Gain is inner tranquillity. Attainment is spiritual realisation. It is an exciting journey... into YOU!

The Prime Characters

Shesha or Adishesha

Also sometimes called *Ananta* or "the Infinite One", *Shesha* enjoys the honour of being the reposing bed of *Vishnu,* his beloved Master and teacher. He is thousand-headed and floats on the expansive waters of time and space. *Shesha* is the Lord and the noblest of *nagas* or reptiles granted the ability to stand firmly on *dharma* or duty by *Brahma* the Father of Creation. *Shesha* supports and carries the weight of the Earth, and serves as the axle on the Spirit of Creation or *Shiva's* chariot. The epic *Mahabharata* details how *Shesha* dislodged the tortoise-like *Mandara* Mountain of *Puranic* fame while churning the Milky or *Kshirasagara* Ocean for *amrita* or nectar.

Brahma, goes the tale, had to swallow an extraordinary amount of *amrita,* this nectar of immortality, but could not confine it all inside him. From the excess that unloaded out of his mouth, *Surabhi,* the heavenly cow, was born. Quickly, *Surabhi's* milk gathered at the bottom of the ocean, the *Kshirasagara.*

Angels and demons, both were eager to get their hands on this *amrita* – laced milk but were seemingly unable to do so on their own. They made an agreement to haul it out together and divide up the nectar. They decided to use *Shesha's* rope-like span to stir up the sea for the sunken treasure. A difficult task lay ahead before both the angels and the demons. *Shesha's* tail was too slimy to come to grips with and his head breathed an inferno of flames every time he breathed out. So, the angelic and malicious spirits arranged to take turns grasping *Shesha's* tail and head.

The churning began. Before the *amrita* surfaced, wonderful treasures materialized. They are used even to this day, for greater well being and contentment. Priceless potions and medicinal extracts materialized. Other celestial beings ascended, all promising to be of assistance, if called upon. Finally, after immense sweat and exertion, there at last emerged the *amrita*. At this instant, the angelic celestials, who were watching the churning of *Kshirasagara*, became circumspect. What would happen to Creation if demons became undying and established in eternal *amrita?* Surely, their evil mental state would give birth to a new dawn of turmoil, if they became immortal. The noble angels petitioned the Son of the Creator, *Vishnu*, to transform this impending emergency.

Vishnu decided to help. By transforming himself into *Mohini*, the heavenly maiden of extraordinary beauty, 'she' proceeded downward along the stepladder from heaven. She arrived at the spot of churning. Both angels and demons saw *Mohini* come down the heavenly staircase. Only the angels recognised that 'she' was in fact *Vishnu*.

The demons announced her arrival with a gasp. The sight of such astonishing beauty left them speechless. Every mischievous spirit there wanted her for his playmate. *Mohini* contracted to wed the very last person getting the *amrita*. She now asked both angels and demons to put on the shutters of their eyes, while she evenly divided the *amrita* between them.

Gonika

Gonika was *Patanjali's* mother. A daughter of a great sage whose wisdom she inherited, *Gonika* begged the Sun for a son, to whom she would entrust the wisdom of her father. The erudition harvested from her spiritual journey also needed a location for protective custody.

Suddenly a tiny wriggling *Shesha* tumbled and then rested quietly in her cupped palms. Then, right before her eyes, the serpent turned into a newborn. *Gonika* named him *Patanjali* ... '*pat*' for he who 'fell' from heaven and '*anjali*', as an offering while appealing for posterity with "folded hands in prayer".

Over time, *Patanjali* received many years of tutoring structured by his mother. Eventually, he traveled to *Chidambara,* the home of *Shiva.* Here he requested the Lord to sanctify him with the required knowledge to put pen to paper, a commentary on *Katyayana's* informative *Sanskrit* rules, based on writings by the grammarian *Panini. Shiva* blessed *Patanjali.* He then went on to evaluate these older explanations. His erudition became known far and wide.

When seven mountain sages asked *Patanjali,* to choose and tutor one scholarly apprentice from each *ashram,* he expressed hesitation. *Gonika* however advised him to receive the disciples.

Patanjali agreed, promising to coach the students provided they remained faithful to one condition. He would place a screen between him and the scholars. His discussions would always remain hidden from the students by an impermanent barrier. *Gonika* directed *Patanjali* to restore the students to contemplate for self-nurturing. Resolving their uncertainties must be distinctive without any ambiguity. *Gonika,* however, departed before *Patanjali* set into motion, the assembly with the chosen seven.

Pakva

Pakva was the son of a widowed minister in a King's court. The learned minister spent much time teaching *Pakva* personally during his early childhood. At the same time, *Pakva* spent his youth under the guardianship of an eminent sage living in a Himalayan cave. He asked *Patanjali* to accept *Pakva* as a disciple.

Of *Patanjali's* seven disciples, *Pakva* was the wisest and most patient. He had learned the scriptures well under his preceptor and was able to "cross-reference" many of the spiritual discussions.

Pushya

A renunciate King but a learned warrior, *Pushya* left for the Himalayas in his fifties. As a child, *Pushya* had traveled to the forest of *Shatashriga* with his brother. The forest monks who lived in the woods baptized and initiated them into religious studies. They coached them in academics and in artillery. *Pushya* spent his youth, with his younger brother, nurturing the higher values of duty or *dharma.* When their father died prematurely, he was crowned king.

The heir apparent did not start ruling until he had successfully achieved diligence in comprehensive warfare, good conduct, virtue and administrative efficiency. *Pushya* excelled his father and the kingdom thrived and prospered under his reign.

Once, while traveling with his brothers through a forest, they lost their way. They were tired, hungry and thirsty. There was no water to be found anywhere. All of a sudden, they saw a deer running off in a westerly direction.

Pushya directed his brother, *Chandra,* to follow the deer, hoping it would lead them to water. Many exhausting hours later, *Chandra* had still not returned. To look over and explore, *Pushya* climbed a tree to get a sense of where they were.

He noticed a pond not too far from their campsite. He hurried to the pool, only to discover that his brother lay dead on the banks of the small lake. *Pushya* wept bitterly. He entered the lagoon to carry water back to camp. To his astonishment, he heard a voice addressing him, from above: "*Pushya,* I am a waterfowl, a crane and this pond is my hereditary property. It is I who killed your brother, because he refused to obey me. I must ask you the same questions. If you can answer them accurately, you can take some of my water. If not, you will meet the same destruction as *Chandra.*"

"I do not believe you are a mere bird," replied *Pushya*, as he calmed himself. "My brother was brave and seasoned in warfare. He had fought many battles, both physical and moral. He was capable of fortifying himself. Please announce your true self to me."

"I am a *yaksha* from the court of god of wealth and possessions. I am not just a bird," the stork replied. "I forbade your brother to take water from my pond without sanction but he paid no heed."

Saddened but intrigued, *Pushya* agreed to answer the *yaksha's* questions. He was imperative to take water to the thirsty campers.

"Now, these are my questions," said the *yaksha*, "First, who carries the Sun and who are his followers? Who makes the Sun set? On whom does the Sun exist?"

"It is *AUM* who carries the Sun. *Devas* or divine souls are his followers. *Dharma* or his duty makes the Sun set. He exists on Truth or *satya*," answered *Pushya*.

"How does *siddhi* or perfection come to students of scriptures?" asked the *yaksha*.

"It happens by deep penance," replied *Pushya*.

"How can a student of these mighty scriptures achieve divinity? Which deed equals good conduct? What makes Man a mortal, and what makes him evil?"

"A learned student gets divinity by meditation. Austerity is equal to good conduct. Death makes Man a mortal and abusive words make him evil," answered *Pushya*

The *yaksha* persisted. "What is the soul of Man? Who is his companion, given by God? How do you become rich? How do you become happy?"

"The spirit of Man is his son. The companion, given by God, is his wife. If you abandon lust, you will become rich. If you abandon want, you will be happy," replied *Pushya*.

The *yaksha* was pleased. And, to the king's surprise,

the stork revitalized the dead *Chandra.* He confessed it was he who, in the form of a deer, led them to the pond. With that, he blessed the family and disappeared.

Menander

Menander was the foster son of *Vishwakarma,* the medical and engineering scientist who was a renunciant committed to serving and learning. Once, while searching for herbs and roots, *Vishwakarma* became thirsty. He saw a girl coming his way, with a pitcher of water perched precariously on her head. He asked for some water. *Dipti* the forest maiden offered him the drink to quench his thirst."

"May you have a noble son who will one day gain admittance into my medical knowledge. He will support his parents in their old age. Call him *Menander.*"

In time, *Dipti* gave birth to a boy, whom she called *Menander.* She could not afford to feed or educate him. Five years after he was born, she was forced to leave the child at *Vishwakarma's* doorstep,

Vishwakarma adopted *Menander* and gifted him with the medical science of long life or *Ayurveda.* He also taught *Menander* that Fire is a friend. The Moon, he was told, gives plants life-giving nectar, and plants, in turn, allow Man to survive on them. He explained that Air surrounding all Creation is for all. The Sun, he said, circles alone, while the Moon is born again and again. He taught *Menander,* the Earth is usually under a dull camouflage. It allows Man time to bring it to bear fruit when it is ploughed for food. In its never-ending structure, Earth can be challenged by Man's intellect.

As far as relationships go, *Vishwakarma* the renunciant discussed that desire ends friendships. And domestic attachments and possessiveness obstruct the path to heaven. On poverty, *Vishwakarma* was of the opinion that a poor penniless Man is outfitted like a barren woman, just as a mob-ruled country is already dead. Lust is the cause of a worldly life which is steeped in materialism, and jealousy is the cause of unending anxiety.

Straightforward like his teacher, *Menander* became a famous doctor like *Vishwakarma.* He continued recognising his birth parents. On his mother's deathbed, *Menander* made an inquiry about an annoying issue.

"Mother, wealth and lust are incompatible with one another, especially in charity. When do they come together?"

As she breathed her last, *Dipti* answered, "When charity and wife find a middle ground, these three blend, harmoniously."

After his mother's death, *Menander* was alone. With no wish to marry or to earn wealth, he embarked on a search to reach heaven. He reached the Himalayan foothills in the realm of sages. He lingered outside their caves in meditation, until an agreeable sage willing to take a disciple found him.

Chandra

Pushya's younger brother, *Chandra* was killed by a *yaksha.*

Awakened from his deathlike sleep, the *yaksha* asked him a set of questions *Chandra* had paid no heed to before.

"What is the divinity of a warrior? What is equal to good nature? Who is lifeless even though he breathes?" began the *yaksha.*

This time, appreciative of the stork, *Chandra* replied, "His tool of war is a warrior's divinity. Sacrifice is good conduct. He who never offers oblations to celestials, guests or servants is dead even though he breathes."

Continued the *yaksha,* "Who is a friend to one who lives outside his country? Who is a friend to a householder, to a patient and to one who is dead?"

"For one who leaves his country, the person he meets

on his travels is his friend. To a householder, his wife is his companion. To a patient, his doctor is his confidant. And to one who is dead, charity is his well-wisher," answered *Chandra* thoughtfully.

The *yaksha* was pleased, and predicted that *Chandra* would, someday, command watchfulness as a student of divinity.

Bhratahari

A learned student, *Bhratahari* learned *Sanskrit* grammar from *Patanjali.* He had a unique gift, granted by *Shiva.* As *Shiva* was once traveling with his wife, *Parvati,* he said, "This boy, in his previous birth, was poor, but he would beg to feed me and worshipped me with great devotion. He should enjoy wealth in this lifetime."

That night, *Shiva* appeared to *Bhratahari* in a dream and blessed him, "Whenever you rise, may gold coins fall on the ground wherever you stand."

So, every morning, *Bhratahari* collected all the fallen coins and stockpiled them under his bed. Over time he became rich. Generous by nature, he gave away his wealth. The news of his generosity spread far and wide. Many came for financial help. Among the visitors came his father and two brothers. Filled with covetousness, they disapproved of *Bhratahari's* generosity.

One day, they coaxed him to a lonely temple in the heart of the *Vindhya* mountains. They employed assassins to kill *Bhratahari.* The would-be murderers were paid off with *Bhratahari's* expensive clothes and jewelery.

Unknown to the family, *Bhratahari* escaped. He lost his way as he fled the temple. Stranded by a frightful hurricane, he somehow managed to find shelter in a truth-seeker's cave. He took him into his sanctuary and agreed to teach *Bhratahari* the scriptures. Fed up with material wealth, *Bhratahari* discovered he was thirsting for true wealth and knowledge.

Ujjaini

The child of a king and a commoner, *Ujjaini* was a great devotee of *Shiva.* As a child, he could have played and frolicked with many people in the royal household, but had no interest in such childish sport. He preferred to be a loner, staying deep in thought. This attitude pained his mother, who urged him to get married, as he grew older. But *Ujjaini* would have none of it.

The turning point in *Ujjaini's* life was when he narrowly escaped death. While bathing in the river one day, a crocodile seized his leg, but he managed to pull free. It was a custom that one could take up the life of renunciation if one was threatened by the danger of death, or *apatsanyasa. Ujjaini* begged his mother for permission to embrace life of a roving monk in forests and mountains. He wished living off roots and berries and spending time in meditation and prayer. With a heavy heart, his mother agreed.

According to records, *Ujjaini* finally ended up in the holy city of *Kashi,* where the sage *Sanandana* tutored him. *Ujjaini* proved to be an exceptional student of many talents and merits, especially in conserving rare plants and herbs. He is said to have encouraged villagers not to disturb the natural microenvironments of these delicate creations of Nature.

Saleta

A Brahmin boy, *Saleta* was born in *Avanti.* Abandoning his duties as dictated by the scriptures, he sinned and strayed from the fold of Brahmins. As he was once traveling on business, he joined a group of villagers, leaving for the city of *Mahismati* to follow the *Kartika Vrata.* After the fast, he was bitten by a cobra and died instantly.

A *Yamadoot,* the Angel of Death, descended to take away his soul, but saw *Saleta* recovering. *Yamadoot* was perplexed, and asked *Narada,* the visiting celestial teacher, to explain. The ever-smiling *Narada* explained that *Saleta* had his sins washed way, since he had spent time in *Mahismati.* With people following the *Kartika Vrata* on the eve of his death *Saleta* won life. Thus, *Saleta* did not deserve an accidental death.

Malini

Malini, from a tribe of forest dwellers, was married to *Chitrakacha,* a savant immersed in contemplation of AUM. The scholar had no time for his bride. *Malini,* young and lonesome, succumbed to a relationship with a hunter. Her enraged husband cursed her to a life of a hunter-woman, directing her to roam the forests.

Wandering around, she chanced on the *ashram* of the great sage *Matangi.* Seeking to be redeemed from the curse, *Malini* took a special liking to this place, where the flowers had a special fragrance. *Matangi* had blessed the flowers with a power never to fade. Once, the sage overcome with emotion for his labouring and sweating disciples blessed them. He wished the sweat of toil would fall on everlasting fragrant flowers. *Matangi* also blessed the trees and the creepers that sprouted from the ground where their toil dropped beads of moisture. It was an enchanting place.

Malini spent her life serving and cooking for the disciples of the *ashram,* as well as the monks who settled in the caves in the mountains. *Matangi* promised *Malini* that she would some day serve *Shesha.* Redemption from her husband's curse would happen. While at the *ashram, Malini* also befriended *Gonika, Patanjali's* mother. *Malini* nursed *Gonika* when she was failing in health. Following *Gonika's* death, she nurtured *Patanjali.*

Malini was the only person *Patanjali* visited before returning to *Vishnu's* home. *Malini* died a peaceful death. She discovered *Patanjali's* true identity. She'd been freed of her husband's curse.

The Story of Meditation

Vishnu, the Lord of Continued Existence, was within himself, meditating on top of the quiet and motionless Ocean. He remained reclined but afloat on *Shesha,* the Lord of Serpents. The circuitous coils remained balanced on the widespread waters of Origin. Time and Space, the essence of melted Existence remained cloaked as dormant creation.

Suddenly, *Vishnu* heard the haunting echo of AUM within himself. In that instant a pulsation awakened in him recollections of the final vision of Mother Nature, before *pralaya* or cosmic dissolution. It was during the last Epoch of Time or *yuga.* Still in meditation, he heard the summoning voices of souls wanting reawakening. They desired to serve Nature. Asleep in invisible Creation, they articulated collectively, humming and infinitely contained within a symphony of *Om.*

Vishnu opened his beautiful, lotus-shaped eyes and saw *Lakshmi,* the Goddess of True Wealth, at his feet. She spoke gently, with a smile, "Awaken, my Lord."

There was no response from her Lord, but she continued, "No person has ever grasped, by intellectual understanding, the limits of your Cosmic Being. Awaken from your contemplation, for Mother Nature awaits your Will. The first day of Creation has started with the rising Sun. He has already embodied daybreak with Light. The vibrating Energy permeates Infinity with its concerto of Om. The dazzling Light has specified *Prana,* the life force to Space, to enliven Creation. Awaken, O Lord of Sustenance, for Primal Creation waits with the essence of Elements. Formation awaits your pleasure."

He awakened with a smile on his face. *Vishnu* raised his eyes and saw *Brahma,* the Lord of Creation, seated on a large lotus. Levitating in space, beside *Brahma* floated another lotus with *Sarasvati,* the goddess of True Knowledge, who takes Man beyond ignorance and darkness.

Both of them spoke to *Vishnu,* in unison, "Greetings, O resplendent parents of Palpable Creation, *Vishnu* and *Lakshmi.* The Sun shines for the benefit of all gods. Now become the innermost Self of all. Day and Night are your two sides. Grant all the voices of desire whatever they ask. They all ask for true Happiness."

Vishnu and *Lakshmi* replied, "Resplendent Nature is indeed re-born. She begins Creation, and carries with Her the mysterious delusion of *Maya.* In her golden womb, *Hiranyagarbha,* lie seeds deeply embedded. There is in them all the paraphernalia to authenticate heaven and earth. May we therefore pay homage to the inexplicable *Maya.* Her *gunas* or qualities are without doubt, efficient as Laws of Existence. As sovereign of all Creation, both living and existing, She controls all with indwelling Awareness, be they object, plant, creature or human. But we must also awaken *Shiva* and *Parvati.*"

The four set out for the beautiful mountain of *Kailash,* the home of *Shiva's* Light and *Parvati's* Energy. Without the essence of the five elements – space, air, fire, waters, and earth – it would be impossible for Creation to happen. *Shiva* was deep in meditation, absorbed in the vibration less *Brahman. Parvati,* sitting beside *Shiva,* contemplated on her husband.

Urged by the call of their visitors, *Shiva* and *Parvati* awakened to the refrain of the guests, "Stir from your meditation. You alone give strength as nourishment to food. Able to command receptive gods, you always offer them immortality or death. They observe all demands and resemble shadows of constant companions. The Himalayan Mountains declare your glory. The rivers proclaim the greatness of your ocean. Your hands dispense justice in all eight directions."

"Man asks for your protection because you are the dual-deity of Cosmic Intelligence. The sovereign state of the Total Mind is the source of your greatness. Make stronger the sky and the terrestrial region. Saturate the middle region with your *rajasic* creativity. Unleash the powers of the resourceful original waters. Recreate the 'indeterminate' with your fire. With one breath of life force or *prana,* enliven all and will the Cosmos into existence."

"*Hiranyagarbha* is your womb. The entire Universe is embodied in your nest. As one whose face is everywhere, as one who remains as the Self in all creatures, awaken. Take control of the senses, the eyes, hands and feet of every creature in every part of the universe. Authorize and point in the right direction, their merits and demerits as differentiated and dispensed by your two hands. Supply them with the biological causes that create the universe and their tangible essence. You, who exist in all created beings, appoint yourselves as Understanding. Because of powers achieved many have reached immortality. Give each their wish. Let each understand their fitting position, according to *karmic* laws."

To this, *Shiva* and *Parvati* replied, "O deities, watch over us and help the Invisible Universe become the coveted Cosmic Being. We will enliven it as energy infused Matter and Spirit of *prana.* It will be worthy of reverence. We will empower it with mental and intellectual capability. It will gain and recognise enjoyment of all kinds. Nature will provide it nourishment, longevity and a suitable home in all and any direction."

They continued, addressing the Lords and Goddesses, "Let us all unite our gift with True Wealth. May Humankind reach the Knowledge entrenched in the Thousand-eyed One. May you motivate Humanity towards meditation. May you keep under surveillance Man's need for Infinity."

With that, *Shiva* and *Parvati* begin the Dance of Creation. By weaving a tapestry of one Universe after another, each more marvelous than the one before, the audience marveled.

Vishnu watched, enthralled. So absorbed was he in the dance that his body began to vibrate with the lure of the *Shiva's* productive cadence. The more *Vishnu* relished the dance, the heavier he became. Bearing down on *Shesha* became increasingly painful.

Since both were used to floating weightlessly on the expansive waters, *Shesha* was uncomfortable, never having experienced such heaviness before. At that moment, the Dance ended and *Vishnu* returned to his buoyant self.

Creation had come to a satisfactory conclusion. First came the vast ocean, with seas of many waters. The year of existence was created. Next came the sun, moon, sky and earth. Ordained rulers of the sentient and insentient beings controlled day and night. The atmosphere and blissful heaven also came to be – as did the Supreme Light, which projected itself as the Universe. Like in previous *yugas,* each had its distinct duty, its own place and ordinance.

Shesha marveled at what had just happened. He asked *Vishnu,* "O Master, you grew heavier, burgeoning with each beat. Your compactness grew unceasingly. As soon as the Dance ended, you withdrew into your normal self again. What does this extraordinary transformation mean?"

Explained *Vishnu,* with a serene smile, "The beauty, grandeur, grace and majesty of the Dance was firmly set in Nature. Therefore the triple talents or *gunas* of Matter became part of the dance by *Shiva-Parvati.* Each *guna* creates vibrations of contagious sensory happiness. That made my body denser and heavier as I looked outwards at the Dance of Creation."

Drifting into a trance, *Vishnu* marvels, "I take refuge in Nature, who is radiant and fiery in luster. She is the Power that belongs to the One Supreme Light, but is visible as

Many. She is the Talent that lives in all actions. We have to watch ourselves alongside Nature's mystical strength and solve the mystery with Her blessings. Man gains Her guardianship through higher planes of meditation. We must shield ourselves from wrong inclinations and indulgence. May we encourage Man to perform every action as a sacrifice for a Common Good."

Shesha was fascinated. He had never seen or experienced anything in this fashion before. He immediately decided, he too must learn the art of dancing from *Shiva,* so he might please his Master. Humbly, he voiced this request. *Vishnu* listened patiently but became silent. After a few moments, *Vishnu* told *Shesha* that his wish would be granted. He unequivocally stated *Shiva* himself would teach *Shesha* everything about the Natural World, Dance, and *Vedic* Grammar.

Thus blessed, *Shesha* wondered about his future Mother and new Environment. He wanted his wish fulfilled. He began meditating and waited for a special moment of a new beginning.

In the caves of the Himalayas lived a *yogini, Gonika,* who had spent a lifetime in meditation in search of True Knowledge. She had the benefit of receiving the wisdom of her father, a great sage.

But as her earthly life approached its end, she prayed for a son, resembling *Vishnu.* He would have to be worthy of receiving the combined knowledge and wisdom of her father and hers.

She became saddened when her prayers went unanswered. It appeared she would leave her human body without making known the eternal wisdom for humanity's benefit. Finally, *Gonika* called on the Sun, the living witness of God, and asked him to fulfill her desire.

She plunged into the river, picked up water in the cup of her palms, closed her eyes and uttered a prayer, "I make this oblation to Earth, Fire, Atmosphere, Air and

Water. I also make this offering to the Sun and Heaven, and the Moon in all its four quarters. May the deities approve my wish with my declaration of *AUM.*"

Upon opening her eyes to offer water to the Sun, she noticed a tiny snake lying in the palms of her hands. It was *Shesha. Vishnu* sent him for his worldly experience. Then right before *Gonika's* eyes, the snake took on the form of human baby boy.

He begged her to accept him as her son. *Gonika,* overjoyed that her prayers had been answered, called him *Patanjali.* Since her hands had been folded in the *anjali mudra,* the name held significance for the child's future.

In his early life, *Patanjali* was often constrained by a vague memory of his soul. It predisposed his awareness to ascend and descend a spiral stairway of wakefulness. He sought his wise mother's assistance for relief.

She taught him to retreat into an astral passageway connecting the brain and spinal cord. She approved his lingering in the hum of his *pranic* life force. *Patanjali's* ascent to blessedness went through increasing levels of consciousness and intrinsic tranquility. The loftier his self became, the more organized was the efficacy of his life force. And the more centred the energy, the quieter and more persistent was the inner call of his soul.

Unlike reincarnating mortals born with paraphernalia of past births, *Patanjali* did not undergo the flawed human modeling. Erasure of what was previously not understood was not necessary. Present-life experiences were novel happenings. Distortion of experiences never captured the law of *karma.*

His mind and intellect were clear of human frailties. Unknowingly, *Patanjali* used his stopover as a mortal to achieve a human existence. By encouraging his inherent creativity, he improved his desired performance and communication. Not burdened by old habits born of long association with Matter, he instead spent his time learning to be a perfect human being.

Unlike an ordinary Man, he was not mutated to think his body was his true identity. Tutored by his mother, *Patanjali* realised that Man is in eternal conflict. His intimacy with the physical body and an indistinct recollection of his more noble desirability has caused a disconnection between him and God.

In his early teens, *Patanjali* identified the cause of Man's affliction. Hesitations of mind and intellect triggered untamed thinking and an ailing body. He approached his mother, who was by now failing in health, and said in a reverential voice, "O Mother, you taught me to recognise the energy of matter and the *pranava,* which permeates the entire universe. The Universe and *Vedas* also embody Om. You have intellectually taught me to identify the link between Matter and Spirit. I adore you, for teaching me to find this through contemplation. O Mother, you, and you alone, are skillful with teaching this Knowledge. Having removed obstacles from my path, please explain how I can show others to become One with both Energy and Light in meditation."

The enfeebled Gonika responded. She felt inspired to speak, "To undertake unfailing recollection of his divine origin, Man must remove over-enjoyment of the senses. Virtue and Truth is the path to austerity. Let me tell you more about austerity."

"Understanding the scriptures is skillfulness. Subduing one's senses is asceticism. Cultivation of a peaceful disposition is solemnity. Giving without selfishness is sharpness. *Yama* and *niyama,* the moral injunctions on attitude and ethics of spiritual living, represent austerity. *Abhyas* of these injunctions is rigorousness."

Gonika reached for some water, and *Patanjali* helped her take a few sips. She continued, "Man must practice *ashtanga yoga.* All eight parts of *yoga* must be practiced together, for that is the correct way to practice the *yoga* of meditation. It is also the only path to Truth. Many thousands of years ago *Krishna* explained it to *Arjuna,* the *Pandava* prince. Its description exists in the *Bhagavad Gita* and in reality is penned by *Ved Vyasa.* It explains the descent and ascent of Man from Spirit to Matter. You must affirm it to those who wish to become serious practitioners of contemplation and meditation."

By now, the prodigy that was *Patanjali,* had sages and pundits in the surrounding Himalayan caves convinced, that he too would some day become a celebrated sage. He would lead Man all the way through the maze of human existence. Even as they spoke, as days ended into evenings, sages and monks gathered at the *Gonika's* cave to listen to *Patanjali's* commentaries on the sacred scriptures.

He began traveling in his search of education. Much to the joy of *Gonika,* his fame spread as a celebrated commentator in *Sanskrit.* She was pleased, for her son's progress meant her wisdom over Time, will stand up to scrutiny.

One day, *Patanjali* set off to visit *Chidambara,* where, it is said, *Shiva* lives. He returned many months later. Upon meeting her he excitedly said to *Gonika,* "*mma,* I called on the great *Shiva* in the caves of *Chidambara.* There, I asked the Lord to bless me with knowledge or *gyana* as well as wisdom or *vigyana.* After explaining I wished to write a commentary on the grammar rules of *Sanskrit* as illustrated in *Panini's sutras.* The Lord blessed me."

After a brief pause, he continued, "I must tell you about an interesting meeting I had while I was in the caves. As I was leaving the caves, I met a Chinese sage, Huen Tsang, who has traveled far and wide. During our conversation, he told me all languages in this world have their origin in *Paniniya.* How fascinating!"

Gonika smiled knowingly, and despite her ill health, encouraged *Patanjali* to write a commentary on *Sanskrit* grammar over the next few months. *Patanjali* spent hours looking for birch bark to make parchments on which he could write his commentary. He searched for berries from which he could make ink and collected peacock feathers for quills. Having gathered the necessary materials, he seldom rose from the stone slab he used as a desk.

Patanjali showed remarkable grasp of the Laws of *Sanskrit* Grammar, and was swiftly on his way to finishing the commentary on *Paniniya* in the *Mahabhashya. Gonika,* however, became concerned that *Patanjali* was spending less time at meditation. One day, she called him and said, "Son, let me remind you about austerity once more. Hermits must have a lifelong dedication to the practice of *asana, pranayama* and *pratyahara.* These three practices are a must for physical stillness, and *dharana* and *dhyana* are for inner silence. They are the highest austerity."

Pausing for a moment to catch her breath, *Gonika* spoke again, as a gentle smile crossed her lips. "And, finally, there is the eighth ingredient of *ashtanga yoga,* which is *samadhi.* This, my son, is for a subjective journey of the self to become One with the Self. It is what will yield the highest perfection in a pursuit of spirituality."

Patanjali realised his mother was gently reprimanding him. It struck him that he had spent too much time giving in to the demands of his inquisitive intellect. He was immediately submissive, "Mother, I understand you want me to lessen the distance between God and me through the eight units of *ashtanga yoga.* I also wish to enlighten myself with Nature I must learn to accommodate Her Laws of Matter and Energy. You have already taught me the science of religious duty through Laws of Being, found in the *dharma shastras.* I understand Matter has an inherent *dharma* to support the duties of Nature. I also recognise that *yoga* is itself based on this *dharma.*"

Patanjali paused, waiting for a response from *Gonika.* She said nothing. And so he continued, "You have defined the irrevocable laws that have survived ages. You have given me *mantras* that seed and germinate into *yoga* and *mantras* that lead mortals to freedom or *kaivalya.* With you I have seen *yogis* free themselves of motive, desire and worldly ambition. To my amazement these *yogis* are free of the Laws of Matter, Relativity and Karma. Their tendencies do not emerge as *vasanas.* Freed of compulsions, they are not ruled by the Laws of relativity or *raaga-dvesha.* Effects of past births do not burden these mortals; I understand the cause of unhappiness. Although effects of past *karmas* bind them in this life, they know ways to free themselves in future. Some seem to have renounced action and others have relinquished their effects. How then do these *yogis* free themselves from quality compulsions of Nature's *gunas*?"

Gonika nodded patiently. This was not the first time such discussions had taken place. *Patanjali* asked questions but was able to talk into them without her help. Continued *Patanjali,* "Mother, I need to understand how they achieve this without *ashtanga yoga.* How does an upward movement of a progressively changing awareness display in Man with an unenlightened *chitta* personality? There must, surely be disciplines through *sadhana,* which can sedate the various *vrittis* that cause swings in thought. Their consequence is on pure awareness."

Gonika waited to see if *Patanjali* had anything more to say. Then, she responded, "Meditation makes Man aware of his complete *samskaras.* These prenatal tendencies are earned and recorded through his many reincarnations. Meditation through recitation of devotional *mantras* and performance of *karma yoga* are also measures to achieve happiness through contemplation. These practices discipline every day behaviour and thinking. Man will not stand up to feeling incomplete. He embraces every second to ensure he is complete. By every means possible, he searches for a way to reach Wholeness."

Patanjali had never experienced incompleteness. This was his first manifestation as a mortal. He asked, "Why does

Man feel incomplete, Mother?" And *Gonika* replied, "Mistaken application of 'for what reason Man is a mortal' is the cause of incompleteness Therefore it is this ignorance or *avidya* that leads him astray. Man needs persuasion and indoctrination into Truth. This is consummated by understanding the processes he uses to reject genuine knowledge."

"What is the origin of such *avidya* that strays him from his birthright of Completeness?" *interrupted Patanjali*. Smiling his mother replied, "To start with, Man uses his musings to erase what he does not understand or is incapable of an agreeable grasp. He then generalises on imagined theories he knows a little about. Now he begins to give credence to the little he knows. Next, he registers his flawed experiences, which are distortions of genuine Knowledge. And these ideas become embedded in his psyche as ignorance."

Asked *Patanjali,* "What, then, is the cure, Mother?"

Replied *Gonika,* "Superimposition on Truth is erased through the study of sacred Knowledge. That way, Man can distinguish the false from the real and, intuitively, see the One in Many." Continuing, "With consistency and hard work, he learns to intensify important assets by seeing, feeling and thinking. In this way he begins to like himself. The distance between the self and Self gradually narrows into Wholeness."

There was silence between mother and son. The cave glowed with natural light coming from the setting sun. *Gonika,* frail with age, reached for water again, and *Patanjali* helped her lift the cup to her lips. After clearing her throat, she lay back on the pillow. She then continued, as if speaking to heavenly spirits she met in meditation. "*Sadhana* is only possible if the seeker has amassed proper prenatal tendencies or *samskaras*. These are fruits of noble actions from previous incarnations. Just as the wind carries the fragrance of a tree in full blossom even if it is in the distance, the fragrance of meritorious deeds spreads to great distances. This is true even if they must travel as far as heaven."

Asked *Patanjali* eagerly, "Man seems exposed to admissible and unknown sins. How can he guard himself from them? Then, how can he aim for Immortality?"

Gonika answered, "All mortals are subject to the delusory effects of *Maya* inherent in Nature's physical manifestation as *gunas.* As *tamas,* Nature exerts its negative schism on Man's psyche as inertia. As *rajas,* Nature exerts its positive polarity through activity and creativity. As *sattva,* Nature's compulsions on an unenlightened *chitta* are to balance *tamas* and *rajas.* Only through the disciplines of *yoga* can Man go beyond the compulsions of Her *gunas.* On a spiritual journey, *sadhana* takes Man on a pilgrimage towards the harmony of *sattva.* He is taught to linger his attention at the *kutasha* between the eyebrows until he experience untainted Awareness. Freed of ego, his awareness one day becomes unalloyed Consciousness."

"And this is the goal of *yoga.* It promises to consummate the self with the Self until it is One with the Spirit in *samadhi,*" completed *Gonika,* with protected effort.

By now, it was late. The sun had set and a chill rolled into *Gonika's* cave. As *Patanjali* draped more blankets over *Gonika,* he heard someone clear her throat at the cave's entrance. It was *Malini.* She came to visit with *Gonika,* her dear friend of many years. In her hand she held a tumbler of hot milk, enriched with honey and mountain herbs.

Patanjali walked towards the cave entrance to welcome *Malini.* "Come in, *Amma,*" he said, "What brings you here tonight?" He pulled up a *charpai* made of sturdy rope lace tied over a bed frame. He invited *Malini* to sit close to *Gonika.* To protect her from the cold breeze he spread a woollen shawl across her legs.

"This morning, while washing cooking vessels by the River, I heard your mother coughing. I thought to bring her some hot milk before she retired for the night," said *Malini.* Then added sadly, "She is becoming feebler by the day, my dear friend!"

"How considerate and thoughtful of you," said *Gonika,* overwhelmed by emotion, "You have always been good-hearted to me, *Malini,* even when I was younger. Whenever I forgot to eat or drink during my austerity periods in *tapas,* you were there to provide for my body. When I became too old to run after *Patanjali,* you were there too."

Malini looked at them lovingly, "*Patanjali* is as much my son as he is yours, *Gonika Amma,*" said *Malini,* her eyes brimming with tears.

"When I am gone, please continue to care for my son," said *Gonika,* "For he too forgets to eat when he is deep in study or in contemplation."

Malini looked from *Gonika* to *Patanjali,* and then said to *Gonika,* in a mock stern voice, "*Amma,* drink up the milk before it goes cold."

Patanjali and *Malini* helped *Gonika* sit up, and encouraged her to drink every precious drop. After that, they chatted leisurely and laughed a great deal, before realising it was time to sleep. *Malini* took her leave, saying she still had chores to do. Cleaning copper pots for breakfast would be overdue otherwise. Renunciates and spiritual seekers of the *ashram,* for whom she cleaned and cooked, will need an early breakfast.

Patanjali could not fall asleep. He reviewed the remedial discussions with *Gonika.* He recorded them in his daily journal. He used this understanding of *Vedic* knowledge for further clarification while in meditation. He remained in the *kutastha* until he distinguished his individualistic self-reaching out for self-unfoldment. Self-realisation would come. He knew he had the grace of *Gonika.* Unable to find any trace of his past existence as *Shesha,* he wondered why. He had no recollection of his life with *Vishnu* and *Shiva*. *Patanjali* decided to peep into his own past births to understand fully all he had been told, but could not.

As the night wore on, he revisited one experience only. That morning, while deep in meditation, he saw himself displaying a mortal desire to learn the art of dancing. While wanting competence over Nature's qualities his preference for knowledge of the scriptures emerged in him. Now he could guide other men. Before *Patanjali* lived through this experience, it was dawn.

He heard his *Amma* stir from a peaceful night's slumber. He felt happy and greeted her cheerfully. As he helped ready her with morning ablutions, he described his night's experience.

Gonika then told him he had come to her as a tiny snake that transformed into a human boy. As they sat down for breakfast, *Patanjali* asked her sturdily accompany him in meditation. She promised she'd follow him.

With her permission, *Patanjali* retreated into the cave, and *Gonika* followed him several hours later. She had told *Malini* that she and *Patanjali* would be in meditative earnestness and should not be disturbed. They remained in the cave for seventy-two hours. Both became integrated with each other as well as the Universe. The experience left them hushed. She glanced at her son and both felt an unspoken ascertion, "I am THAT which is impossible to define." They then allowed *Malini* to look out for them. She also fasted for three days, but *Malini* nonetheless, attended to their needs with great love.

Patanjali, who had started out as a spiritual novice, now continued to aspire for an exalted existence. He practiced the eightfold yogic discipline his mother had described. He discovered he had an ability to think and act with clarity of feeling and purpose. The more he grew spiritually, the more deeply he mourned for seekers burdened with past births and individuality.

He developed an intuitive aspiration to find the cause of tribulations in the lives of mortals He investigated *yama,* and decided these universal moral commandments can change daily attitudes. He determined that those abiding in *niyama,* had outlined for them, rules of living for self-purification through abstinence from over-indulgence. After many hours in different *yogic* postures, he decided that practice of *asana* purifies the body and mind, through long-drawn-out stillness of body parts.

Patanjali studied the scriptures and exposed that *swasayama* was physical breathing but *pranayama* was controlled *pranic* breathing for experience of "no-breath". His guidance under *Gonika* continued, even though using reduced intensity. "Breath control is self control," *Gonika* would say. She initially taught him to equalize the duration of both inspiration and expiration until his breathing was well regulated. She then asked him to concentrate on the inspiration and expiration and again between expiration and inspiration. She asked him to pause at the silent intervals for as long as it is comfortable while watching the silence within and looking at the *kutastha,* while listening to the vibration of the *pranava.*

Gonika explained that it is the Cosmic Mother who draws in the life force to enliven and energise the body with each breath. *Gonika* found *Patanjali* easy to teach. She was pleased with his progress. When *Patanjali* reached the age of seventeen, his mother taught him healing through energisation of bodily matter through *pranayama.* He understood every atom of every cell in his body is colored with pure *pranic* life force.

He studied, acknowledged and then surrendered to the meaning and function of the seven physiological *pranas.* He then witnessed seven flames stirring inside the physical body like seven tongues touching the seven worlds where life-breath eventually migrated at the end of corporal existence. In the living, these sevenfold flames moved towards the secret place of the heart. Each then deposited themselves in their respective places within the divine astral cave.

In the brain, *Patanjali* saw the soul seated in atoms of the subtle body. Concentrated in between and behind the two eyebrows, in the *kutastha,* he saw the resplendent Cosmic Being. He had withdrawn all his senses into himself like a crouching tortoise. In this state of *pratyahara* he was able to rest in his own centre of Awareness.

As *Patanjali* discussed his progress and his experiences with *Gonika,* she realised it was time to teach him the various stages of meditation. She had taught him concentration in *dharana* by integrative attention in the *kutastha. Patanjali* easily learned the art of contemplation in *dhyana* by continuous concentration on his ideal, *Vishnu.*

It was not long before *Patanjali* experienced complete absorption in *samadhi.* In this preoccupation, *Patanjali* lost all awareness of his body, breath, mind, intelligence and *chitta*-personality. He discovered the essence of the "*ham sa so ham*" *mantra. Gonika* had told *Patanjali rishis* give this to aspiring spiritual candidates, to find out the unity of bodily Energy and the life-force or *prana* of the soul.

Once *pranayama* is understood as a personal experience in meditation, there is dawn of true knowledge or *gyana.* The wisdom about this connection of soul with Cosmic Soul leads one to renunciation [*tyaga*] from earthly dealings. Tranquility and happiness results from steadiness such spiritual practices afterwards.

While still under the tutelage of his mother, *Patanjali* saw his *Amma* suffer the afflictions of an ageing body. He saw the emotional consequences of such changes for him as a son. It pained the young man to see his beloved mother decay with age and over time. The seeker taught himself the art of transcending such pain and pleasure through disciplines of yoga.

As a result, *Patanjali* developed rapidly, discovering the

vagaries of human existence. Breath control taught him thought control.

By now, the sages in the Himalayan caves were convinced that *Patanjali* should start instructing their students, but *Gonika* disagreed. She felt her son must spend more time studying, experiencing and analyzing the duality of likes and dislikes, pain and pleasure, heat and cold, earthly happiness and unhappiness.

One night *Gonika* warned her son and *Malini* that her end was near. She was now acutely aware that *Patanjali* must spread the knowledge she had given him. She commanded him to begin with seven disciples from seven neighbouring ashrams. He was to teach them *ashtanga yoga*. With that final instruction, *Gonika* receded into herself, on the lookout for the crowning *samadhi*.

Gonika died before sunrise. *Patanjali* overcome by the anguish of separation became troubled by the experience. True to her promise, however, *Malini Amma* was there to nurture the young man until he could resume his life as an academic. *Patanjali* remained immersed in study and meditation for many months, perfecting his information.

He had understood the reason for his birth in Gonika's hands, and now knew he was an incarnation of *Shesha*. He felt an intuitive urgency his days among mortals were ending. *Patanjali* had gained all he wanted as a mortal. He was ready to close his journey. He grieved for his lost mother, *Gonika,* and even though she was for eternity there, *Malini* could not pacify him. *Patanjali* would see *Malini* spend her evenings alone. Always in deep thought, he knew she, too, missed *Gonika Amma.* The cheer of the three chatting and laughing was no more. *Patanjali* became more distant also.

Before long, *Malini* persuaded the sages to encourage *Patanjali* to accept seven disciples seeing that *Gonika* had so counseled. *Patanjali* was ready to conform. He had entered the world of seeking-mortals for knowledge of dance, science of meditation, health and *Vedic* grammar. He succeeded in articulating concisely the *Sutras* and described *Raja Yoga.* He focused his dynamism on urging earnestly the importance of life's efforts. Whether living an ordinary life, working or dancing, Man's mental, intellectual and spiritual evolution must be aimed at consummating the search of the Self for true happiness.

The Himalayan caves were filled with seekers in various stages of evolution. They were all beings born of the same Cosmic Spirit and Nature's Matter. *Patanjali* saw them invoke the Creator, who comforts Creation in so many ways, and who is seeing their thoughts and deeds. He observed their offerings to Nature and Spirit. They were aptly granted with plenty. He saw the Supreme fountain creating waves to yield enjoyment for all beings. He secretly thanked symphonic waves humming syllables of AUM.

He decided all his seven disciples be taught contemplation of AUM through *mantric* repetition. Promising himself that some day each seeker would arrive at immortality, he decided they the seekers would learn competence of *ashtanga yoga.*

On an appointed day, *Patanjali* started his classes by saying, "May we always repeat, in our contemplative sacrifices, the name AUM, which has created this Cosmic Reality. May we hold *Vishnu* in our hearts with greetings. With the Creator, *Brahma,* and the Repository of Energy, *Shiva,* may we praise him," *Patanjali* said.

He continued, "I will teach from my cave, separated from you by a hanging drape. My voice will carry the teachings of Masters before me. Make no attempt to watch me in person.

May He, the Lord, join us. Let favorable remembrance with He who reveals the *Vedas* be with us always. May this supreme seer, who is the first among the gods and who is born before the rest allow us to understand his words."

Having said that, *Patanjali* started the instruction about reaching a transcendental state of isolation. This final beatitude would be a gift of liberation earned through knowledge and wisdom. He warned his students that these sessions would go on for many days and nights.

As the sessions ran, he taught them the path, and responded to their reservations. Some disciples found his replies extraordinary and, at times, equivocal. Some were disappointed, but persisted to hear the statements *Patanjali* made. These seven disciples would, eventually, record his statements as the *Yoga Sutras.*

In the millenniums to come, *Patanjali's* endeavours with the seven apostles would blossom. These 196-recorded *sutras* are now researched, studied and discussed for thousands of years. As wished by *Gònika* they would lead mortals, even mortals of today, to cultured thought, speech and action. *Patanjali's* endeavours would become the necessary norm of refined knowledge, in a cultured body and a civilised mind. They are the *musts* for gaining tranquility and reaching self-unfoldment and Self-realisation.

Book One – On Contemplation

Dharana Pada

The natural underground chamber *Patanjali* had shared with his mother ran at least twenty feet deep into the side of a mountain. It had an unexplainable luminous affluence to it, which redeemed it from complete darkness. Even the light of a tiny lamp became augmented many times. A heavy drapery a few feet inside the grotto marked the entrance. It also protected the cave from natural elements. In the centre of the cavern was a natural slab of rock, which *Gonika* and *Patanjali* used as their seat for meditation. It also served as a desk, which *Patanjali* used to write his commentary. An oil lamp on the left of the slab threw softened light across the cave. A woolen shawl lay, neatly folded, on the right. On the far end of the cave were two beds, piled with quilted bedspreads for protection against nightly chills. This was what *Patanjali* called home, where he had lived since he was born.

Once emotionally ready after *Gonika's* death, *Patanjali* accepted seven learned students of *Vedanta.* The disciples were students of seven dissimilar sages from the various caves of Himalayan foothills. *Patanjali* had noticed, watched and surveyed these would-be disciples over the years. Each had a unique strength of character. He was sure there would be some interesting meetings of the wise at his *satsangs.*

For the first session, *Patanjali* drew the curtain and sat on the slab. It was dawn and the occasional chirping of awakening birds broke the silence of the Himalayan valley. The disciples – *Pakva, Ujjaini, Chandra, Pushya, Menander, Bhratahari* and *Saleta* – felt apprehensive because of the curtain that separated them from *Patanjali.* But they realised the tutoring is by one of the best. They accepted *Patanjali's* condition and this arrangement.

The students huddled together. It was a chilly morning. Pulling their shawls tightly around them, they hoped the rising sun would soon warm them. There was also the promise of *Malini Amma's* warm breakfast. Separated from his students, *Patanjali* had drifted into his thoughts, when a faint voice interrupted the silence.

"What is *samadhi yoga*?" asked *Pakva,* a seeker who had gained advanced scholarship under tutelage of several masters. *Pakva's* widowed father, who understood duty, responsibility and relationships of human birth had tutored him until he was seven years old. He repeatedly told *Pakva* attainment of human birth was a privilege. The highest knowledge of Self-realisation, he was told early in his life, is reached through the efforts made by a human body.

Pakva had spent the next twenty years at a *brahmacharya ashram,* where he lived a life of study and celibacy with a learned sage. He taught him methods of arriving at peace in daily living. He prepared him to achieve Man's highest goal.

Unlike the other six disciples, *Pakva* had already come to the realisation that joy gurgled from his inner depths, even if in fleeting moments. He had learned the world of objects, emotions and thoughts had no place in inner growth. He found perfect happiness within. He rejected expectations from others. *Pakva* felt no loneliness and had no longing. He instead felt complete and fulfilled.

With *Pakva's* question, the inner upheaval and transformation of each disciple began. Replied *Patanjali,* "With divine blessing, let us begin." After momentary silence, he continued, "Let us begin by explaining *yoga.* With reference to your present question, *yoga* is cultivating awareness. Its eventual transcendence is towards unalloyed consciousness. It is the path to being one with AUM."

After that, *Patanjali* started his discussion by tracing Man's flawed emergence from physical and mental enslavement. He analysed the ingredients of awareness and its behavioural patterns expressed as thoughts. He explained the need for calming physical agitation and thought swings for purposes of inner integration and silence.

The seven disciples, unfamiliar with *Patanjali's* style of teaching, allowed him to speak while they listened. They worked at coordinating their minds with the young Master. A great sense of anticipation and expectation flooded their hearts. Later, of course, there would be days when they could interact freely with the eloquent sage.

Continuing, Patanjali expounded the discipline of *ashtanga yoga,* drawing from his experiences with his mother. *Patanjali* knew this discussion was beyond the understanding of their senses. Worldly interaction also could not intimate the disciples about this yoga. Nevertheless, he sought to test them, and fathom how serious they were. "*Yoga* is concerned with ending disturbances in awareness," said *Patanjali,* as he mentally sought to define meditation.

Continuing he said, "*Yoga* can also be defined as control of outgoing awareness that sees, wants and gains. It highlights ways in which Man can understand the mind and its roles. It helps Man still the mind's oscillations, and leads to an undisturbed state of silence. Awareness of silence, in turn, sits in the centre of the heart of consciousness. All of this is seated within the brain."

Continued *Patanjali,* after a pause, "Once Man has achieved and stopped every mutation of his *chitta* personality, he learns to ignore it, and the body's agitation. He already knows, through personal experience, that his mortal afflictions are not of the Self. He learns to separate the disturbances of the body and personality from the blessedness of the Self."

This was how *Patanjali* began his *Yoga Sutras.* He explained meditation by defining *yoga* and identifying meditation as a neutralization of both negative and positive thoughts.

The sun was rising and the cosmic furnace slowly warmed the valley. The curtain swayed in a gentle breeze. The disciples waited expectantly. Again, *Pakva,* seated nearest to the curtain, said, "Master, tell us where the Soul or Self lives, if not in the body?"

Patanjali continued, "You will discover the Soul remains in its own perfect self-contained grandeur. With the act of meditation, a negation of *chitta*-personality takes place. Then, a *yogi* can continue in his own undeniable character – the Self."

Patanjali understood his student and although he recognised *Pakva's* question, he had answered as if omitting some details. He continued with his thought flow. *Patanjali* knew intuitively, that *Pakva* understands already for he was, perhaps, the most evolved of the seven apostles.

But all the disciples understood what *Patanjali* had just explained. If a seeker is able to endure in him in meditation, it is possible to experience a sense of being One with the Cosmic Self.

Patanjali tried to continue, but also wanted to break the ice between teacher and students. *Pakva* sensed the young Master's discomfort. He therefore asked the teacher to explain how thoughts distracted seekers.

Patanjali, becoming uncomfortable with his monologue, was grateful for the interruption. "Mental whirlpools are *Vrittis.* They have the ability to distract the seeker from his own eternal peace," started *Patanjali,* and added, "The Soul or Self however is an eternal, indestructible, self-sufficient, self-contained entity. It embraces both pure Awareness and Consciousness. In its freed meditative state, the Soul is disassociated and the seeker's awareness is undisturbed. When the *chitta* personality is not self-contained, it becomes embroiled in its own disturbance. This happens because it engages thoughts."

Ujjaini found the Master's statement unclear. The son of a royal father and a commoner, *Ujjaini* had grown up among children of royalty, but spent his time away from them. He had shown signs of being a self-eradicating thinker early in his life. *Ujjaini* had nearly lost his life in a fight with a crocodile. As was the tradition, his new life started when snatched from the jaws of death. This credited him the choice of spending his life in the discovery of the Self. Although his mother wanted him to marry, *Ujjaini* chose the principles of *apatsanyasa* because, to him, a denial of worldly life appeared like a gift from heaven.

Ujjaini asked *Patanjali* to explain what he meant by mental 'disturbances'. The renunciate was single-pointed in intent and thought. His interest in the environment and Nature's delicate creations left him emotionally susceptible. But he never allowed any disturbance defeat his inner peace. *Patanjali* understood this young student too and explained that when the Soul was self-centred – meaning when *chitta*-personality identified with objects, emotions and thoughts – it forgets its own radiance as the untainted Self. Said *Patanjali,* "Looking outwards, the thinking-*chitta* links its intellect, mind and ego with an object. It now takes on the object's reflection. The unenlightened *Chitta,* sheathed in this cloud of ignorance, loses its legitimate brilliance. The purpose of *yoga* is to disconnect *chitta* from the object-directed mind and intellect. This, through breath control and thought restraint."

Ujjaini had another question, "Master *Patanjali,* what is this harassment that capsizes Man's need for true happiness? The Universe is so carefully and intricately created by the Cosmic Mother and worthy of being served and loved. What turns Man away from his duty? Why is She plundered instead?"

Though the sun had risen, it was still wintry in the valley. *Saleta,* a third disciple, surveyed his own visible exhalation in the chill. He wondered if it was perhaps warmer in the cave? After a moment of silence, *Patanjali* replied, "These disturbances, whether or not distressing, are of five kinds. The unenlightened *chitta*-personality may or may not recognise them as agonizing or objectionable."

A discussion broke out among the disciples. *Patanjali*

was pleased. The ice had broken. After many debates, the seven spiritual hopefuls decided that some disturbances of the blind *chitta* were enjoyable. They were pleasure rousing, desire stimulating and favorable to instinctive and innate striving. On the other hand, upheavals that were not gratifying, provoked, exasperated and restrained *chitta,,* causing it suffering. Each disciple clarified himself with illustrations of personally distressing as well as entertaining experiences. Finally, they all agreed that both pleasure and pain disturbed them. It distracted them from achieving a self-contained state. The blind *chitta,* therefore, comes with undesirable thoughts or *vrittis.* "We should be making notes of these discussions," said *Pushya,* the eldest and fourth disciple. Then continuing said, "So at the end of our deliberations with the Master, we can measure up our initial stages of understanding with what we finally assimilate and incorporate. For there is bound to be transformation in each one of us."

It was resolved that *Pushya's* younger brother, *Chandra,* would take down notes and the older brother would edit them. *Chandra* agreed absentmindedly. His mind was preoccupied with asking *Patanjali* to describe the five kinds of thought disturbances in *chitta.* But before *Chandra* could say anything, *Patanjali* had pre-adjusted his own thoughts and answered, "The fivefold swings in the *chitta* are the result of knowledge, illusion, delusion, sleep and memory."

With that, *Patanjali* appeared from behind the curtain, and seen standing in front of the cave. The sun had lifted its golden head in the sky. It was time for breakfast. He led the disciples to Malini Amma's hut by the riverbank. The disciples were deep in thought as they followed the Master. When they sat down to eat, *Patanjali* sat near *Amma,* some distance away. All of them chanted grace and the disciples ate in silence, quite preoccupied.

Suddenly, peels of laughter disturbed the peace. Village children were bathing downstream, having a caper in the water. This broke the silence and the seven students began discussing *Patanjali's* last statement. When they had finished feasting on breakfast, they came to intense conclusions. As if in support of their rational effort, the laughter downstream solemnly stopped instantly.

Said *Bhratahari*, "*Chitta* can be drawn into a so-called 'true' opinion of knowledge, which is based more on provisional assessment than on substantiality."

Added *Saleta*, "I know that awareness can also be lured by illusions due to contrary understanding. Even though inbred with uprightness, my awareness is tormented by curiosity.

Deluded by what already appeared to be of dubious quality, I nonetheless abandoned duty or *dharma* for a life of want or *kama*. I was bitten by a cobra and left to die. My life, however, was returned to me just because I had unintentionally spent a night with fasting villagers. They kept *Kartika Vrata* for *Shiva's* son in the village of *Mahismati*."

After a pause, *Menander* added, "Obviously, awareness as *chitta* can become enraptured by delusions of fanciful and imagined idealism or illusions. The moon looks as if it encircles the earth and emerges as if it is reborn each month. But it is the sun alone that encircles the earth."

Added *Saleta*, "*Chitta* can be seized by sluggish or *tamasic* thoughts of pessimism, especially when the mind is sleepy, and subtle."

The resolute *Pushya* added, "Then, there is memory. Recollecting personal experiences remembered correctly or wrongly, can convince *chitta* to accept as true its continuity, and permanence. Now it becomes embedded as 'truth', in its very substance."

The discussion led the disciples to make reference to their study of the *Bhagavad Gita*. *Patanjali*, sitting with *Malini Amma*, listened carefully and smiled at each other, approvingly. He looked at *Amma*, and she nodded her endorsement. *Pakva* began by quoting *Krishna,* who asserts in the *Gita* that a *yogi* who ignores the temptations of his senses and constantly practices *yoga* with a humble spirit, can see the indwelling Spirit. To transcend and lay open the *chitta,* Man needs concentration in the *kutastha,* while at the same time watching his breath.

Pakva explained how he silences the breath and slides his awareness into the centre of the Self, behind and between the eyebrows. Arrested breath erases all thought. *Pakva* said he intuitively, experiences thoughtlessness and breathlessness. Here worldly knowledge seems inexplicably irrelevant and dissolved.

While referring to knowledge and wisdom, *Pakva* again quoted *Krishna.* He reminded them *Arjuna* cautioned men who merely read the scriptures but do not necessarily follow moral rules nor do they meditate with deep devotion. They therefore never reach their Goal.

However, the disciples argued, but concluded that objective reading of scriptures is also knowledge but decided that this 'knowledge' was of doubtful value because it lacked convention. And it was this ambiguity that made the subject of 'predetermined' Knowledge questionable.

When *Patanjali* heard this, he unexpectedly stood up and after thanking *Malini Amma* for breakfast, took his leave. Taking his cue, the disciples also thanked *Amma* and followed the Master to the cave. As *Patanjali* took his seat behind the curtain, he decided to enlarge upon their subject of knowledge, after having heard their discussion.

Patanjali started, "Knowledge, meaning real knowledge, is based on three kinds of confirmation – direct view, correct inference or deduction and testimony of authoritative scriptures written by experienced sages." With that, he became silent, throwing the territory open to his students. He sat back to heed them as they authenticated his statement.

The valley was still rather frigid, as though the sun had

cloaked its heat waves. The disciples now sat under the peepal tree, just outside the cavern. They began by agreeing that Man remains sympathetic to conclusions and inferences as a logical extension of any *gained objective knowledge,* whether by reading or studying. They also highlighted *yoga philosophy.* Five senses offered a way and means for Man to make out worldly objects. Through them, Man expanded his knowledge of every bits and pieces. Man obviously resolved all thought disturbances by sketching conclusions.

"Why is Man compelled to do that?" asked *Saleta.*

Answered *Pushya,* "To feel complete. Man increases his personal knowledge to feel whole and undiminished. As we have predetermined, Man is an inquisitive animal. He reaches out for causes and infers."

The quiet, thoughtful *Chandra* added, "The more scientific the Man, the more his attention is devoted to discovering added intricacies, to satisfy his ego."

Menander came to a decision, "This, as we know, is the first disturbance of the intellect."

The disciples agreed. They went on to discuss the qualities of the intellect, which lies dormant in Man. Said *Chandra* absentmindedly, "Intellectual quality is concerned with information, analysis and awakening. Man hopes that enlightening intellect through singled out knowledge will lead to development of the power of discrimination."

"And the student simply cannot do this by himself," *Pushya* said.

There was silence. Suddenly *Ujjaini* quipped, "Processing the intellect needs apprenticeship. And being a teacher's disciple is the only way to culture the inner layers of human personality."

Pakva had the last word about 'book' knowledge, "When the mind, senses and ego retreat through reading, the intellect becomes clear. If culturing is spiritual, the intellect gains wisdom." With this, the disciples had defined *knowledge, both objective and subjective.*

Asked *Bhratahari,* "Are you saying subjective knowledge is wisdom?"

Pakva replied, "By definition, *wisdom* is intuitive knowledge." *Pushya* added, "Wisdom has the quality to realise only a clear state of being One. There is no duality in its view."

Said *Chandra,* "There is only 'right'. There is no 'wrong'. In all honesty, wisdom knows only what IS. It has no doubts; and it will defuse all memories of past opinions of relativity, or dualism, and of time."

Probed *Bhratahari* even further, "What, then, about *questionable knowledge,* Master?" This time, he had asked *Patanjali* the question, to which the teacher replied, "Illusory knowledge or doubt is based on 'non-real' and non-fact. It is based on distortion of reality."

The disciples felt it was easier to understand "knowledge and wisdom" than to understand '*doubt*', believing that it was more complex. It was still cold in the valley, and the subject under discussion made them huddle closer together. *Pakva* cleared his throat, and started the discussion with, "Doubt is 'wrong understanding' that creates wrong feelings and taints the *chitta.*"

"That is true," *Saleta* responded, knowingly.

Added *Pushya,* "In the search of Truth, a seeker's effort about doubt should not be thought as true-knowledge. If false knowledge about doubt becomes his experience, further effort to experience the *chit* or Consciousness is hindered."

Chandra said, "Such experiences lead Man into a trap. The Law of Relativity or *raaga-dvesha* will grip the *chitta* and imprison it. Here in a deep-seated, persistent anxiety, the *chitta* is led towards relentless thought disturbances or *vrittis.*"

Saleta thoughtfully finished with, "This, then, is the second disturbance of the intellect."

This time, it was *Menander* who asked the Master, "What happens to Man when he lives with intellect that is ingrained with disturbance? Can he live in reality?"

Replied *Patanjali,* "Living one's own fanciful thoughts and ideals, which have no factual basis, is *vikalpa.* It is vague, uncertain knowledge that does not match with reality."

Ujjaini was in deep thought, as he leaned against the peepal tree. He had experienced recurring fanciful imagination. Uncontrollable fantasy or *vikalpa* often disturb his *chitta* personality. He often wonders what his life would be if he was still in his palace. Had he not rejected the comforts of royalty and refused marriage, where would he be today?

Memories of his childhood occasionally disturbed his usually tranquil mind. Retrospection led him to analyse an imagined life. *Patanjali* knew of *Ujjainis* recurring mental disturbance and wished him to discriminate against all fanciful existence. *Patanjali* recognised such imagery caused *Ujjaini* disturbance in thought. His concern was that imagination or *vikalpa* could concentrate itself in the *chitta.* He may act it out someday.

He knew, through trial and error, *Ujjaini* would apprehend thought disturbances. *Ujjaini* needed to awaken his intellect and transform his delusions and illusions into attentiveness and absorption into the *kutastha.* *Patanjali* also recognised that *Ujjaini* thirsted for true subjective Knowledge. If he could live a genuine life, his purified thought would necessarily discover this different vision.

Ujjaini realized the Master was addressing him and immediately joined the discussion. The seven admitted that in *vikalpa* lay an imagined world they reminisced about. They had, at one time or another, dreamed of more pleasure, wealth, and greater esteem, in an imagined heaven. *Pushya,* a widower in his fifties and renunciate king, had experienced this life. He said, "Heaven is the wrong place to look for, while living as a mortal. As long as Man attaches himself to such externalised ideals, including heaven, he will, and must, suffer anxiety displaying as *vrittis* of restless thought."

Menander declared the personality of a thought-free state seems *tamasic* and inert. He questioned why this 'dull' state of existence was desirable. He asked *Patanjali,* "Master, do you subscribe to lethargy, rather than a creative or *rajasic* existence while awake?"

Replied *Patanjali,* "Dreamless sleep is an inert state of the *chitta* personality. In this state, Man does not feel the sense of reality."

The seven analysed *Patanjali* statement. *Pushya* knew there was more to this answer. *Pakva* stood up, and paced the earth below him. *Patanjali* watched them, and then heard them describe Matter's nature as a *dharma.*

All of them have experienced, She – the Cosmic Mother. She compels both the wise and the ignorant with her qualities of inertia, creativity and harmony. *Chandra* said, "If compelled and forced by pessimism, Man is forced to accept and agree to the iniquity of *tamasic* void of sleep, which by nature is inert. But inertia can be substituted with a positive state of mind in meditation."

He added, "Many seekers succumb to *tamasic* pessimism whenever things alter. They are forced to be what they are not used to. We willfully make situations worse than they are, through imagination and flawed conclusions. Instead of gaining insight into the intrinsic value of Supreme Reality, we allow our vision to be blunted. Then, overwhelmed with disgust, fear or horror, pessimism raises negative thought disturbances in the soul as disturbed *vrittis.*"

At this point, *Pakva* reminded them that thought disturbances were recognisable because Man has experienced them before. The disciples concluded, therefore, that although these experiences have no reality, they have a "persistent value" in Man's memory. *Patanjali* elucidated this further, "Memory is an adjustment of awareness in *chitta,* and it allows us to recollect all past words and experiences."

Chandra, of course, was busy taking notes. He had experienced mortality when a *yaksha* had fatally wounded him as a young man. Now, wiser and placid, he watched more than he spoke. He was an expert in worldly interaction. As a deep thinker he understood the after-effects of Matter's compulsions on Man. He also rationalized how these effects were ingrained as memories. "The present is what the past was, and the future is what the present is," he spoke up, continuing, "Man must free himself from the compulsions of Matter in the present. Because Matter's compulsions are innate in Nature's character, they must be contended with. Analysing effects of qualities on every thing, plant and creature is important. Man has never taken the time to admit the 'cause' of these effects on Creation."

It was almost midday. As the sun showered warmth over the valley, a cool breeze blew around them. *Pakva* and *Ujjaini* sat under the peepal tree, while *Chandra* and *Pushya* sat closer to the mouth of the cave. *Patanjali* remained behind the curtain, as his disciples discussed Authenticity of the Power of Matter. He was confident the group of seven would reach the right conclusion. *Menander, Saleta* and *Bhŕatahari* were now discussing some texts.

Patanjali had tutored his private apprentice *Bhratahari* about the *Mahabhashya.* They deliberated in *Patanjali's* cave while *Gonika Amma* was still alive. On his own initiative and consecrated by *Shiva, Bhratahari* had chosen a life of renunciation and thrown away unimaginable treasures. He understood the effects of Matter's magnetism on those who live in ignorance of Her powers. *Bhratahari* said, "Only *Prakriti* is the supreme authenticity, which perseveres eternally," adding, "Names and forms are temporary offspring and special effects of Her compulsions. They do not persist beyond their transient appearances and are experienced as memory. Such temporary awareness exists only in the individualised self as unenlightened *chitta.* In fact, the state of personalised ego is a deluded state, where names and forms appear real."

Saleta analyses the seeming reality of possessions. Their imagined substantiality made demands on the *chitta.* With *Pakva's* help, he divided these into principles and classes. He assigned each a life of empirical value that was, of course, also imagined and therefore deceptive. As they delved deeper into the subject, they realised *chitta* does not wish to be influenced. But everyone wished to reach this perfect state of emancipation, even if the conclusion was flawed. *Saleta* sighed, for he longed to be free from these demands that were expressed as disturbances in thought. *Pakva* consoled *Saleta,* saying, "Identified with a purified divine *chitta,* Man can become the inward-seeing ego."

His companion disciples knew and understood *Pakva* to be free from excessive thought disturbance. Man has to practice detachment from want and demands made by the body-mind-intellect sheaths, on the Soul. Added *Patanjali,*

"Freedom from the disturbances of desire in the *chitta* needs consistent practice and detached patience." *Pakva* understood *Patanjali* instantly. There was an unspoken truth in this *sutra.* He and the others leaned closer to unravel this statement.

Pakva initiated the discussion, "Other than the Spirit, there is nothing higher, and nothing more minute. It is only Matter supported by Spirit that exists as the visible Universe. Not by work, not by progeny, nor by wealth can Man reach Immortality."

Added *Pushya,* "Many have reached immortality by renunciation."

Interjected *Menander,* with passion, "But we seek That which is beyond even the heavens."

"That which you seek already shines brilliantly within your own purified hearts," said *Patanjali*. He told the disciples to strive clearly to understand the body, mind and Soul. That is the only path to purify *chitta's* awareness. Stilling the *chitta* personality needs constant practice of breath and thought control, he added. From this point on the disciples, acknowledged that evolutionary path to self-unfoldment must be through the practices of *yama, niyama, abhyas* and *pranayama*.

Having identified the pathway as one of renunciation starting with restraint, they validated adherance to observances through constant practice. *Pranayama* matured to breathlessness and, therefore also, the experience of automatic sense withdrawal in *pratyahara*. Together this allowed for concentration or *dharana*, while in contemplation or *dhyana* which matured into meditation or *samadhi*. The disciples agreed upon an inward journey to experience perfect contentment. The promise was a detachment of the *chitta* personality of mind-intellect-ego, from external objects.

Ujjaini defined the unambiguous secret of continued success. "When practitioners fall from the grace after meditative successes, each can and should, revisit the practice, starting with *yama* and *niyama*," he said adding, "When re-starting from the beginning, all spiritual endeavour promise enduring success. Success is ensured through *abhyas*." *Chandra* interjected, reminding them they had been discussing the eight steps of *ashtanga yoga*.

Bhratahari added, "It is logical to involve *ashtanga yoga*. Correctly understanding it is the means to still intellectual reasoning or *buddhi's vritti*. *Vairagya*, as dispassion, reigns supreme after that."

Added *Pakva*, "Immortality, then, is identifying with the Supreme."

Bhratahari added, "All seekers come to nothing when *Vedanta* on its own does not free the intellect through book knowledge. They arrive at purity of mind by practicing the disciplines indicated, but seekers fail to reach their desired destination. Only by *yoga* and practicing steadfastness can Man reach God through meditation."

Pushya concluded, "Freed from want and passion, *yoga* helps cultivate nonattachment to things and persons, which hinder progress in the *yoga* of meditation."

At this, *Patanjali* entered the conversation on the subject of meditation, "Practice, in meditation, means an unrelenting experiment to still the *chitta's* swings and to regain silence." After a pause, *Patanjali* added, "Long hours of persistence are needed, for alert practice is the foundation of restraining the unenlightened *chitta's* swings."

Pakva and *Pushya* both sighed deeply. They knew the great wisdom of deep meditation is gained only through dedicated effort. They had learned through personal experience that success in spiritual practices or *sadhana* can inflate the seeker's ego. This is something seekers need to guard themselves against. Only humility allows for the dawn of spiritual wisdom. *Patanjali* read their minds, and wanted to remind them that desire must also be surrendered. And he said, "Patience and a willingness to abandon and detach oneself from want is renunciation."

Saleta found detachment difficult to master. He stated in dismay that disentanglement or *vairagya* is a learned quality. The *chitta* personality must be taught to remain unmoved by temptation. He felt that freeing the senses, one after the other, perhaps allows seekers to gain proficiency over all senses entrenched in the physical body or *sthula sharira*. *Menander,* the *ayurvedic* physician agreed, but with reservation, stating the seeker must learn to enter his *sukshma sharira*. He was of the opinion it is easier to subdue desire for sensuous pleasures, through the subtle body.

All the disciples agreed. Desire cannot be conquered unless it is sublimated for a higher and more-satisfying experience. They all nodded in agreement. *Pushya* and *Chandra* had succeeded in walking away from the eleven wits of five senses, five organs of action and mind/intellect, while under the tutelage of forest monks, with whom they had spent their childhood.

They had identified five types of indifference or *vairagya*, functioning from five personality levels. Together, the brothers recalled their experiences. The monks had, at first, engaged the princes on a physical level – for instance, *Pushya* had the habit of relishing meals being prepared for the royal table – he licked the spoons used for stirring. *Chandra* regularly pocketed *imli*, or sour tamarind, that was held in reserve for cooking. The cooks would complain to their parents, who'd forgive this strange behaviour. The monks, however, warned the young princes to disconnect from their sense of taste, which had led to these bad habits. They obeyed, but could disengage only for short periods. They confirmed eventually, that as long as desire persists involvement is bound to rekindle attachment to old habits.

The forest monks ordered *Pushya* and *Chandra* to physically stay away from the objects of their want. Distancing themselves from the object of desire would allow their ego to become self-conscious. Over time, the brothers were convinced that their habits had diminished. Because of persuasive restraint on willpower, they had temporarily become indifferent. But when the monks exposed them to their desired objects of the past, memories of old habit and pleasurable experience still existed. That is when the monks ordered them to silence their emotional demands and rethink from an intellectual level. The monks impressed on them that any indulgence can be given logic of virtue. Ultimately, the young princes understood the authority of the body, mind and intellect.

After that, the monks taught them the art of physical and mental transformation during energisation of the different bodies, through breath control in *asana* rejuvenating and healing decayed cells of the body. When breathing became subtle, the princes learned to withdraw into the divine cave where, by concentration, contemplation and meditation, they were taught to listen to their own inner sound of the reverberating AUM. They found they could withdraw into themselves. This was complete *pratyahara.* Engaged in this experience, the monks made them realise that they were within the citadel of the *chitta.*

Pushya told his companion disciples that he first had to comprehend *chitta.* He discovered that mastering desire-thoughts is possible in this citadel. When the eleven senses had receded into a single thought, he had found, within himself, the sinless pure lotus of his heart. This, he discovered is the unspoken, home of the Spirit. *Pushya* learned to convert the gross physical body into subtle life, the energy of the astral body. This was the easiest way to withdraw from the senses. Through the help of willpower, *Pushya* himself was able to move into his *karana sharira.* Here he was able to modify the effects of ingrained tendencies from past births. *Chandra,* too, came to the same conclusion, but only after many weeks of *dharana-dhyana.*

The forest monks were patient. By encouraging that only an unrelenting virtuous ruler made honest kings, the brothers were put on a righteous path. Eventually, *Pushya* and *Chandra* experienced self-unfoldment. They understood, instinctively, Nature's compulsions are observable as illusory name and form. The oldest of the monks explained that unless there was supreme detachment from objects, there can be no escape from *Prakrit's* influence and compulsions. Personal want, the monk said, for what is already theirs, stems from a lack of understanding and a false sense of separation from the Cosmic Mother. Desire results in entanglement with Her qualitative compulsions and reverses the natural flow of *prana* towards indulgences and devolution. Armed with this understanding of Nature and Her powers, *Pushya* and *Chandra* ruled their kingdoms without being influenced by personal desires but, rather, ruling as if serving Nature like devoted sons. The divine Mother Nature, in turn, ceased to manipulate them with Her *gunas.*

The monks had succeeded. The brothers had involuntarily discarded their bondage to birth and death, name and form, likes and dislikes, and entrenched habits. They ruled till they were ready for seclusion and disengagement from possessions. "Once within the realms of the Soul's underlying existence, I realised and experienced the essence of thought," *Chandra* said, as if reliving his amazement. "In this stillness and silence, with subdued senses, it was automatic renunciation of all want. I felt free from all compulsions of Matter." He paused, and then added, "I am occasionally able to delve deeper into myself through regularity or *abhyas.*

Pakva and *Ujjaini* stated, almost in unison, "*Vairagya* or dispassion is a personal experience and privileged realisation. There is no need to smother desire. The ecstasy of meditation takes the seeker to sublime heights. The understanding transcends all wants." *Saleta* now understood that only *abhyas* purifies the mind and intellect. And once this transformation is launched, there is momentum to travel even deeper. He also understood dispassion must be born of a personal coherence and experience.

All disciples were deeply moved with this discussion. In agreement, they abruptly broke into a unanimous expression of: 'AUM'. Rising into their ancient cause, they remained in an unbroken contemplation of AUM.

The sun was setting and the creatures of the forest were settling in for the night. The valley was ready to sleep. The disciples were engrossed in the sound effects of AUM within and without. Their receptivity to being one with Bliss in togetherness was exhilarating. Experiencing the Universe as a Cosmic Divine Person is a blessing they must wait for. To connect with the foundation of humanity was their aspiration. Uncontaminated by an unenlightened *chitta,* the disciples silently understood the unstated objective of humanity. They must think through and realize the purpose of such an experience. Their Awareness had transcended body, mind, intellect and ego to become the nearly purified individualised soul.

Patanjali was delighted with this unplanned event. *Pushya* and *Chandra* had shared their tales as if in a casual manner, which triggered forgotten reminiscences of Self-experience. Satisfied with all he had heard, he said, "The purest form of renunciation is achieved when one transcends the qualities or *gunas* of Nature. One can, then, enjoy the soul itself, which is in an eternally undisturbed state. Clarity of intellect and heart lead to this." He also took this opportunity to describe the characteristics of the enlightened *chitta* personality sheaths. This again provoked another discussion.

This time, however, *Patanjali* wanted the disciples to recognise normal consciousness, which is usually preoccupied with investigation, personal enjoyment and asserting the ego when self-conscious. And he said abruptly, "Through practice and detachment, four types of awareness develop for the purposes of self-analysis, integration, ecstasy and the experience of the pure being."

Saleta, Bhratahari and *Menander* were good friends. They often confided in each other. They spent hours together to experience the changes that come to pass from deep meditation. Through *yoga* practice, they had discovered the four types of growth and change during heightening Awareness. The 'seeker' in them had progressively become the 'seer' when looking at a 'seen' experience. In this awareness, the 'seeker' looks as if it has 'seen' it all while the 'seer' watches, until all become One. This encounter was a recurring observable fact when tested by each one of them.

Started *Saleta,* "After awakening from a swoon of death, I was overwhelmed by a chance to live life for the second time. Born and brought up a *Brahmin* who was taught laws of virtuous living which I disobeyed. This second chance led me to analyse the purpose of my life. An inner awakening gave me a chance to harvest parts of this knowledge. The futility of my experiences of worldliness seemed obvious."

Menander commented, "Such realisation is wisdom. It is bound to lead to a changed inner happiness." To this, *Bhratahari* added, "Freed from materialism and extroversion, the discovery of the Fountain of Bliss, within, is true disclosure."

Pushya was listening intently. He had encountered changes similar to what the three had individually and collectively experienced. As the dialogue continued, the curtain lifted slightly. A corner of the screen had wedged itself in a crevice in the cave's wall. From behind the curtain, *Patanjali* had moved closer to his disciples. He was sitting on an unstable three-legged stool, away from the slab where he usually sat. The disciples saw his bare feet underneath the curtain.

Pushya, trying to define the bliss of being One with Consciousness, said, "This experience of being One feels like an overloaded attentiveness."

Asked *Ujjaini,* "Why, then, are there levels of awareness, before one can reach the shores of a perfect sense of One Attentiveness?"

Answered *Menander,* knowingly, "Awareness, as understood by physicians, occurs as levels of thinking, originating from different areas of the functioning brain." As doctor, *Menander* had analysed all levels of thinking in the different parts of the brain.

Suddenly, the disciples heard *Patanjali* clear his throat, a hint that he approved the direction in which the dialogue is headed. *Menander,* thus approved, began by defining '**discussion**' or *vitarka.* First, there is *vitarka.* This is a deliberate discussion about a seeker's thinking, based on study and practice of a subject, such as *ashtanga yoga,* for instance," he said. Then continuing he said, "This leads a seeker to the root of his intellectual understanding. Having satisfied his curiosity, his thought is stilled and silenced. The seeker now makes an intellectual analysis of his new found state. From the halls of his intellectual being, he assesses this knowledge from his personal perspective."

"He peels off thoughts from his gross physical and subtle or astral body sheaths, layer by layer. He reaches a subtle understanding of this 'learned' knowledge. By viewing his inner circumstances, both past and present, he makes conclusions. These discoveries are relative. Therefore this reprogrammed knowledge lacks erudition. Man uses the forebrain in the frontal lobe for this *vitarka.*"

Menander next analysed '**inquiry**', or *vichara.* He said, "To change knowledge, one must launch into self-investigation, from a stored image of impressions and thoughtfulness. This is the second level of thinking. When seekers can still the mind at this level of inquiry, it thinks from the occipital lobe in the back of the brain." He explained how the ever-present impression of the 'why' and 'wherefore' of effects grant seekers discriminatory powers to make out real from the unreal.

After that, *Menander* described the "**Bliss of Self discovery**", or *ananda.* "This is the third level of serious thinking. It is a progressive unearthing of proper knowledge that leads to self-development. From self-unfoldment, there is Soul-fulfillment. With it comes the discovery of *ananda.* Because of such pure insight, the learning seeker remains in the enlightening *chitta* itself. Here he is temporarily empty of ego. The base of the brain, in the insula of the parietal lobe, is the seat of *ananda.*"

Finally, *Menander* described the pure Soul, or *asmitarupa*: "This state of pure being is of the **enlightened *chitta* – the soul or Self**. To reach this state needs the guardianship of an enlightened teacher. He must have the ability to nurture the student through study, discussion, investigation and fulfillment." He added, "When the seeker finally remains in the enlightened *chitta,* the teacher has the ability to support the seeker within the limbic cortex of the temporal lobe. In this state, the student learns to draw from the four sides of the brain, and converge into the stem of the brain. Man reaches here by enduring in the *kutastha* for a long time."

Pakva interrupted suddenly, saying, "Once Awareness is synchronised, a seeker can receive the transitory state of *manolaya.* This is dissolution of the mind in its own cause. *Menander* is describing this point, where seekers reach a plateau in spiritual practice."

Menander had, indeed, experienced this plateau but had never voiced it. *Pakva* continued, "With persistent practice, *chitta* can be made to move up towards the source of the mind, in the heart of Consciousness. And here, the *chitta* personality must merge into a mindless, 'unbeginning' and endless *chit.* This is a conquest of the Spirit. *Chitta* becomes *chit.* Awareness merges in His embrace and becomes Consciousness!"

Saleta and *Bhratahari* were surprised to learn that all levels of evolution and dissolution worked from different physical locations in the brain. Even *Menander* was surprised at *Pakva's* disclosure. Said the scholarly *Bhratahari,* a champion of devotion, "The rise of Man can be scientifically traced. Through constant practice or *abhyas* and withdrawal by *pratyahara,* it is possible to move from physical coverings to the core of bodily cells. Deeper entry is possible only through *pranayama.* When egoistic awareness perseveres until it penetrates and discards mundane thought and intellect, this enlightening *chitta* enters and rests in the hall of Awareness. Here while abiding in the *kutastha* behind and between the two eyebrows, he waits to experience complete happiness."

Ujjaini, feeling the discussion had missed *yama* and

niyama, said, "Triumphant existing as a seeking mortal is always possible. But it is first necessary to get acquainted with the self, or unenlightened *chitta.*"

Chandra asked, "What is the purpose of this expertise?"

Ujjaini replied, "The intellect in the *chitta* personality can be made to understand that it is the mind and intellect that spread selfish awareness within and around the body. The egoistic self must undergo self-unfoldment through scriptural study and contemplation. It is the only method to reach Self-realisation."

Added *Menander,* "It is possible to teach Man to remodel every molecule of every cell of the body into healthful dynamism, through the radiant life force of *prana.* But he must discover the connection between Energy in matter and Life Force. A seeker must see and understand these effects clearly, by unburdening past tendencies."

He continues, "When within a state of *savikalpa samadhi,* a blissful seeker in an ecstasy of *ananda,* sees no disparity between the 'seer' or Consciousness in *chit,* the 'seen' or Awareness of *chitta* and the 'seeing'. The triad of knower, knowledge and known are absorbed in an experience Oneness. The meditator, the subject and the meditated or object are in perfect absorption within the mind."

Patanjali was growing increasingly thrilled with the discussion. In his commentaries of classical learning, *Patanjali* had analysed superconsciousness. He defined the experience by merging the triad of meditator, meditation and meditated as *samprajnata samadhi.* He described four levels. In *savitarka samadhi,* there is an experience of *samadhi* or Oneness, but the practitioner has a doubting argumentative mind. In *savichara samadhi,* the experience is of intuitive Oneness, but after deliberation, reasoning and inquiring of a pondering intellect. In *sananda samadhi,* the internalised experience of *chitta* interprets Oneness with a feeling of elation. In *sasmita samadhi,* the experience of

Oneness is with a feeling of individuality. It asserts 'I exist as *anand*'."

Patanjali, who authored *Ayurveda,* understood *Menander* and confirmed the anatomical analysis of the brain and its four levels of thinking. He found this trend of discussion encouraging.

Suddenly *Pushya* exclaimed, "*Shivoham! Shivoham!*"

The disciples responded by chanting also in togetherness, "*Shivoham! Shivoham!*" and drifted into deep meditation.

It was almost twilight, and dusk had begun to spread its sails over the valley. The disciples were awakened from deep contemplation by *Malini Amma's* call. As usual, she thrilled her copper *thali* or plate, with a wooden spoon. But they were still eager to build on their earlier discussion.

They addressed their experiences of super-consciousness. Fixed in sense-withdrawal of *pratyahara, Saleta, Bhratahari, Chandra* and *Pushya* concentrated through heightening access through concentration in *dharana.* They recognised sound and light from the five spiritual centres of the subtle bodies. They corroborated their experience of awareness in the *kutastha* as a personal realisation. They accepted this intuitive experience as a progression towards a cognitive trance characteristic in *samprajnata.* This experience, they said, was transcendent and needed no instruments of opinion. The super-consciousness experienced mingled the knower, knowledge and knowing into a single state. Said *Pushya,* suddenly, "Being One is experienced only in a Void, filled with vibrations of AUM."

There was an unexpected realisation that AUM was the link between Matter and Spirit. Starting with an atom, to every molecule in the Universe, AUM was the substructure as well as the consolidation. The disciples had experienced this connection, but had not made the conclusion. AUM is the common thread that links Matter in a wide-ranging array. The Holy Spirit bonds every atom, creature and Man to the Universal Being. *Pushya* continued, "The knowledge of AUM allows Man to climb into the divine cave and attune himself to deepening calls. The symphony allows Man to enter higher states of understanding and realisation." Instinctively, the rest knew *Pushya* had experienced this Infinite Void filled with AUM.

Malini Amma made the plate call again. It was dark now. *Patanjali* appeared from behind the curtain. The disciples, immersed in their own thought, followed him silently to the river to freshen up, and then to *Amma's* hut for supper. The apostles' had not realised it, but they were all hungry. *Amma* had prepared a meal of rice and vegetables, and sweet yogurt or *dahi* for dessert. After dinner, *Patanjali* thanked *Amma* for the meal and left the cottage first. As he walked to the door, he said to his disciples, "We will discuss 'Void' in the morning."

The disciples thanked *Malini* and withdrew to their respective huts or caves, for the night. At the crack of dawn, the village rooster downstream shouted his persistent cockcrow. The seven disciples hurried to the river to bathe. It was a frosty morning. Shivering they readied for another discussion with the young Master. They scurried towards *Patanjali's* cave and saw the oil lamp was already lit. They saw *Patanjali's* shadow already sitting on the stone slab. They sat around the grotto entrance, wrapped up in shawls and clustered close together.

Started *Patanjali,* "In the experience of Void, in *savikalpa samadhi* you discussed in detail yesterday, that the seed of the past is not destroyed and is therefore termed *sabija.* The seed is latent in the *chittamaya kosha* of the mind and intellect. Such subconsciousness is experienced in unconscious deep sleep. Dormant impressions are hidden. They spring forth during moments of insensibility."

"Agitation in Awareness create swings and disturb the purity of Consciousness. The agitation recedes in *chitmaya kosha* of Universal Intelligence. The experience is of *navikalpa samadhi* or *nirbija.* Here the experience is only Awareness and Consciousness, without any seed of past births."

He, then, spoke on internalised meditative states, which he called *samadhi. Patanjali* was referring to two states of being One with Consciousness.

The disciples intellectually understood that *savikalpa samadhi* is experienced as a divine union with Awareness. This state is a merging of the triad of Knower, Known and Knowledge. They understood the 'Known' was Matter, the 'Knower' was the Spirit – both the subject of their search. They are to be interpreted through 'Knowledge' using Nature's instruments of perception.

They estimated this inner meditative experience is an intercommunication of the 'Knower', 'Known' and 'Knowledge' experienced by an individualised but enlightening *chitta.* The disciples also knew, from experience, that this was a plateau stage in spiritual practice. They affirmed it as an incomplete knowing or *virama pratyaya.* Unless one intensifies one's spiritual effort, they understood, they cannot experience the higher state of a sought after destination or *upaya pratyaya.*

With that, a new day had begun. *Menander* had already pointed out that once the brain is stilled, only *samskaras* or past tendencies are detectable. The disciples agree that in this state, the seeker is temporarily freed of passion, want and appetite, without too much effort. The need to practice *ashtanga yoga* helps transcending tendencies as well.

Menander had told his comrade disciples the nearest one comes to this state of *samadhi* is in the few moments ahead of falling asleep. This is when the intellect in *chitta* relaxes its hold on thought. The mind is silent and the ego loses its identity. At this, *Patanjali* clarified the condition of the enlightening *chitta.* He said, "From those who arrive at this superior seed-awareness or the *sabija* of *chitta,* some may experience a 'bodiless' view of oneself and merge in *Prakriti's* Awareness. This may lead to isolation, but not of emancipation." The young teacher asked his seven followers to discuss and describe *sabija samadhi.*

Pakva started the discussion, "In this state, Awareness in the *chitta* is poised between the seed and seedless state of being. Caught in this bodiless state of being, *chitta* merges with *Prakriti,* and experiences isolation." To this, *Pushya* added, "Unless reminded, Man forgets to climb the topmost rung of the spiritual ladder, to the *nirbija* state of emancipation."

Chandra said, "In *nirbija samadhi,* as Consciousness and Awareness merge to become the *chit* or Universal Intelligence, the self easily becomes the Self and enters the Cosmic Soul."

Patanjali, however, warned his disciples, to remain careful and meditate with consideration, "Practice endurance in meditation. The purpose must be aimed at even added trust, confidence, vigour, keen memory and a power to understand. Crush spiritual complacency, with constant practice or *abhyas.* This is the key to success."

"Despite gains at spiritual practice, seekers are always in danger of slipping back into habituated old ways," *Saleta* said, who was himself a living example of having fallen, despite a righteous upbringing. Added *Ujjaini,* "One needs the ability to discriminate between isolation and emancipation to reach the *chit.*"

The scholarly *Bhratahari* added, from experience, "We must not feel elated because we have conquered the five elements, nor should we seek delight because we move without heeding demands of the body. All must adopt a newer form of self-absorption." *Ujjaini* agreed, "We need to leap even further into the core of our being." *Bhratahari* decided, "We need to harness wisdom, with complete attention and awareness. By harnessing decisions with frigid and serious intent we must leap towards Final Emancipation."

The disciples heard *Patanjali* clear his throat. Encouraged by the urgency in his disciples' voices, *Patanjali* said, "The goal is near for those who are intensely vigourous in the practice of *ashtanga yoga.*"

Pakva returned to the experience of a Void, which *Pushya* had referred to. "Dormant impressions of past lives are out of sight in *savikalpa samadhi* in the *chittamaya kosha.* These have a habit of springing up during moments of pure Awareness. As the Master said, such intrusions create fluctuations and disturb the purity of *chit.* Universal Intelligence is *navikalpa samadhi* experienced in the *chitmaya kosha,* in the *kutastha.* Although some describe this as a void, the image of the Cosmic Being is reflected here."

Pushya referred to *Vyasa's Bhagavad Gita,* thus enriching the discussion. Said *Pushya,* "*Krishna* describes a true *yogi* as one who endlessly follows the meditative path with nonattachment and intense need for God communion. Such a *yogi* is described as fully severed from physical, astral and causal bodies, including tendencies. Having reached the fourth permanent state within the altar, the Cosmic Being becomes plainly visible at the *kutastha.*"

Added *Bhratahari,* "*Vyasa* has been recorded as saying that if a *yogi* is able to strengthen his union with the Cosmic Being, he reaches Final Emancipation." *Chandra* interjected, "Master *Patanjali* has also defined such a *yogi.* He is one who makes intense effort without impatience. He owns devotion, energy, recollection of his true Self, through discrimination. With calm persistence in deep meditation, such a *yogi* achieves emancipation in a short time." As *Chandra* finished, *Ujjaini* said pensively, "Only a supremely energetic seeker reaches the highest goal of *yoga* quickly. And, of course, a *yogi* of such calibre is guided by amassed virtues from former lives."

There was complete silence, as each disciple grasped the importance of *Ujjaini's* statement. Seemingly closing the discussion, *Pakva* said, "Progress is, therefore, certain for such a seeker."

Patanjali, however, wanted to clarify this further. "Progress even from this level may differ. Results may be mild, moderate or intense, depending on the *yogi's* eagerness and intensity of perseverance in the *kutastha.*" This statement triggered another discussion. *Saleta* said, "Whether the seeker's eagerness and intensity of effort towards emancipation is *mrdu* [mild and gentle], *madhya* [medium], *adhimatra* [causing dispassion] or *tivra* [intense], the goal for Self-realisation becomes time-bound."

Said *Menander,* "Master *Patanjali's* declaration that *savikalpa samadhi,* the state of being One within a changing *chitta* of Awareness, is arrived at by penetrating faithful meditation to *Ishvara* or, Lord as Universal Being."

"*Ishvara pranidhana* is devotion to the Lord while waking, dreaming and sleeping. This allows the seeker to efface himself as the egoistic self. He awaits His grace for Self-realisation," added *Ujjaini,* who had experienced such exhilaration.

As an environmentalist, he had worshipped the Cosmic Mother with very old helpful rites of *ishtapurta* to shelter plants and creatures in sanctuaries. So intense was his devotion to Her creatures that wild beasts sat around him when he was in meditation. There was no fear. Neither Man feared Beast, nor did Beast fear Man.

Stressed *Patanjali,* "*Chitta*-personality of body-mind-ego may be restrained by sincerely meditating on *Chit,* at the centre of Universal Intelligence and surrendering to It." He wanted the disciples to understand that Time and devotional Surrender were of equal importance for Self-realisation.

Once he was convinced, they all knew that Known was Matter or *prakriti* made familiar by means of earning real Knowledge. They should know the Knower pervaded them, as the Spirit of *Purusha*.

Patanjali now altered the direction of this discussion. He said, "The *chit* is *Ishvara*. This Universal Being is free from conflict, unaffected by action and untainted by cause and effect." He had already spoken to them about afflictions and reactions to action that affect Man while on a spiritual journey. These he said had no effect on *Ishvara* within or without. *Patanjali* said a seeker must reach this state of "being unaffected" by *klesha* [pain], *karma* [action], *vipaka* [aging], and *ashnaya* [hunger].

Pushy said, "The Master cited *karma* as one of six obstacles Man faces on a spiritual journey," and added *Bhratahari*, "This is so only if *karma* is a materialistic act, provoked by egoistic desire for fruit. Only then does it set into motion action and reaction. If an act is not desire-motivated or dedicated with renunciation and surrender of fruit, this law is not triggered. Reactions bind themselves to the doer, until the cause is fulfilled."

Impatiently, *Saleta* asked his fellow-disciples, "Why are we discussing hardships of living again?"

Replied *Chandra*, who was busy taking notes, "Every discussion is valuable, because it is aimed at developing higher states of understanding and awareness. It is worth the time." To this, his brother *Pushya* added, "Time and discussion are needed to digest the teachings of Masters." And then concluded *Ujjaini*, "It is a precondition, even if the theme is repetitive."

Saleta held his ground saying, "Master *Patanjali* has agreed to teach us the arrangement of this great Knowledge. Obviously, he waits for us to digest these statements, some of which we already know. And I think nothing in this world is more purifying than such unalloyed Knowledge."

Pakva had been deep in thought throughout this exchange, and others noticed this. They also became quiet. At length, *Pakva* said, "Armed with Knowledge by itself, the self cannot of itself be perfected in *yoga.* Man needs to know the workings of the self to find, in time, the Self."

There was silence again. The sun had risen and a warm gust of a breeze burst through the leaves. High up in the *peepal* tree, cooing doves pleasantly punctuated the pregnant silence. Said *Patanjali,* speaking this time about AUM, "In Aum is entrenched the unrivaled source and seed of all Knowledge – omniscient, omnipresent and omnipotent."

The disciples listened intently, but *Chandra's* attention had wandered. He was thinking about his childhood in the forest. The monks had spent hours allowing his young mind to understand ideas. Now, he suddenly realised, *Patanjali,* a teenager, was building on this old knowledge, and adding maturity to understanding. The young Master, he thought fondly, was showering them with Eternal Knowledge. As this thought peaked within him, *Chandra* realised his story must be told. He asked *Patanjali,* abruptly, "Master, please define a true *guru.*"

Patanjali replied, "God is the first, the leading, the absolute *guru,* unconditioned by Time." There was a long pause. *Patanjali* then continued, "God is represented by the sacred syllable 'AUM', also called the *pranava.*" *Chandra* agreed, his mind now clear. The Supreme Spirit is the first and main teacher, bound neither by space, time, nor place. *Chandra* sighed, "He is all, and all is He." In his heart, he prostrated at *Patanjali's* feet.

Patanjali had celebrated *Ishvara* and a perfect *guru* with one symbol, the sacred *pranava* AUM, also the unifying symbol of divinity. The disciples were well versed with *pranava,* which is chanted in His praise and for sacred fulfillment. They all recognised AUM as the sound vibration of *Ishvara* and the source of all Creation, before, within and beyond Creation. They understood that *Purushotama* was before and beyond this vibration. They also understood this vibration is the nearest way to *Ishvara,* the Cosmic Being of Universal Intelligence. *Ujjaini* explained, "I think of AUM as the impersonal source of all beings hidden in the Cosmic Egg of *Hiranyagarbha.*" To this, *Saleta* said, "I am more comfortable thinking of AUM as *Brahman,* remaining within the sea of each heart."

Menander said, "To me, the symbol AUM is the eversteady faithful bow, while *chitta* is the arrow. Together they allow us to strike the Supreme cause of Happiness in the world." *Pakva* and *Chandra* in particular were elated with *Menander's* use of the symbol AUM. Said *Chandra,* "Every seeker should try to use Awareness of enlightened *chitta,* and aim at and merge with Consciousness of *chit* to reach *Brahman,* the *Purushotama.*" *Pushya* added, "Universal Intelligence or *Chit,* can target *chidakasha,* aiming to become One with Infinity."

Patanjali was pleased with these renderings, and said, "Repetition of AUM and contemplation of its meaning evokes feelings that lead the seeker to the highest state of *yoga.* The seeker can, then, understand the significance of His Word, the Universal Sound." The disciples were aware the aim of meditative practice is for Consciousness and Awareness to merge in a single experience of *chit.*

The experience should be free from the impediments of present and past, whether conscious, subconscious or unconscious. For that was the only way to the Goal into the Cosmic Being. Added *Patanjali,* "Meditation on this *Ishvara* by repeating AUM removes obstacles and leads to the unearthing of the *chitta.* This helps remove all impediments to *chit* in Selfrealisation." *Patanjali* had thus expressed the power and use of AUM as a *mantra.*

Patanjali, next elaborated upon the obstacles a seeker faces while on a spiritual journey, "These obstacles are impediments. They are physical diseases born of *inertia.* They become evident as mental doubt, carelessness, laziness and non-subjugation of the senses. Intellectual and inaccurate views of the world and causal obstacles are because of lack of perseverance to hang on to decisions. Inability to continue progress because of pride and stagnation causes sliding back." Warning his disciples that such impediments must not hinder a seeker's spiritual journey, *Patanjali* added, "These impediments are often with sorrow, despair, restlessness of the body and irregular breathing, which further distract the *chitta*."

With this, the disciples began analysing such obstacles. Starting with *Chandra*, "These obstacles and impediments come from three sources – *adhyatmika* [earthly], *adhibhautika* [astral] and *adhidevika* [heavenly]. All of these need to be conquered through *yogic* discipline."

Pakva, the most advanced of the seven gifted disciples, was quick to realise they were back where they had started. To practice *Raja Yoga*, seekers of spirituality have to practice *ashtanga yoga*. This is the only way to take care of obstacles *Patanjali* had just discussed. *Pakva* said, "Adherence to single-minded effort can prevent these impediments."

The disciples knew they were, like all seekers, subject to losses and gains made during meditation. They knew, from personal experience, that only when body, mind and intellect are fully purified is it possible to surrender to *chitta* first and then *chit*. This submission has to be without expectations. They recollected, as *Patanjali* had plainly stated, that submission to *chit* is beyond the reach of ordinary mortals. All eight steps of *Raja Yoga* should be practiced. Enduring in the *kutastha* is the only way to meet with the Being of Universal Intelligence. At their request, *Patanjali* agreed to review *ashtanga yoga*.

Patanjali began with the necessary practical groundwork.

He counted the qualities that kept mind in comfort, through control of want for indulgence. He explained when *chitta* is enmeshed in the senses, the seeker is in a web of indulgence. He urged his disciples to rejoice with the happy, and compassionate with the sad, friendly to the virtuous and indifferent to those who live in vice. Mental adjustments, through *yama* and *niyama,* were essential for a seeker's social and individual health. Following social virtues of *yama* keeps the seeker's mind serene and pure. "Through cultivation of friendliness, compassion, joy, and indifference to pleasure or pain, and virtue or vice, the *chitta* becomes favourably disposed. Live in serenity and benevolence," *Patanjali* said. He, then, commented on *asana-pranayama* saying, "The seeker can earn single-minded calmness by safeguarding the long silence at the end of expiration, as also at the end of inspiration."

At first *Pakva* recognised *pranayama* as a technique to arrive at a serene thought-free state. But by harmonizing inspiration and expiration, as well as the pauses in between, *Pakva* told the disciples, there is the experience of bliss. *Pakva* advised them to make a note of the Master who is referring to all phases of breathing.

Stabilisation and control of breath is within the range of a seeker's individual comfort zone. He reminded them that though they must watch and feel the breath with awareness they will eventually, transfer their attention into the *kutastha. Patanjali* had expected his disciples to grasp what he was saying. Only a novice, he thought, would fail to understand that he was speaking about *swasayama* becoming *pranayama.* At least twenty per cent of a physical breath is pure life force or *prana* used for energizing the physical and astral being. *Patanjali* continued, "Single-pointedness is earned by contemplating and becoming engrossed in the object of interest. Dedication and devotion keep the mind and *chitta* steady."

There was silence. To the disciples, the statement sounded ambiguous. But *Menander* elaborated, describing his own experience of *pratyahara* as a natural after-effect of *asana* and *pranayama.* "While in a comfortable *asana,* it is possible to move awareness away from body-awareness. Once entrenched in breath control, it is easy to withdraw into the *kutastha,* behind and between the eyebrows. *Swasayama* swaps to become *pranayama.* Breathed in life force enlivens the body-mind-intellect which is now in suspended animation."

"In this centre of awareness, *prana* permeates in all bodily directions. In the brainstem from the "Mouth of God" life force or *prana* energises as it travels along *nadis* or channels from seven spinal centres to seven physiological systems of the body," said *Menander.* Adding, "When the *chitta* personality is withdrawn into the centre of awareness, the senses is dormant – in *pratyahara.* There is a total loss of body-mind-intellect awareness."

"Such an existence is like being in hibernation, but fully aware," exclaimed *Saleta* excitedly.

Said *Pushya,* 'Right!' He continued, "Developing intellectual sensitivity in *chitta* depends on the integrity and intensity of concentration-contemplation in *dharana-dhyana.*" Added *Bhratahari,* "For only perfect *chitta*-clarity allows the seeker to gain this insight." Interjected *Ujjaini,* from his own experiences with the Cosmic Mother, "When the refined *chitta* is conspicuous, you find yourself face to face with *Prakriti.* Movement from Mother Nature's Awareness to the Spirit of *Purusha* is a *chit* experience."

Patanjali, pleased with their sincerity, said about *pratyahara-dharana,* "An inner stability is gained while engrossed in contemplative brilliance of the 'sorrow-free' effulgent light within the core of one's being." Hearing this, *Bhratahari* wanted to comment on his experience in concentration or *dharana,* "I have almost reached the innermost core in the *kutastha.* Sometimes it is possible to see the effulgent light of the three bodily sheaths. This reflecting "third eye" is short-lived. The mind is so engrossed with the brilliance that delving into its source is impossible. As the thought waves become still and the *chitta* becomes silent, one only sees an ocean of pure Awareness."

Pakva added, "Every seeker must learn to silence the *chitta* personality by unifying attentiveness at the *kutastha.* When the *chitta* is stilled and silenced, it unloads the "remorse-free" light of the Soul." The disciples, themselves serious practitioners, had reached the shores of the enlightening *chitta.* They sought to focus on the heart of infinitude, in the *kutastha.*

Said *Patanjąli,* about concentration-contemplation or *dharana-dhyana,* "This is done by focusing the mind. Enlightened sages who are freed of desire and attachment are calm and tranquil. Or are made so by reflecting on divine materiality."

Pakva had occasionally experienced the radiance of the *kutastha chaitanya.* Consciousness that knows itself knows others and he said, "In the *kutastha* is found the Soul. We are told we must enter It. *Chitta's* delight at this innermost vision is so engrossing that one forgets to penetrate the Light," *Pakva* said. He understands how he had failed to identify his source. He confessed, "I am still and bask in a silence where none experience thought waves. *Chitta* endures incremental enlightenment while by it. I wanted emancipation." Even as he reflected on this pure state, *Pakva* gained confidence the seeker in him would, someday, arrive at a balance. His mind will someday mature into a 'desireless' state. But for this, would his 'need' for emancipation must be erased." Having said that, *Pakva* became silent.

Said *Ujjaini,* compassionately, "Try concentrating on feeling the breath stalking in and out through the nostrils, while watching Awareness of Infinity in the *kutastha.* In the process of breathing, listen to the heavenly sound AUM rising from all spiritual centres of the divine cave. Thus removed from the physical body, remain beyond astral physiological-psychological-intellectual sheaths. You will surely reach the purity of Awareness."

It became all too obvious to the disciples that even advanced students need a compassionate teacher, and sincere brother-disciples, willing to share experiences of their obstacle and victory. *Patanjali,* happy with the encouragement, confirmed they were worthy students. He completed his commentary on contemplation-meditation or *dhyana-samadhi,* "Success is achieved by recollecting and reflecting on experiences of conscious, subconscious, unconscious and superconscious states, as a waker, dreamer, sleeper and in awareness."

With that, the Master emerged from behind the curtain. As he walked downhill from the cave, he asked the disciples to discuss his last statement. *Pakva* repeated the subject and *Menander* started first by defining *chitta,* "The *chitta* exists through four states of being. In the sleeper or *Nidra State,* a seekers experiences existence and Bliss. In the dream or *Svapna State,* he experiences wandering thoughts of present and past happenings. In the waker or *Jagrata State,* the meditating seeker witnesses rising thoughts. In deep awareness or *Chitta State* he experiences universal awareness." He paused, only to find his fellow-disciples deep in meditation. *Chandra,* for one, was oblivious to everything and was experiencing a superconscious or *turiya state.* Having channeled his thought into silence, *Chandra* had transcended all conditions into a single Awareness. He was already in *samadhi,* experiencing Oneness with the Whole.

The rest were still walking their awareness through the steps of *ashtanga yoga* that *Patanjali* had just described. Each, however, was acutely aware that individualised *chitta* was moving towards self-unfoldment and soul awareness. The *chitta's* desire is to merge with the *chit.* Said *Pakva,* suddenly, "Even in deeper and deeper meditation, one is able to identify various states and levels of awareness." There was another long spell of silence, as *Menander* and *Pakva* lapsed into a collective trance.

As *Patanjali* walked back to the cave, returning from

Malini's hut he noticed an absence of the usual chatter of discussions. Intrigued, he reached the cave and found his disciples deep in meditation. *Saleta* stirred, because he was finding it difficult to concentrate on the void filled with *On Contemplation*

Patanjali smiled within himself as he walked back to the cave. He wanted all his disciples to experience oneness in *samadhi.* He knew they were swinging between two depths of oneness – *sabija samadhi* and *nirbija samadhi.* Because *Patanjali* wanted to continue discussions, he stepped behind the curtain. As he sat, he cleared his throat, making known the session is to begin.

Some disciples had stilled their minds and felt rejuvenated. They were refreshingly receptive for the Master to begin. For the benefit of *Saleta,* who had difficulty concentrating on objectless AUM in a void, *Patanjali* spoke as if he had not paused. "Or, meditate by fixing attention on any object that is conducive to steadiness of awareness," said *Patanjali,* outlining a steadying meditation technique using objective contemplation. *Patanjali* knew *Saleta* would benefit from this technique. The rest of the apostles seemed comfortable with subjective meditation.

Said *Menander,* "O Master, you have described first six steps to reach Consciousness through *ashtanga yoga.* You have repeatedly highlighted we know whatever exists through the senses. Sensing through nearness and informational input are only the triggers. If all of this and all of that is pervaded by AUM within and without, why do some of us find it difficult to reach our core?"

Added *Saleta,* almost pleading, "By stilling and silencing the *chitta,* we expect to discover, within ourselves, the living Supreme Spirit. It promises us the experience of limitless, unchanging, all-knowing happiness. Why is it so difficult to stabilize the thought-free mind in Awareness? Master, if the Supreme lingers in the sea of my heart, why does it engage in camouflage?"

Patanjali was silent. His mother qualified this – Man's quest, repeatedly. Finding the Supreme within is the ultimate goal as well as every mortal's struggle. He too had experienced the Supreme, but had witnessed the suffering, the pain of birth, growth, decay, pleasure and separation. He observed with anguish the short-lived presence of his beloved mother *Gonika.* She had given him the Crowning Knowledge of Matter and Spirit. She ensured the teachings of *Raja Yoga* would continue for posterity. Like his mother, *Patanjali* felt compelled to pass on what he had learned. To live effectively as a mortal, his disciples must learn the process. By now, he knew about his past life as *Shesha.* He wished to return home. But his commitment to his disciples was not as yet achieved. He knew he must encourage them to meditate on the Supreme in the heart and in the *kutastha.*

Pakva, like the others, was familiar with the *Vedic* tradition of finding the spiritual heart in this space in the chest. His mother had taught him the spiritual heart is comparable to an inverted lotus bud. As long as Man is engrossed in 'senses' and seeks external pleasure, his heart remains like an inverted lotus bud at night, turning away from the light of the Sun.

Pakva interrupted *Patanjali's* thoughts, "By turning away from distractions of materialism, we should enter the chambers of our hearts, where the lotus can become a heliotrope, ready to receive Life from the Divine Sun?"

Added *Chandra,* "The forest monks told us the space below the throat and above the navel is territory of the Total Universe." *Pushya* recalled this too, "I remember them telling us the narrow space within of the spinal cord near the heart exists the *sushumna nadi* and it supports every faculty of body-mind-intellect."

Said *Ujjaini,* "When the mind enters this space through *yoga,* the seeker intuitively senses the Cosmic Being, the source of the entire universe."

Continued *Chandra*, "The monks explained to us the middle of this space, between the heart and the *sushumna*, is occupied by the non-decaying, all-knowing, multifaceted Fire of *Prana..*" Chimed in *Pushya*, "They also spoke of flames coming from every side. This Fire enjoys the food Man presents to it. Assimilated food is then delivered like spreading rays, vertically and horizontally." The royal brothers were immersed in each other's thoughts.

Menander was intrigued with this explanation of *prana* that controls the physiological-psychological-intellectual workings of the body. *Bhratahari* unexpectedly remembered his previous life as an illiterate devotee of *Shiva*. He was told by an aged monk, "The centre of Fire permeates the whole body. From the core, the blaze of Fire dazzles like a flash of lightning. The Soul remains in the middle of this flame. Though limited, this Fire is the Trinity of *Brahma, Vishnu* and *Shiva*, who are the material and efficient cause of both Man and the Universe. They are also Supreme Pure Consciousness."

Chandra also recalled the monks describe the Supreme as the orb of the Sun. "Its Light is AUM. Its Fire is the flame-like radiance of *Prana*. According to the monks, these can be realised by purifying *Chitta*," said *Chandra*. Finally, *Pakva* said, "Competence over the *chitta* is a powerful feat, even if told through children's stories. Once it is controlled, disciples of the Truth transform every atom of its expression. The purity of awareness allows penetration of atom, as well as, the mighty Cosmos." *Chandra* added, "Pure transformed *chitta* can penetrate space and the deepest regions within, according to the monks."

From behind the curtain, *Patanjali* finally said, "Mastery in contemplation fetches powers over the finest particle to the largest mountain." The disciples were silent. *Patanjali* confirmed their many stories and discussions on purifying the *chitta*. Understanding heightens as veils strip away ignorance, stage-by-stage, layer-by-layer. *Patanjali* continued, "The *yogi* realises the 'Knower' Spirit, eleven instruments of 'Knowing' [the five senses, five organs of action and *chitta]* and the 'Known' Nature, are one and the same. He realises, he alone, is the one unified 'seer'. Like a transparent crystal, he can then reflect unsullied purity."

Pakva and *Pushya* began another discussion, showing the disciples had come a full circle. They began by asserting the human form is comprised of three bodies [physical-astral-causal] and five sheaths [physical-physiological-psychological-intellectual-causal]. They moved to talk about the unenlightened *chitta* that requires enlightening through meditation. Finally, they talked about Universal Intelligence, as *chit.*

Chandra and *Pushya* moved towards comparing opinions about the lively *Prana* as a Fire that controlled all bodily works and the Energy of Matter. These were ideas introduced to them when they were children. Intuitively, *Ujjaini* reminded the disciples, "It takes refinement, through intense practice of *ashtanga yoga,* for *chitta* to become stainless, pure and sensitive." And *Menander* added, "Unless all these bodies and sheaths are made to merge, it is impossible to experience the Perceiver who watches, Perception that merely looks and Perceiving Knowledge. All should be One. This merger comes together in the 'seer' alone."

Commented *Chandra,* "This merging and transparency of the enlightened *chitta* is *samapattih.*" At this, *Pushya* added, "I prefer to call this state *samadhi* because it radiates its own pure state."

Saleta, however, was silent. He was wondering if the enlightened *Chitta* state "the newfound Self" personality is like experiencing the Soul. *Saleta* scrutinized *Patanjali* over these many days and to him, *Patanjali* embodied truth, purity and love. This gave *Patanjali* subtle, but substantial, clues to the questions the students were asking. *Saleta* thought, "The nature of such true sages is transparent and possessed of flawless awareness." He decided he needed more time to think through his own statements before attainment of the Truth.

As the disciples pondered over *Patanjali's* words, *Pushya* quoted the *Bhagavad Gita*, "*Krishna* declares in the *Gita*, "Under my presidency, my Nature performs. Through the processes of self-referral, the transformed mortal expresses all natural laws of *Prakriti*". That is how *Krishna* declares his might and transparency."

Patanjali was pleased with the depth of knowledge. He said, "At this stage of *savikalpa samadhi*, its meaning and content mingle to become 'special' knowledge in a harmonious blend of understanding. The seeker, therefore, is engrossed in this new knowledge – its understanding becomes a logical conclusion."

The disciples understood. They had reached a refined state of awareness under the Master's tutelage, where words and their meaning blend into a fresh understanding. It becomes a new wisdom, with which they become preoccupied. Amongst the layers that cloud their refined *chitta*, there remain veils, each of which must be separated and understood by intense concentration and contemplation or *dharana-dhyana*. The disciples realised that as long as these solutions are inadequate, they must face problems of manifestation of past births.

But *Patanjali* addressed a cure for this obstacle, "In *nirvitarka samapattih*, the difference between memory and intellectual illumination is disclosed. When memory is cleaned, *chitta* shines without any reflection."

Chandra realised that cleansing and erasing is needed for mind to be purified of *smriti*. In meditation, the mind and memory have to stop working as distinct entities. The seeker must reach a "no-mind-no-memory" state. Only then will Awareness manifest itself in an unblemished state, without any reflection or recollections of objects and thoughts. *Chandra* thought, "That would be *nirvitarka samapattih,* where awareness needs no logic for expansion." *Pushya* interrupted Chandra's thoughts, saying, "*Smriti* is a storehouse of all recollection, whether of past thoughts, experiences, even past impressions. It is difficult to sublimate *smriti*!"

Saleta said, "Memory is reflected knowledge and impacts the intellect. Unless *chitta* is purified, it is impossible to arrive at a transparent intellect." *Pakva,* however, saw no problem in clearing the mind of its memory bank. He said, "Through intense practice of *yoga,* new experiences replace old ones. And these new understandings are free of memories. They can then purge memories. Once memory ends as a separate entity, it merges with awareness and gives prominence to new experiences." Agreed *Menander,* "A strategy such as this, to erase old thoughts and memories through deeper meditation, would bring clarity to the intellect."

Pushya finally agreed. Purging *chitta* by discrimination would separate bad habits of faulty opinion. He said, "Through *asana* and *pranayama,* a new virtuous character is built. The body and brain then, move together because there is integrity between them." All this time, *Saleta* was leaning against the *peepal* tree, listening to the others distinguish intellect from intelligence. Then there was the effect of memory on an intellect's transparency. He decided old memory supports Man's unenlightened *chitta.* If old memory is erased, new recollections gained during meditation will work on a transparent intellect. Now a purified intellect becomes his true *guru.*

Patanjali was listening in with great interest, and was, at the same time, aware of *Saleta's* private thoughts. He said, "Through this transformation of awareness by contemplation on ego, the intellect is deliberately cleared of doubts in *savichara samapattih.*"

The disciples understood *Patanjali*. He spoke of inner contemplation. Intellectual reasoning leads to awareness of self-luminosity. Its characteristic vibrancy or *rajas* of Nature within becomes *sattvic* or dormant. Inner understanding of Man's new conditioning leads to awareness of space, time and cause. Of course, this realisation is beyond words and is very personal. In *savichara samapattih*, transformation of awareness happens through observation and reflection during *asana, pranayama, pratyahara, dharana* and *dhyana*. In *nirvichara samapattih*, the experienced transformation stifles *savichara samapattih*.

The disciples realise that *Raja Yoga* takes the body and brain on a return journey towards integrity. At the end of this journey, the seeker is promised the bliss of *ananda*. But the tainted *chitta* experiences egoism or *asmita*.

As they heard *Patanjali*, the disciples became increasingly pensive. For the Master spoke of matters that could be understood, realised and experienced only through an inner intuitive understanding.

Said *Patanjali*, "The subtlest part of *Prakriti* is intelligence as Awareness. When qualities dissolve in Nature, it loses every stain and becomes unadulterated." At this juncture, the disciples had less to say and more to think about. The Master asked them to delve deep into themselves, beyond Matter's envelopment. Only by exploring the subtlest particles of Nature can they reach their goal. For that, there must be an ending to all swings of the mind, intellect and ego.

Only then can they arrive at the subtlest state of the primal intellect, the *mahat*. When meditation hushes ego in the *chitta, Prakriti* achieves Her end and merges with *Purusha* to become Intelligence or *chit*. Matter and Spirit become Universal Intelligence experienced in the *kutastha*. The disciples knew this would be a subjective experience. They realized their understanding has reached crossroads of self-unfoldment for Self-realisation.

Pakva broke the silence, as the disciple in him desired to realise this Awareness, with a seed of "I-ness", as well as 'desireless' Awareness. *Pakva* felt these are two states of the mind. He also felt the experience of *samadhi* is a function of the intellect.

Patanjali clarified, "So far, all writings have referred to *samadhi,* as hinging on the support of a seed, termed *sabija.*" There was silence again. The stillness of the body and the silence of emotion and thought, including ego or *asmita,* has to be a role of the brain, they thought.

The disciples turned to *Menander,* the physician, to explain this subject since he has dealt with it in his past. *Menander* understood that experience of the six *sampattis* or virtues is born at specific anatomical locations of the brain. Said *Menander,* "Logic or *savitarka,* and even non-inquiry or *nirvitarka,* are tasks of the frontal lobe, which is also concerned with memory, intelligence, sex-drive, foresight, insight, mood and logic."

"For inquiry or *savichara,* or even non-inquiry or *nirvichara,* the resource is the back of the brain, in the occipital lobe. *Ananda* or bliss is experienced at the base of the brain, in the limbic cortex of the temporal lobe." *Menander* then pointed out the location of *asmita,* or individuality. "The 'I' – state is on the top of the brain," he said, "Here, at the fontanel, on the top of the brain in the parietal lobe, lives the pure Self!"

Ujjaini and *Pushya* understood that it was impossible to unify the four quarters of the brain and their virtues or *samapattis* without intense practice at *ashtanga yoga.* "Only through determined *yogic* practice can the physical atom be transformed to thought essence," said *Ujjaini.*

Added *Menander,* "The seeker thus reaches the summit of his own Nature, as a single thought or seed. He can, then, control all of awareness. He also stops the brain's oscillations at will."

"This, we agree, is *samadhi* with seed, or *sabija samadhi*. In this state, the petals of the lotus unfold. The Sun of Awareness rises," *Pakva* said.

Saleta was pensive. He said, at length, "The petals of the lotus, the *sahasrahara* in the brain, unfolds while the seeker is awake, and closes when he retreats to the centre of the brain-stem."

Pushya came to a sudden realisation, and exclaimed, "Once the seeker has retreated from the brain's works and remains in the brain-stem, causal seed-thought, too, stop."

'This,' said *Saleta,* completely understanding *Pushya's* outburst, "is *nirbija samadhi.*" Asserted *Chandra,* "If we can get to this level, we would be on the threshold of Final Emancipation."

Said *Pakva,* as if in protest, "If stagnating at this level means remaining at a threshold, one only conquers the elements of earth, water, fire, air and space." And added *Chandra,* in line with *Pakva's* thought, "If the seeker plunges into his past, he reenters the web of pleasure and pain. But if he crosses over, *chitta* merges into *Chit,* and he reaches freedom and beatitude."

Patanjali was delighted with this intellectual drama. The disciples had to conquer the impulsion and compulsion of Nature, and realise the truth of their understanding. "With proficiency in *nirvichara samapattih* comes purity. When *sattva's* luminosity flows undisturbed, it kindles the spiritual light of *chitta,*" said *Patanjali.*

The disciples understood. When intellect and awareness wait at the non-reflective *kutastha chaitanya,* the vehicle of the soul illumines spontaneously. Knowledge and understanding of *chitta's* real state is then obvious as the luminosity of Consciousness. *Patanjali* clarified this idea, "When awareness remains in wisdom, there is a direct spiritual view of Man's true state of being. He has earned this spiritual wisdom. The enlightened *chitta* is observable in insight and powerful luminosity. This great knowledge and wisdom emanates from Truth. It is different from and is beyond the knowledge Man gains, through books, testimony and inference."

The seven disciples agreed that wisdom is 'earned' only through insight. *Pakva* commented, "Such knowledge springs from an intuitive knowing of *chitta.*"

"Wisdom is also gained by listening to the vibrating inner *pranava* of AUM," said *Pushya.*

"This is a *sattvic* intellect," added *Menander.*

"Nature's Total Will, in this state, instinctively guides such changed seekers," said *Ujjaini.*

Chandra added, "An evolved seeker senses and recognises no duality."

Said *Patanjali,* seeking to further describe this state of being, "A new life begins, ingrained with truth-bearing wisdom. Previous impressions are left behind. New impressions are not allowed to emerge. All that was wished before is lost. Any new desire is cancelled. All doubt is resolved. *Chitta* is clear, pure and serene."

Patanjali paused. Did the Master have more to say, wondered the disciples? Indeed he did.

Patanjali continued, "When this new light or thought of wisdom is also surrendered, seedless *samadhi* dawns."

With that, *Patanjali* had ended the day's session. The disciples were unaware an entire day had passed in discussion. What they did realise, however, is that they must learn to restrain even new impressions. *Pushya* mentally reinforced the Master's assertion. One reaches *nirbija samadhi* only when both old and new impressions are dissolved. *Saleta* realised that insights must be restrained also. Thought-flames need smothering in all the states of expression, whether waking, dreaming, or in blissful sleep. The 'Me' displaying as unenlightened *chitta* and 'I' revealing as enlightened *chitta* must be stifled, without a trace. Awareness as enlightened *chitta* must merge with *Purusha's*

Spirit of Consciousness to become Universal Intelligence or *chit.* This is to be found in the *Christ/Krishna* Centre in the *kutastha.* Enduring here for a long time in meditation is the path to the Cosmic Being in *chidakasha.*

Book Two – On Practice

Sadhana Pada

Patanjali had exposed his disciples to the *sadhana* of *yogic* self-discipline. He outlined how a balanced mind is essential in reaching the state of an enlightened *chitta.* He was pleased with the quality of his seven disciples. Together, they strengthened unfolding each other's thoughts through natural adaptation. They also realised they could not consider themselves 'evolved' students, despite their extensive learning. The science of *Vedanta* is too subtle. They understood they must always learn by starting from the beginning, even if the purpose is completed time and again. *Patanjali* stressed they must start with basics of *sadhana* and work towards freeing oneself from oppression of humankind. He prescribed repetitive practice or *abhyas,* and uninterrupted spiritual practice or *sadhana.* He took them through pitfalls faced along journeys of self-effort.

Patanjali insisted that *abhyas* and dispassion or *vairagya* were musts, if one seeks to still swings of thought. Seekers disbelieve the power of meditative practice, he said, because they encounter confusion caused by impressions embedded in the subconscious and unconscious minds. Students are familiar with this sense of unbalance, despite sincere spiritual practice. For uninterrupted meditation, *Patanjali* recommended all seekers, whether admitted or not, must begin with the basics, again and again, for reorientation with the Goal. He also outlined that a comeback compels a review of the basics of this science. Identification of human credentials is also necessary for successful meditation.

With the discipline on *sadhana, Patanjali* told the disciples to discover the identity of their inclinations and dislodge them, a few at a time. Through the practice of *yama,* the first limb of *ashtanga yoga,* each disciple teaches himself and develops honest humane living, said *Patanjali. Niyama* cleans the *chitta* personality of impurities embedded in the human psyche. Steady postures of *asana* relieve seekers of physical and mental disarray. Simultaneously this stabilises him in the divine cave of brain and spinal cord. *Patanjali* insisted *pranayama* prevents scattering of *prana*. By transfiguring mind into quietness at its core, it becomes competent for meditation. *Pratyahara* is an automatic conquering of senses and mind when immersed in *pranayama*. Transforming physical atoms to energy and life force or *prana* is the purpose of *pranayama* as opposed to *swasayama*.

When these deliberations ended, silence had enveloped the valley. The evening had a fresh crispness. The disciples followed *Patanjali* to *Malini Amma's* cottage for dinner. Having eaten nothing after breakfast, they were all famished. *Amma* welcomed them. She served them a hot meal of rice-lentil gruel or *khichri* and yogurt soup or *kadhi*. A few fresh vegetables on the side made it a meal fit for a King!

Over dinner, *Patanjali* told them the next session would begin the following morning. As they ate, the disciples realised they were in for a treat. *Amma* was hiding a steaming pot full of wonder. She prepared an unanticipated milk pudding or *kheer*. The two cows in the *ashram* were generous giving them milk this day. The meal was eaten in silence, punctuated with the noise of dining together. *Malini Amma* scurried around to make sure everyone was fed.

Saleta asked suddenly, "Why do so few take to spiritual training?"

The question stopped *Malini Amma* in her tracks. Though she continued to stir gently the *kheer*, her thoughts went back in time. When married to *Chitrakacha*, a *yogi* who preferred to live in the forest preoccupied with *sadhana*, *Malini* refused to recognise her husband's ways. Inexperienced, isolated and lonely, *Malini's* passionate needs drove her into a young hunter's arms. One day, after his morning dip in the river, *Chitrakacha* returned home to find *Malini* in the hunter's embrace. Enraged, *Chitrakacha* said, "I banish you from your marital home, woman. May you wander the forests as a hunter woman!" Though he said this quietly, the enormity of this curse stunned *Malini*. She begged forgiveness. Said *Chitrakacha,* dismissing her with finality, "You will live until *Shesha* himself forgives you. Only then will you be able to leave this mortal coil you presently occupy!"

With that, *Chitrakacha* walked away. *Malini,* filled with remorse and sorrow, spent months wandering the groves. She needed shelter. Where was she to find *Shesha*? One day stranded in a storm, it rapidly became dark, before she could find shelter. Forced to look for safety, she singled out a *ber* tree. Its ripe fruit had fallen in plenty all around. She ate them and thanked the Lord. Enervated by exhaustion she fell asleep under the generous fruit tree. By daybreak, the squall had passed and skies cleared. *Malini* explored her surroundings. She found the *ber* tree had a large deep hollow she could call home. A nearby, a river gurgled a welcome. She now had home, shelter and food in the safety of the fruit bearing tree.

Malini stopped wandering the woods and settled into her intended home. She unpacked her tiny bundle of belongings and washed her hair and clothes. As she sat down for breakfast of berries, she saw a group of *sadhus* or monks clearing an area of the forest. As the eight *sadhus* toiled, sweat dripped from their bodies to the ground.

Suddenly, a voice from the interior of the deep forest, said, "May every drop of sweat that lands on this earth you so lovingly clear for me, turn to ever-blooming fragrant flowers." It was *Matangi,* an old sage who had spent decades in penance to erase his own demonic tendencies. In fact, this forest was acclaimed for its distinguished inhabitant. Even as *Malini* marveled at the *sadhus'* focused effort and at *Matangi's* approval, she realised she had found her Master. Understanding her remorse and her need for forgiveness, *Matangi* agreed to let her stay in her fruit tree. He taught *Malini ashtanga yoga.* She cooked for and served the *sadhus* of his *ashram.*

One day, *Matangi* sent for her. As she entered his hut, he said, "Sit, my child." *Malini's* mind was racing. She had a worried look on her face. *Matang* laughed, *"Malini,* I am now old. You too, have aged with me. My time has come. I leave this body tomorrow. Before that happens, I want you to go to *Gonika's ashram."* *Malini's* heart sank. She was gripped with fear. Would she again have to wander the forest to crack the curse? Would she have to flounder again? *Matangi* read her thoughts, and said, "Do not be alarmed. I have arranged for you to serve *Gonika Amma* and the *sadhus* who live in the Himalayan caves. My child, there you will meet *Shesha.* You will find your deliverance there." With that, *Matangi* stood up and walked away. A young *sadhu* assigned to take *Malini* to her next home stood outside. She followed him through the forest, down valleys and over the mountains. She finally arrived at the cave where *Gonika* and little *Patanjali,* then a two-year old, lived.

Now, as she stirred the *kheer, Malini* remembered the patter of little feet and the jingle of his tiny anklets. She smiled to herself as she remembered little *Patanjali.* And she saw *Gonika* in her mind, encouraging *Patanjali* to walk to the beat of the tinkle of his anklets. *Patanjali* was quick to learn, but intolerant of his clumsy child-body.

The disciples had finished their meal. *Menander* interrupted *Malini's* thoughts, "*Amma,* is the dessert ready yet?" It had been a couple of minutes since *Saleta* had posed a question earlier. But *Malini* had just relived a lifetime of space and time. She smiled, and served dessert. *Menander* exclaimed gratefully, "This is delicious!"

Malini repeated *Saleta's* question to herself. "Who, indeed, is fit to embark on the spiritual path?" She knew from her own experience that both teacher and disciple must have certain qualifications. She wondered what *Patanjali* would say. *Patanjali* answered, "A burning need to practice, self-study, analysing the scriptures and surrendering to God are all acts of *yoga."* Again, there was silence. After he finished his meal, *Patanjali* thanked *Amma* and walked back to his cavern. The disciples conformed with the Master's move. The next day would see a new area for discussion, and debate.

After the meal, *Malini* completed her routine tasks and went to bed. She realised she had seen *Gonika* coach her students, as she now sees *Patanjali* with his apostles. She also knew *Patanjali* as a disciple. When admitted into *yogic* practice *Gonika* impressed on self-restraint, self-study and scriptural learning or *svadhyaya.*

Now the teacher *Patanjali* made sure his disciples learned how to stabilise the mind, and purify the body, speech and mind. He demanded they use the three paths to spirituality – *karma yoga, gyana yoga* and *bhakti yoga.* Through *karma yoga,* a disciplined life of service in a spirit of renunciation and surrender would transform the body, mind and intellect. Through *gyana yoga,* they could inculcate study of the scriptures or *svadhyaya.* It would help them withdraw from the surface into the Inner Being.

And finally, through *bhakti yoga,* self-surrender or *pranidhana,* should loosen the grip of ego. *Chitta* would surrender to Self-will. Thus empowered by control over their daily lives and enlightened by inner understanding, the ego transforms. Focus on Inner Light, of the *kutastha,* becomes easier.

The next day began with a sunrise. The seven disciples were eager to start. It was chilly and as always, they clustered together, wrapping themselves with cloaks. The hill women wove the shawls from wool of mountain goats on looms. Beyond the curtain, *Patanjali* sat on the slab. He started where they had left off the previous evening, "The practice of *yoga* lessens the body's afflictions and leads to absorption or *samadhi.*" He, then, asked the disciples to discuss the need for strict and intense spiritual practice, as described and taught in *ashtanga yoga.* Started *Pakva,* "The eight steps are to downgrade all obstacles to meditation, be they physical, physiological, psychological-intellectual or causal."

Pushya added, "The practice involves a *yoga* described in many an aphorism or *sutra* in the *Vedas.* Obeying the rules of restraint and to their adherence or *yama-niyama* allow seekers to control lust and yearn for sensibility. Once reprogrammed the practice of action without wish for fruit or *karma yoga* becomes easier. Self-propelling transformation in personality results from surrender and giving up of fruits of action." He paused to clear his throat, and continued, "Energising and healing *mudras* or yogic exercises with *asanas* belong to realms of *hatha yoga.* This is especially thought for those who need taming the material body."

"*Pranayama* and *pratyahara* are also practices of *hatha yoga,*" *Chandra* reminded *Pushya,* who nodded consent, but said, "What we are discussing here is *gyana yoga.* The 'self' realising it is the Self is the purpose of *yoga* of knowledge."

Said *Ujjaini,* "Master *Patanjali's ashtanga yoga* anchors seekers to wisdom and intuition through *gyana yoga,* but it takes *bhakti yoga* to continue the search."

"The eightfold *ashtanga yoga* is a *Raja Yoga,*" said *Menander* impatiently, "It draws from all four *yogas.*"

"Through deepening *pranayama,* withdrawing bodily senses and mind into the inner core is *pratyahara.* Seekers still their bodies and sheaths and enter silence. There they hear the *pranava* – AUM," proclaimed *Ujjaini,* his eyes shut but feeling his inspiratory breath extinguishing in the *kutastha.* There was no expiratory breath as he withdrew above the *kutastha.*

Ujjaini stilled his normal heartbeat and breathing. He sat peacefully, but seemed dispossessed of all life. The other disciples watched this, quietly. *Saleta* marveled silently at the sight. *Bhratahari* commented, "*Ujjaini* has crawled away and remains suspended in the centre of Awareness." *Menander,* the learned doctor, confirmed the autonomic nervous system governing breathing and heartbeat can be deliberately controlled with intense *pranayama.*

Said *Menander*, "Synchronised breath dedicated at the nerve confluence of the hypothalamus, below the centre of awareness in the *kutastha,* is the secret of absorption. The milk of life, *prana* is drawn off Nature's oxygen, to enliven the body at each inspiration."

Exclaimed *Saleta*, "*Prana* in breath is the sinew that fastens Man to Cosmic Mother!" He could not fully understand this scientific fact *Menander* had just summarized, but was happy with what he achieved in understanding.

Said *Bhratahari*, "This knowledge on 'breath-offering' is also how *chitta*-personality reaches significance." *Saleta* added, "Breathlessness defines *svadhyaya* – a perfected learning of knowledge. Submission to learning from a Master and scriptures is hastened by remaining out of flow of air."

Pushya said, "Only devotion or *bhakti* for this wisdom has the authority to approve merits of contemplation or *dhyana*. To experience Self the self needs trust and devotion also. Unless seekers reach the shores of a causal seed-state, it is impossible to achieve self-transformation." At this, *Menander* reminded them that meditation involves the scientific processing of the body-mind-intellect. Unifying thought already intrinsic in four lobes of the brain needs practice. Unless they experience an ascent into the centre of Universal Intelligence in the pineal gland and into the spiritual heart, the thoughtless state of *samadhi* remains a fiction. *Menander* said, none can hope or merely wish to enfeeble physical, mental and intellectual obstacles that enshrine the soul.

As the discussion continued, *Pushya* became silent. The disciples turned towards him. His silence appeared unbearably long. Suddenly, *Pushya* snapped out of his preoccupation and let out a heart rending plea "O Death, do not cut off our lives just yet. Let not poor health cripple us. While living in the luxuriant lap of your blessed mountains, O Cosmic Mother, may we not falter. Let us not be subjected to privation while we offer our oblations. For all of us, I beg Death to tarry until all have succeeded. May we meet Oneness with the Universal Being."

In the cave, *Patanjali* too was strikingly subdued. He heard the prayer. He shifted in his cavern but remained silent. The curtain fluttered carelessly in the breeze. The disciples could see his unmoving feet. After a long pause, *Patanjali* listed the afflictions or *kleshas* that imprint on spiritual journeys. Said *Patanjali,* "Five afflictions disturb the equilibrium in Awareness-ignorance or lack of wisdom, Ego about 'Me' and 'I', attachment to wish motivated pleasure, distaste to pain and fear of death. A tenacious attachment to living is the motivation for such behaviour."

Pakva sat up straight. He realised he was given a recipe to spiritual success. Inspired, *Pakva* opened the discussion, stating the Master had listed five thought disturbances or *vrittis* that were, five *kleshas* embedded in Man's psyche. He mentally analysed these afflictions and said, "These *kleshas* occur from three levels – intellectual, emotional and instinctive." *Menander* quickly added, "They originate from the four lobes of the brain."

Interrupted *Bhratahari,* "Early understanding comes from the frontal lobe. Logical reasoning is made in the occipital lobe. The seat of memories of habits is in the temporal-lingular lobes. And the seat of individuality is in the parietal lobe. Have I understood anatomy of the brain correctly, *Menander*?"

Menander nodded, continuing, "*Avidya* or ignorance and *asmita* or "I-ness" are intellectual afflictions of the frontal lobe. The seat of true I-Consciousness is found on top of the brain, in the parietal lobe." *Pushya,* the royal renunciant who had no medical knowledge, asked, "But where do thoughts of likes-and-dislikes and habits of past births rest? Please show exactly where such thoughts spring from." He had recovered from his earlier outburst.

Answered *Menander,*. pointing to his head above and between the ears, "These are thoughts of an emotional mind. The plane of *raaga-dvesha* and habits from past births are etched in the depths of the brain, within the temporal-lingular lobes."

At this, *Chandra* let out a soft moan and asked, "Deep within the brain?" And *Saleta* complained, "No wonder Man continues to be a victim of his yearnings, since it is so deeply embedded in his brain."

Bhratahari added, woefully, "Man performs under the spell of subconscious expressions – hatred for what he does not like, and attraction for what he likes." However, he added with enthusiasm, "I guess the secret of this affliction is profound. Man must relearn to love the Cosmic Mother. Until he makes the Cosmic Connection with Her Universal Body, Man will remain an orphan in his mother's womb. Until this connection happens, *raaga-dvesha* cannot dissolve. Once resolved, the opportunity to serve the Cosmic Mother becomes a privilege."

"Such mental agitation, causing disharmony between body and mind, cause psychosomatic diseases," warned *Menander,* "Such afflictions originate in the hypothalamus, the nucleus in the midbrain, controlled by the planet *Chandra.*"

After *Pushya's* outburst for Existence – at least until Man has experienced Self-realisation – *Saleta* asked, "Did *Pushya's* plea come from an instinctive clinging for earthly life or *abhinivesha*? Does such a plea lead to cynicism when exchanging ideas with others? Does desire to live longer make Man selfish and self-centred?"

Answered *Menander,* "This affliction, or desire for long life, is tied to the causal centres of the brain, within the medulla." Added *Pakva,* who logically identified this person's anatomy, even though he had no medical training, "This part of the brain is an unconscious brain."

"But it retains past birth-impressions or *samskaras.*

Therefore, they are obstacles to meditative effort," *Pushya* was quick to point out. *Chandra* came up with a logical conclusion, "If the brain's four lobes are combined into a single experience in the brainstem, seekers must meet with thoughtless superconsciousness. Where is Universal Intelligence experienced?"

Laughed *Ujjaini,* "Very good, *Chandra.* A logical conclusion to an anatomical discussion."

Menander replied, "The union of Matter and Spirit is experienced as Universal Intelligence or *chit.* The star in the *kutastha* is the entrance to this domain, which is in the pineal gland.

Patanjali listened carefully to discussions on types of thoughts that cause disturbance. Medical facts about roles of the brain gave the discussions a scientific breakdown. Said *Patanjali,* "Ignorance about self and Self or *avidya* is the source and arena of all pain and sorrow, whether dormant, attenuated, interrupted, halted, or fully active." He wanted the disciples to move away from the anatomical brain. *Patanjali* had already given *avidya* the status of "consecrated" place or *kshetram* for human affliction, revealing as arrogance, desire, attraction-aversion and a thirst for living.

Said *Pakva,* "But these are the high places or *uttaresham* of imbedded tendencies within the causal being. They might be dormant or *prasupta,* attenuated or *tanu,* hidden or*vichinna* or active or *udaranam.* They are still hindrances, because they disturb inner peace, even when a seeker is in an advanced state of transformation. They say even mighty sages have been disturbed by such afflictions."

"Make no mistake," said *Menander,* "These are errors and tendencies ingrained into Man's psyche as habits. Seekers who fail to reassess such errors in understanding leave themselves open to problems while on a spiritual journey."

Said *Patanjali,* "Every doubt has to be resolved in the

pursuit of *sadhana.*" The disciples became silent, realising only discriminating intellects make resolutions to correct every opinion. Once armed with knowledge or *vidya,* wisdom or *vigyana* adapts thoughts with actions. Continued *Patanjali,* "Mistaking the transient for the permanent, the impure for pure, pain for pleasure and the not-self for the real Self – all this is termed *avidya.*" After a pause, he added, "*Asmita* is mistakenly identified as *chitta* by the body, the mind and the instruments of awareness."

The disciples slipped into deep thought until *Menander* broke the silence, "When the unenlightened *chitta,* as 'Me', identifies with the physical body, the *chitta* personality smells, tastes, sees, hears and touches. The seeker's intellect or *buddhi* naturally directed by false understanding of the frontal lobes gets support from a reasoning occipital lobe. The seeker experiences a false reality from the temporal-lingular lobes, and the ego settles with a misleading identity with its eleven senses – meaning the five senses, five organs of action and the mind. This "I-ness" or *asmita* displays the *chitta* personality of the ego from the parietal lobe."

Saleta was thinking about how Man loses his way. He then thought aloud, "Why, indeed, does Man fall by the wayside and suffer the pains of reincarnation, and endure the Law of Cause and Effect?"

Patanjali answered, "Pleasure leads to desire, which has an emotional attachment to Man's likes. And unhappiness leads to hatred."

There was a pause, and *Chandra* opened the next discussion. He said, "Pleasurable experiences ignite desire and a sense of attraction for things." Interjected *Bhratahari,* "And fulfillment of these wants must create attachments."

Responded *Chandra,* "So Man forgets himself when he is on the path of indulgence. Eventually, he gets enmeshed in the sorrow of bodily illnesses." With this, *Chandra* had identified how a perfect body becomes susceptible to rapid bodily decay. Decided *Saleta,* "Preoccupied with a sickly body, mind and intellect, Man has no time to self-unfold."

Ujjaini, after deep thought, finally said, "*Raaga* is a *karma,* an action. It is a natural, innate tendency to perform, for material gain and pleasure." *Chandra* agreed, and *Ujjaini* continued with his train of thought, "It is born of ingrained past habits and energised by the radiance of awareness. Man can either turn inwards, towards the Light of Sun as AUM – or misuse the radiance of the sun or life force *prana,* for extrovert pleasure and personal gain."

"Man is free to turn either to his inner *guru* for peace, or outwards for material awareness," said *Pakva,* adding, "*Krishna,* in the *Bhagavad Gita,* clarifies that Man justifies both these. Both can be restated as duty."

Saleta interjected, "Interaction with the outer world, almost always, causes pain, sorrow and misery. And this is bound to trigger a chain of *raaga* and *dvesha.*" *Saleta,* who still remembered how 'pleasures he could have had' tormented him and saw them as ideas of desire that were yet unfulfilled. He confided that, sometimes, he is overcome by feelings – hating himself, his family, his neighbours and his surroundings. He is, in those moments, overcome by a sense of worthlessness. The Master had defined *dvesha* as aversion to something that brought suffering. He called it a reactively disagreeable response to names, forms and situations. As he reminded the group of this, *Pakva,* the most discriminating of the disciples, cautioned *Saleta,* "In such situations, the right attitude is to apply one's discriminative free choice. Follow and decide what is right and best for oneself. A discriminating person can balance his life between contentment or *sukha* and sorrow or *dukha.* A discriminating person does not have to live life at the mercy of compulsions of pain or pleasure."

Menander preferred to talk about Man's love for long life or *abhinivesha.* His scientific mind had analysed this habitual thought. Love for *abhinivesha* is supported by a wish for materialistic pleasure. He said, "Attachment to life is helped by one's own life force or *prana.*"

Added *Pushya,* "The urge is self-perpetuating. It can be so strong that it does not spare even the Wise. Each one of us has sampled death in previous lives. The seed of fear of mortal death is ingrained in the causal personality. Little wonder, then, the wish to keep living is so strong."

Behind the curtain, *Patanjali* was pleased with this progress, for he could now discuss an innate affliction of mankind. The Master said, "Self-preservation or *abhinivesha* is an instinctive attachment to life. It is the subtlest of afflictions, and is found even in the Wise." He asked the disciples to define *abhinivesha* explaining the desire to live forever has both power and tenacity. He directed their discussion, so they'd come to view *abhinivesha* as "clinging to life because of bodily attachment".

This inclination is ingrained in the causal memory, where it multiplies itself as a fondness for living. The disciples agreed. They first wondered how *ashtanga yoga* could reverse this friendship with the obvious body. *Saleta* opened the discussion, "Through *asana, pranayama, pratyahara* and *dharana,* the seeker delves deep within himself."

Confessed *Bhratahari,* "I trained myself to watch the inward movement of *prana* renovating energy of physical atoms, from the surface of the skin and throughout all bodily sheaths."

Said *Chandra,* "I have been able to merge physical with energies of the subtle bodies. In my experience, there is no difference, except subtlety of matter's vibrations, across the sheaths that envelop *chitta.*" *Bhratahari* confirmed, his own experience is identical with *Chandra's.* Said *Bhratahari,* "I see no difference between life-and-death from the perspective of expression and its starting point as seed. Both are a continuum of different declarations" Both

Bhratahari and *Chandra* understood that life force or *prana* and the energy of matter were one, even when their display is seemingly different. Merged with AUM, the energy leaves as seed of subtle-causal bodies. Abandoning the physically dead body is to leave it to the infinitude of the five elements. As they said this, *Pakva* commented, "*Chandra* and *Bhratahari* have understood and realised the continuation of life-and-death. All are phases in one perpetuity."

Said *Menander,* "It is, like getting a new shawl, when the one currently being used has decayed." With this simile, *Pushya* bemoaned the fact that seekers aspire for self-unfoldment and Soul-realisation, but cling to the frame of the physique. *Ujjaini* expressed his experience with the power of *abhinivesha,* "Attachment to life and body is like a hypnotic spell. It is what happens when a chronically caged bird does not leave its entrapment, even when the doors are left open for it to fly away."

Saleta said, "Attachment to the coverings of the body – physical-subtle-causal – stem from Man's natural urge for immortality, which expresses as self-preservation. It expresses outwardly, as greed or *lobha* and possessiveness or *moha* for belongings, he gathers in present existences.

Behind the curtain, *Patanjali* was deep in thought. He was not burdened with previous incarnations, habits, tendencies, *raaga* or *dvesha.* But he suffered deeply at the loss of his earthly mother, *Gonika.* His memory of being *Shesha* left him yearning to return to *Vishnu. Patanjali,* the mortal, understood, realised and experienced suffering humankind. He could correlate with his disciples' distress. The five afflictions of ignorance, egoism, lust, malice and attachment to life could be countered and erased through meditation, *Patanjali* thought.

To help his disciples with the effects of these clever misfortunes, *Patanjali* entered into the discussion. Clearing his throat, he said, "These foregoing five subtle hindrances can be lessened and erased by efforts and schedules against retrogression." He paused, waiting for his disciples to grasp what he had said and, of course, for *Chandra* to write. Then, he continued, "The upheavals in awareness, created by gross and subtle hardships, have to be muted through meditation." *Patanjali* then outlined how the Law of *Karma* causes these afflictions, saying, "The collected residual impressions of past lives, whether good or bad, are rooted as suffering. These circumstances of merit or demerit will be experienced in present, and future, lives."

The students know the Law of *Karma* is the Law of Justice. Every self-centred action crystallises as a reaction. They understand they are facing them at this moment in time, will do so later in the current lifetime or in future lives. Potential reactions exist as seeds of future afflictions in the causal being, the cause of expression for new lives. They also knew that actions rooted in desire, greed, anger, lust, pride and malice call up such afflictions.

Patanjali prescribed the practice of *Raja Yoga* to purge mortal existence and encouraged the disciples to perform cleaning actions or *tapas,* surrender in *Ishvara pranidhana* and reeducate the intellect with knowledge or *svadhyaya.* Said *Patanjali,* "So long as the foundation of action remains, it results in one's assemblage of ancestry, span of life and the hidden past one has to live."

The drapes to the cave fluttered in the afternoon breeze. The disciples' concentration was drawn to a grasshopper landing on the earth between two rocks, they were using as seats. The grasshopper positioned itself into the soft soil as if wanting to brace itself after a long day in the sun. While watching this play, a bird swooped down, trying to grab it for food. But the grasshopper jumped to safety, leaving an imprint in the dirt. The disciples silently surveyed the melodrama. In front of them was an example of self-preservation or *abhinivesha,* for life or *ayur* stemming from a love and hunger for living or *bhoga.* The disciples just witnessed a reaction to affliction, prevailing, even in the life of a grasshopper.

Pakva started the discussion, "Life springs from both good and bad actions, which leave favourable and unfavourable imprints. The fruits that are gathered in the present life will leave residual impressions, as *samskaras,* as the grasshopper just did." *Pushya* wanted to discuss imprints and impressions in a better context. Said *Pushya,* "The fruits of all actions from previous lives are recycled from memory of past knowledge. These imprints languish in the unconscious mind, within the causal being, as *vasanas.*" *Chandra* agreed and so did *Saleta,* who added, "The unfulfilled fruits of action remain dormant within the causal being, as *karma-phala.* If deeds were performed frequently in previous lives, they remain in the causal being as *habits* or innate prenatal tendencies, or *samskaras.*"

Hearing this, *Patanjali* continued. He classified habits that are uncultured when based upon incorrect knowledge or *vipaka. Patanjali* stressed the stamp of misdeeds have their causal roots in the five obstacles or *kleshas.* Every disciple has experienced such reactions to past-life actions in their present life. They recognised these reactions are unsuspected and lie dormant. They wait for the right condition to show up in future lives. *Patanjali* again stated it was from these roots that specifics of future births are determined.

He, therefore, defined reactions to action saying, "Joys are the fruits of meritorious action or *punyas,* whereas sorrows and a short, miserable life are the fruits of *paapas.*" *Patanjali,* then, went on to discuss *yogic* practices that minimise effects of such imprints. He emphasised on Self-motivated action and avoidance of reaction through surrender. Said he, "The discriminating Man knows that mind changes. Qualities of Nature, and past seed-impressions, even if pleasant, are commingled with the sorrow of future reaction. He, therefore, remains aloof to them."

The disciples know the wise recognise that pleasures eventually, lead to pain, in the form of reactions. This happens within the mechanisms of *karma.* Pure inner peace is reached for real happiness and pleasure by gaining knowledge. This is necessary to scrape out roots of pleasure and pain.

By understanding the inherent motivating *gunas* of Nature, the wise discipline inertia, control creativity and complement *tamas* with *rajas,* towards a neutral field of harmony or *sattva.* The wise intellectually understand Nature's compulsions. He learns to identify and harness life force or *prana.* By moving up the ladder of the divine cave he travels by the *sushumna.*

Pakva started the discussion again. He was of the opinion the wise are empowered by dispassion and 'right' knowledge. He enters the domain of intuitive intelligence. *Pushya* referred to the *Bhagavad Gita* to explain that Nature is the field of knowledge, as well as the battlefield of living. He said, "With the right understanding, it is possible to realise and experience the *gunas* of Mother Nature. Armed with this realisation, it is possible to surrender all future action as a service to the Cosmic Whole."

Saleta sighed in relief. It is possible for seekers to enjoy the treasures of life and living, as long as they distance actions from their fruits. But still, it was clear to all the disciples that past reactions and hurt from past actions must be faced. Nevertheless, *Patanjali's* response was reassuring. The effects of past actions on a person's psyche can be minimised by *yogic* practices. Discriminative knowledge gained through study and meditation can be maximised in the same way. *Patanjali* also promoted *Raja Yoga* as a prophylactic healing skill. It conditions towards a healthy body, mind and intellect. Transformation of the physical body matures into a self-healing energy sheath, deflecting all unperceived afflictions of gross and subtle bodies.

The disciples realised *Menander* has been quiet for far too long. But suddenly, drawing from his vast medical knowledge, *Menander* said, "Energise every physical atom with *prana.* Encourage the healthy physical and physiological bodies to stabilise the mind and intellect. The egoistic self will, then, be fit to deal with the mischief of the unenlightened *chitta.*" At this, *Patanjali* entered the discussion and said, "It is possible to avoid the pain that is yet to come." The disciples' minds were racing. They knew inner composure is disturbed when the mind is lured towards the world. Smiling to himself, *Patanjali* confirmed their thoughts, when he said, "The supreme cause of pain is the mistaken identification of an unenlightened *chitta* of 'seen' personality of *Prakriti* with the 'seer' of *Purusha.* The cure lies in dissociating them."

Saleta found this statement confusing. After all, the intellect of the enlightening *chitta* is so close to the *chit* or Self that a purifying intellect can mistake itself for intelligence. *Bhratahari* entered the discussion, saying, "The intellect in Matter, as *chitta,* has to be diligent. It mustn't become involved in painful relationships with the worldly and at the same time identify itself as the nonworldly." To this, *Chandra* responded, "Intellect must make a choice. It can logically dissociate itself from objects of indulgence through proper understanding. Otherwise, intellect unwittingly enmeshes itself with a false identification with pure intelligence. In fact, intellect must have the knowledge of both *Prakriti's* Awareness and *Purusha's* Consciousness. Embraced together they are Universal Intelligence of *Brahman* or *chit*".

Explained *Menander,* "I am pure Awareness of *Prakriti* while an enlightened *chitta.* And I am also the ever-pure witnessing Consciousness, as *Purusha.* Awareness lodges comfortably in the cup of Consciousness. In the extrovert Man, they seem separated." *Pushya,* recognising *Saleta's* confusion, said, "In Man's mind, the *chitta-chit* can remain connected as one only with a purified, enlightened *chitta.* The Knower of this fact is one in whom the divisions of Knowledge, knowing and knower do not exist. An inner understanding as deep as this is possible only through intuitive and personal inner realisation. The unenlightened *chitta* already lives in the seat of enlightened *chitta*. Pure intelligence of *chit* alone can connect pure Awareness, with pure Consciousness. The 'seen' has to become One with the 'seer', as one unit. The seer is both the knowledge and its experience of seeing that is happening beyond himself."

Pakva explained how swings of the mind enmesh the unenlightened *chitta* with deficient thoughts. He said through *Raja Yoga,* however, it was possible for the intellect to gain right knowledge. This transforms intellect by freeing it from the demands of the world.

After this discussion, *Pakva* and *Menander* explained how master glands in the brain influence transformation of atoms, molecules and tissues. Neurohormones and neurotransmitters patterned and modified in accordance with desired changes are released. The physical body metamorphoses accordingly. Since *chitta* can retrace its steps to its rootstock in the brain, its new identity can be resolved. *Menander,* insisted there is symmetry between the 'seer', 'seen' and 'seeing'.

Chandra saw "seen-seer-seeing" from a different perspective. Through devotion for the Cosmic Mother, he sees himself as a portion of the Whole. He had, logically, conceived the 'seeing' of Nature by the awaring intellect in the 'seen' as inseparable from the Consciousness of the 'seer'. Confirmation came to him in meditation. His intuitive intelligence gave him the Truth. *Pakva* finished the discussion, saying, "When Man transcends the *gunas* of Nature by entering the *kutastha,* he has succeeded in distancing himself from the 'self'. He can merge with the 'seen', 'seer' and 'seeing', as one thought of being the Self. This is meditation."

After this discussion ended, *Patanjali* wanted the group to move to the topic of Nature's compulsions. He said, "*Prakriti* has three *gunas* of *sattva, rajas* and *tamas.*

The eleven senses – five senses, five organs of action and *chitta* – change under this influence. They exist only to serve *Purusha,* either for enjoyment or for emancipation."

Menander opened the discussion, "The Master speaks of Nature's compulsions as if Cosmic Mother encourages Man either to lead a life of unfettered enjoyment, or a restrained life searching for its Source." Responded *Pakva,* stressing what they already knew, "Despite being in high-awareness form in meditation, Man is subjected to temptation of memory of immediate pleasure, both prenatal and postnatal." Moaned *Saleta,* "And because of this, the hard-earned joy of self-control and meditation unravels."

Bhratahari said aloud, "O you Senses why were you not made to devote yourselves to the everlasting rejoicing in *chit?* Why were you not there to ripen until *chitta* developed a permanent habit of enjoying the Soul?"

Said *Pushya,* "My senses were given to promote the real 'I' and not to serve up to insatiable appetites of 'Me'. The body temple was provided for self-control, health and emancipation. Only a healthy body, mind and intellect is fit for spiritual search." *Chandra,* his younger brother, added with conviction, "As soon as Man conquers his delusory habits, he earns intuition, calmness and omniscience. He can then embark on self-unfoldment."

Ujjaini added, seriously, "The compulsions of *Maya* are delusory. Forced subjugation of habits can lead you to believe these compulsions have left. There is a deceptive feeling of victory. But they repossess the mortal." Added *Pakva* ruefully, "This journey is a permanent, uninterrupted struggle for self-control."

Patanjali had not experienced these struggles himself, but he listened with compassion. Finally, he said, "Nature's *gunas* create divisions and collapse in the *chitta* personality. Some of these transformations are distinguishable, and others are not. Some can be prominent, while others cannot." *Patanjali* had, thus, corroborated the controversy on the delusory nature of Matter. He asked the disciples to analyse *Prakriti,* one layer at a time. He wanted them to discuss how they can free themselves from the confines and compulsions of Her *gunas.*

Pushya started the discussion; "Let us start with Nature that is pure Awareness. She also owns innate intelligence or *mahat* ingrained with the qualities of *sattva, rajas* and *tamas.* These are risky qualities that cause cycles of birth and death. The five elements – earth, water, fire, air and space – that make up Nature, are tied in." The disciples were listening attentively. Continued *Pushya,* "Man is the microcosm of the macrocosmic Mother. So Man granted with *chitta* is, in essence, microcosmic *mahat* which, enmeshed in the polarities of creativity or *rajas* and inertia or *tamas,* also compel Man to see-saw between these *gunas.*"

Pakva agreed with a nod of his head, and said. "These *gunas* are not only embedded in Nature, but also in the next eleven layers of Man – the five senses, five organs of action and the mind." Added *Pushya,* "But *Prakriti* is wedded to *Purusha.* As Universal Intelligence or *chit* it grants Man with a free Determination. Will exerted through *Raja Yoga,* harmonises the two polarities in Nature and reach neutrality in *sattva.* These steps are necessary for purposes of emancipation and Soul-realisation," said Ujjaini.

Bhratahari asked quizzically, "Sincere seekers have been able to cross the anatomical, physiological and psychological sheaths of the body. Isn't that part of neutralisation through meditation, too?"

Chandra answered, even as he took notes, "To divest oneself of the human body in meditation and enter the divine cave of the brain and spinal cord, stay at the *kutastha.* That is how one approaches the sanctum of Pure Awareness and Consciousness. By tenaciously persisting here, it is possible to transcend the *gunas* of *prakriti.*"

Ujjaini had, as usual, drifted away into himself. As the

others watched, *Menander* shook him, and asked, "Where have you been, *Ujjaini*?" "I was just drifting into *samadhi* and experiencing my own nature of *ananda*," replied *Ujjaini*, becoming silent again.

Saleta was listening quietly. He found the silence in the valley hypnotic. He had drifted in and out of a trance. He witnessed internally the palpable merge into Unmanifest Nature. His delight knew no bounds. He intuitively saw everything; it all finally, unites into the embrace of *Prakriti* with *Purusha*. *Saleta* exclaimed, as he roused from his contemplation, "Nature merging into the Spirit is a divine marriage. A seeker can realise and experience this nuptial only through *yoga*." The other disciples, especially *Pakva*, *Pushya* and *Chandra*, realised that while busy in discussion, *Saleta* had made a giant leap into his spiritual journey. Inwardly, they rejoiced for him.

Patanjali had spoken of *Prakriti* as *chitta* that merely looks and allows all the changes to happen when desired alterations are punched into Her memory. Adjustments whether beneficial or otherwise, are exactly what Man wants and wills. He understood the discussion had guided his disciples to the witnessing *Purusha* who watches Nature's play. Said *Patanjali*, "The Soul or *chit* is pure Conscious Intelligence. It witnesses *chitta* without relying on it. The intellect of Nature and the consciousness of the Spirit exist only to serve the Soul or *chit*. *Chitta* waits patiently for a desire of emancipation towards *chit*."

The disciples linger on the discussion for a while. It impressed them so deeply they were consumed by it. The enormous importance of this session was making relentless demands on their natural world. It was late in the afternoon. The sun continued to conjure up its dance of high temperatures, despite the fact that it was cool under the peepal tree. *Saleta* and *Ujjaini*, who had drifted into deep meditation, snapped back and felt fully revived. *Ujjaini* opened the discussion, saying, "It is a natural tendency for eleven agents of *chitta* to be attracted to the world."

Added *Saleta,* "The intellect of Man, as *chitta,* thinks it is the pure intelligence of *chit.* Only *yogic* practice can reverse this predisposition. The Soul-seer or *chit* alone can reveal itself. The enlightening of the *chitta* is a journey to this destination."

Menander cautioned the disciples, "A study of the mind and its agents is a precondition to any investigation intellect undertakes. A search for oneself through Knowledge is the only way to enlighten the *chitta* personality of Awareness. Whatever changes noticed from this study can be realised and experienced by the *chitta.* It must then come face-to-face, in meditation, with Consciousness."

Patanjali wanted to comment on Matter and Spirit and the young Master said, "Dysfunctional association with *Prakriti* ends for emancipated beings. For the unrestricted *yogi,* the vehicles of nature – body-mind-intellect – have served the purpose of freeing the *chitta.* The relationship of *chitta-chit* has been fulfilled in emancipation. But, beguiling bondage to objects-emotions-thoughts continues. It manipulates those who are caught up in the world's turmoil." *Patanjali* paused for a moment, and then added, "The juxtaposition of the 'seer' or *Purusha* or Consciousness with the 'seen' or *chitta or Prakriti* or Awareness, is necessary. It is for the 'seeing' through body-mind-intellect, to discover its own nature."

Menander's analytical mind seized this opportunity to warn his companion disciples, "Because of pure knowledge, the perceiver witnesses every analysis recorded in the brain through its association with Nature. If this connection is nourished with ignorance or *avidya,* it sets in motion, only indulgence. Its consequence is physical or mental ailments that bind Man to Matter. However, if this involvement is expedited through *vidya,* Man contracts a debt to serve *Prakriti.*"

Added *Pakva,* "Only intense spiritual practice leads Man to sovereignty from indulging in the outer world.

Devotion to Mother Nature has the ability to free Man from plundering Her wealth for *moha* or possessions"

Saleta was about to ask for ways to destroy *avidya,* but *Patanjali* read his mind. *Patanjali* mentioned, it isn't just lack of knowledge, but absence of spiritual knowledge, that leads Man down the path of indulgence. *Patanjali* said, "Lack of spiritual knowledge is the cause of this misapprehension. It leads to false identification of the *chit* and *chitta.*" *Patanjali* further mentioned the importance for right knowledge, saying, "Obliterating ignorance is possible only through correct understanding. Wisdom alone finally links the 'seer' to the enlightened 'seen'. Remember, the 'seer' is the Spirit or *Purusha* as *chit* and the 'seen' is Matter or *Prakriti* discernible as *chitta.*"

Patanjali's message was clear. *Yoga* has been designed to help the seeker avoid these mistakes of flawed identification. Errors of conduct stored in the causal being enable the emergence of future sorrows. Instinctively, the mind turns more readily to pleasure than to the vision of the Soul. As the Master became silent again, the disciples suddenly recalled that *Patanjali* had delineated the mind as the bridge between the senses and pure Awareness. Said *Pushya,* "The mind is a secret enemy and a treacherous friend."

Chandra said, "The Master advises seekers to train the mind by cultivating perfection with sense interactions. This avoids grasping powers of the mind and senses over external events and objects."

Asked *Saleta,* "How does one ensure that seeds of false thought, that give mind unnecessary potency, are destroyed?"

Pakva answered, "Thought and breath are closely interconnected. If every breath is offered intently, with perfect devotion, to the *chitta* in the *kutastha,* the power of the mind and its false thoughts can be destroyed."

Patanjali reassured his disciples that seeds of false knowledge are destroyed only through intense *yogic* practices. *Pranayama* transcends mind and intellect and *pratyahara* unthinkingly abandons the senses during meditation. An unbroken flow of intellectual discrimination is the only way to erasing ignorance. *Pakva* showed a practical method to rise above thought, by willfully offering every breath to the *kutastha*. Repeated *Patanjali,* confirming what *Pakva* had said, "The constant flow of discriminative knowledge as thought, word and deed – with every breath – is the only way to destroy ignorance, the source of all pain."

As *Patanjali* finished, the disciples asked him to end this session. They were weary and hungry. The intensity of discussions had left them drained. *Patanjali* smiled behind the curtain, and agreed. No sooner had the session come to a close, the disciples hurried to the river to bathe. They each engaged in a short period of meditation. Refreshed they walked towards *Malini's* hut for a meal. *Amma* welcomed her hungry brood. "Sit yourselves down," she said adding, "I can see *Patanjali* coming down the hill."

Patanjali entered the hut and prostrated before *Malini Amma.* Childlike he said, "I am cold and hungry, *Amma.*" *Malini* smiled. Filled with pride she embraced him tightly when a burst of affection filled her heart. Said *Amma,* "I have made your favourite *dal* and rice. The villagers brought me some butter, carrots and sugar. I made your favourite dessert, *gajjar halwa.* Come, sit down and let me feed you like I did when you were a child."

With that, *Malini* spread out eight brass *thalis* or plates and eight golden tumblers of water. She served everyone and told the disciples, "There is more in those pots, over there. Please help yourselves. I am busy with *Patanjali* today." Grace was chanted, after which the teacher and disciples symbolically gave food to the ancestors. They now settled down to eating. An endearingly unusual sight startled the disciples. They saw *Patanjali* lessen himself into a child for *Amma's* sake. They watched, dumbfounded.

Malini sat down in front of *Patanjali.* After carefully mixing the rice and *dal,* she raised portions of the food into *Patanjali's* waiting open mouth. Her strong but withered hands fed *Patanjali,* her heart blazing with warmth. *Patanjali* ate dutifully. He finished his selected share of food. Thankfully he said, "That was delicious, *Amma.* Now, I am ready for your divine dessert." Smiling, *Amma* stood up slowly. She was now sluggish with age. She protested, "I must look after your disciples now."

Seeing the *Malini* and *Patanjali* interaction was an enchanting experience for the disciples. *Pakva,* who had never experienced a mother's love, said, "A mother is a mama, for eternity." *Malini* understood the unstated. She served the disciples *halwa* and kissed every one of them on their brow.

After dinner, *Patanjali* and the students thanked *Amma* for her dedication and kindness. Each retreated to their respective caves and huts to read and, finally, rest. *Malini* saw them to the door, and then ate the little of what was left. After cleaning the pots, she willed her frail frame to the *charpai.* Her eyes felt heavy and irritated from the smoke off the firewood used for cooking. Tired but still lively, she entered the refreshing hall of deep sleep. The sun had set long ago and the crickets had begun their cacophony – only tonight, it seemed a chorus of a lullaby.

As dawn approached, birds twittered enticement to a new day. It was a cold morning. The seven disciples arose at the rooster's reliable and energetic daybreak call. They went down to the river and plunged in. Once accustomed to the icy water, the disciples turned Eastward. Offerings to the rising sun, oblation and reverence, seems like an ancient ritual. Sages followed this traditional offering for aeons. Pledging worshipful detachment to the sun endures to this day and until separated from the earthly body of Mother Earth. Severance should be likened to a ripened fruit falling off its vine. They prayed for an everlasting recollection of their innate Immortality.

Then, dressed and wrapped in shawls, they hurriedly made their way down to *Amma's* cave, only to discover that *Patanjali* had already finished breakfast. The disciples rushed through their breakfast of hot milk and puffed rice. At the end they prayed to the gods to withhold them from sinning, whether by speech, understanding or action. After that, they made their way towards *Patanjali's* cave, where the curtain was already pulled away from the entrance. They saw *Patanjali* sitting on the stone slab. As they approached the cavern, *Patanjali* looked up. He stood up and waited for them to settle in before drawing the curtain. The disciples assembled in front of the cave. They prostrated to *Patanjali's* wisdom and sat down for another session.

Patanjali began the discussion, saying, "Through this method of unbroken discriminative knowledge, the seeker gains the final knowledge of seven frontiers." When *Patanjali* introduced them to the Seven States of Awareness, he expected them to know the subject. He paused, and waited for them to analyse this assertion. *Pakva* said that he had learned there are seven frontiers that need integration. Unless this is done, the experience of Oneness with the 'seer' and 'seen' remains distant. *Menander* wanted to list the seven frontiers, but *Pushya* suggested each of them list one frontier and describe it. In this manner they are equally involved in the discussion. *Pushya* asserted, "Integration of the bodily energy, or *sharira samyama,* has to occur in the wakeful state or *jagran.*"

"There must also be integration of all energies in the five senses, or *indriya samyama,* in a flash and at the same time," *Saleta* said.

"There must be integration of the five physiological energy elements, or *prana samyama.* These five being *prana, apana, vyana, samana* and *udana,*" added *Menander.*

"There is a need for integration of mind energy, or

mano samyama, even while in dream states or *svapna,*" *Bhratahari* said.

"Then, there is the need to integrate the intellect, or *buddhi samyama,* as well," added *Chandra.*

"From this depth, there is need for integration with Awareness, or *chitta samyama,* in sleep or *nidra,*" said *Ujjaini,* thoughtfully.

Finally, *Pakva* described the seventh frontier, "Integrating Self or *chit* with Universal Self or *chidakasha* is *atma samyama.* This union happens in *turiya,* in superconsciousness of deep sleep. But while this integration takes place, each synthesis being realised must be within the frontier of Man's own special identity."

The disciples had read *Vyasa* and *Yoga Vashishta,* and were, now, being taught by *Patanjali.* They realised that all three *yogis* had referred to these seven states of awareness for integrated knowledge. *Patanjali's* experience of these seven states was beyond thought or words. In that state of unity, full enlightenment was realized. Here Awareness preserves its distinguishing and deciding characteristics with Wholeness. *Patanjali* stressed that inner reality can never be overshadowed by any outer experience. He explained that meditation allows Man to conquer the body, calm *pranic* life force, control breath and still the mind. Developing instinctive detection of *pranava* while inward bound towards the Light in the *kutastha,* is the way to God or *Brahman.* All the way through this point, said *Patanjali,* Awareness and Consciousness merge and surrender into the Cosmic Void of *Purushotamma.*

The disciples were spellbound as *Patanjali* shared his experience of *turiya.* They discussed the *yogic* practices that took him throughout the miscellaneous layers of awareness. *Saleta* asked *Patanjali* if it was difficult to conquer the body. He wondered if *Patanjali* had practiced *yama, niyama* and *asana. Patanjali* did not reply. He merely smiled. *Bhratahari* admitted that he is able to manipulate the flow of *prana* during *pranayama* and *pratyahara.* He felt the physiological body is controllable and transforms once the physical atom is converted into its pure energy state. He added these *yogic* practices take a seeker into a 'dormant' state of existence. *Patanjali* nodded in agreement.

Menander told the group he learned to restrain the mind's movements through *dharana* in inspiration. He explained how he feels personal pride in the deeply wished success of his actions.

Once, after successfully saving an unborn child of a dying woman, he emerged from this experience, intensely moved. He hailed the gods of dreams and recognised them as agents of Universal Desire, which transacts action. *Menander* stressed it is longing for a Common Good, which is the ambassador for preferred triumphs. He affirmed his empathy for saving life, plant and creature is such an inclination. He begged the gods to disassociate him from 'agency'. *Menander,* then, confessed he'd sacrificed want, which troubled his egoistic mind, into the fire of oblation. *Patanjali* smiled approvingly.

Pushya became quiet after *Menander's* emotional tale. He realised they were all casualties of mental disruptions born of want, which sneaks into spiritual endeavours. *Pushya* said Man is required to act through the power of *dhyana,* and *Patanjali* nodded. *Chandra* exclaimed he yearned to experience the brilliant transcendental awareness of *samadhi,* which he understood but had not reached. *Patanjali* compassionately assured *Chandra* that he would surely succeed.

Ujjaini too had not experienced this luminosity. It would develop through addition of comprehensive knowledge of *chitta.* But he was aware that knowledge of the self was available within the core of his own being. He recognised the eightfold path must be practiced consistently and continually before one reaches self-unfoldment. *Pakva,* who had been listening quietly, said supreme knowledge of *chit* dawns only when *chitta* surrenders its individuality as the unenlightened self. By merging *chitta* with *chit,* it was possible to experience *chidakasha.*

Patanjali was pleased with the discussion, for the disciples had listed the seven insights that took *yogis* to higher realms of *yoga.* The practice of *Raja Yoga* promised to take them to final stages of their individualised existence. *Menander* had correctly identified the need for restraining the mind and intellect, for without that, it was impossible to restrain the unenlightened *chitta. Patanjali* added that through *Raja Yoga, chitta* automatically sheds outer layers, freeing it of bodily obstacles. After that, the seeker is ready for Soul-realisation. Here the intellect watches, hears, feels and sees AUM in a single experience. The 'Me' becomes 'I'.

But *Patanjali* reminded his disciples, "Before we can reach the final stage of clear discriminative knowledge, we must practice every limb of *yogic* instruction with dedication, and in graduated steps. These practices bring about inner stability." After a pause, *Patanjali* added, "Dedication to the practice of meditation remodels a mature personality in the seeker. *Yoga* cures or lessens all physical, mental, moral and spiritual suffering. And such perfection is only possible through wholehearted love for *yoga.*"

Menander, the physician was a spiritual scientist who had learned to identify the inner movements of how these transformations occur. He said, "The rising and merging of oppositely flowing *pranic* currents neutralise polarities, of downgoing *apanaya* and upgoing *udanaya.* It takes seekers to the core of their divine cave in the *sushumna.*"

Added *Ujjaini,* the devoted environmentalist, "*Pranayama,* practiced while focusing into the *kutastha,* ensures there is complete breath control. Successful *pranayama* is a prelude to winning, effortless *pratyahara* into the divine cave. Concentrated effort clears all blocks in the spinal cord. Astral parasympathetic and sympathetic nerve channels are made to move up towards *kutastha.* Through *dharana* and *dhyana,* every form of transformation – physical, mental, moral and spiritual – takes place in the *kutastha,* the centre of Awareness. Once this individualised template of one's microcosmic self is transformed, it is possible to endorse the macrocosm, be it Man, plant or creature. Now, healing and nurturing Cosmic Mother's body becomes a labour of love." *Ujjaini* wanted to ensure that all disciples understood "one need not harm or exhaust anything in the environment", for egocentric materialism.

Menander then explained how every transformation of the three bodies and five sheaths is recorded in the thalamic-pituitary-hypothalamic nuclei. His explanation, however, became too specialized for the others. They demanded, "*Menander,* speak in words we understand!"

Continued *Menander,* "The planetary system of the Universe is transcribed within the brain and spinal cord."

Bhratahari and *Ujjaini* were already aware of this but the rest weren't. *Patanjali,* from behind the curtain, announced his approval with an encouraging cough, a sign for *Menander* to continue. *Menander* went on, "In the planetary system of the central nervous system, the Sun is the thalamus in the brain, where *Prakriti,* as self, records all actions motivated by desire. And it is from here the self looks at all these changes taking place in the bodies and sheaths of Man."

Asked *Saleta,* "Do you mean that these records are reactions to desire willed by the individualistic self?"

'Yes,' *Ujjaini* interjected, adding, "And whatever is recorded here is in permanent connection with the Total Mind of the Universe, the nuclear Sun."

Said *Pushya,* incredulously, "The effect is in every atom of the self's total memory bank and, also in the Universal Mind?"

Explained *Menander,* "The Sun only 'looks' at all actions: good, bad or indifferent. Once it has scanned the changes, they are accounted for in Nature's memory bank or *chitta.* In Man's brain, the thousand-petaled *sahasrahara* is found at the top in the parietal lobe. From here, *chit* watches and witnesses all changes and transformations taking place, in response to desire and Man's Will. The Spirit watches the changes in individualised Matter, but without interference. The *thalamus,* in the centre of the brain, is the Sun of the individualised creature."

"How are these changes effected through *yoga?*" *Pakva* asked.

Answered *Ujjaini,* "When individualised *Prakriti* is transformed through *yogic* exercises, it instructs the hypothalamus [the Moon] to release *yogically*-transformed neurotransmitters. The thalamus also commands the pituitary gland to release *yogically transformed* neuro-hormones. These are the master glands for the whole endocrine system," said *Bhratahari.*

Chandra finished by saying, "From here on, the cells, molecules and atoms of the body are invigorated and Man is transformed into a new being."

Menander agreed by saying, "Absolutely, and it takes seven years of intense practice to get to this transformed state of being in the brain."

Pakva and *Pushya* were delighted with this scientific explanation of transformation of every atom, molecule, tissue and organ in Man. All the disciples understood *yogic* change penetrates every atomic arrangement starting at disengagement of transformed neurotransmitters and neurohormones. They, in turn, trigger release of transfigured hormones and transmitters, leading Man to a healthier body, more qualified for meditation.

Exclaimed *Saleta,* "Molecular change in the different *koshas* and *shariras* correspond with the seeker's *yogic* Will.

Every change must be understood as the seeker's involvement. When every cell desires emancipation, there is complete transformation in the seekers body."

"Every action, after that, is 'seeing' from a deeply transformed condition. The 'seer', 'seen' and 'seeing' become a single experience of self-unfoldment and emancipation. Self-realisation," said *Chandra,* "Is a truth born of intuitive understanding."

"How long does this take?" asked *Pushya,* again. "Seven years of intense meditation for the brain-transformation and twelve years for the body," replied *Ujjaini.*

At this point, *Patanjali* wanted to remind his disciples the path becomes more difficult as they move forward. Many slide back into old ways. He insisted, therefore, that *ashtanga yoga* must be practiced, in full, at every moment. To stress this point, *Patanjali* reintroduced the eightfold path of *ashtanga yoga.* "Moral injunctions are *yama.* Fixed observance is *niyama.* Posture is *asana.* Control of breath is *pranayama.* Internalization of the senses towards their source is *pratyahara.* Concentration is *dharana.* Meditation is *dhyan* and absorption of Awareness into Consciousness is *samadhi.* These are the eight ingredients of *yoga.*" *Patanjali* continued to state, "The first three limbs, *yama-niyama-asana,* are ingrained in Indian tradition. These codes of ethics even children must learn, before they turn seven, to overcome natural *tamasic* tendencies. Although *Patanjali* discussed *pranayama* and *pratyahara* as separate entities, the disciples knew each depended on the other for full expression. Together they are hidden facets of a single *yogic* meditative-practice.

Said *Ujjaini,* thinking deeply, "*Pranayama* and *pratyahara* combat extreme *rajasic* tendencies ingrained in a seeker. Perfect control of breath and withdrawal from the senses sets you up for an inward journey. The excursion is from atoms on the skin surface to the core of one's being within the spinal cord."

"This shoreline is the divine cave. After this, seekers enter the sanctum of God's altar, in the brain," said *Pakva,* adding, "A seeker who makes spiritual progress through such practices arrives within the core of his being. Harmony between *tamoguna* and *rajoguna* is the first step to *sattvaguna* in the brainstem." *Pakva* had just described the logic of *pranayama* and *pratyahara.* Added *Menander,* "The *yoga* of meditation arms the seeker with whatever he has gained on the battlefield of life."

Ujjaini added, "The changing emancipation-aspiring seeker must, one day, face the ego." At this, *Pakva* explained the ego undergoes four stages of evolution of Awareness in the *chitta.* Said *Pakva,* "These changes expose the seeker to **four psychological battles**. Under control of the egoistic individualistic self, the *chitta* makes restless **bodily** demands, triggered by the senses. This is when the intellect is eclipsed by restlessness. Ego and desire control the sense-mind, but the individualistic unenlightened *chitta* makes no effort to fight back. In the second stage of evolution, the unenlightened *chitta* has begun to fight **psychological** battles with the subtle astral envelopment of *prana-manas.* But these victories are temporary. This happens because of ingrained *avidya* in the seeker's real nature. Calmness is reached. But the self is still restless, because of demands of present and past ingrained desire."

There was silence. *Pakva* continued, confidently, going on to describe the third stage in a seeker's psychological battle. "At this stage, the seeker uses his **Will** and faculty of **persistence** to practice continuous meditation. If he persists, his efforts will allow him to enter the harmonised *sattvic* core at the base of his brain, in the *ajna* spiritual centre," said *Pakva,* adding, "Enlightening *chitta* has begun!" *Pakva* paused, waiting for the disciples to absorb the discussion, as also for *Chandra* to finish taking down his words.

The others remained still, digesting what *Pakva* has said. The valley was absorbing the heat of the sun. The disciples had unfastened their shawls. Some lay in the shade of the *peepal* tree. *Saleta* leaned against a rock and absentmindedly scribbled in the dry sand. *Patanjali,* meanwhile, had moved from the slab to his stool nearer to the curtain, showing active interest. His bare feet became visible under the curtain. Continued *Pakva,* "The seeker can expect to experience longer spells of peace and lessened restlessness. During *dharana-dhyana,* the seeker experiences his seed-state of *chitta* as Awareness."

The disciples were familiar with this part of the discussion, but *Pakva* realised that each understands not all, every time. He continued to explain, "In the fourth stage, the individualistic self, the **ego** must be conquered and executed."

Interrupted *Saleta,* "That is a difficult task." And added *Menander,* "To free oneself from the clutches of all these – ego, desire, anger, fear, greed, attachment, pride, habits, temptation and jealousy – seekers must transfigure every atom of every cell."

Ujjaini noted, "The gross physical body or *sthula sharira* should first be made healthy through energisation, healing and transformation."

Added *Bhratahari,* "And the subtle body or *sukshma sharira* should be made vibrant and brought under control through the practices of *pranayama* and *pratyahara.* The causal or *karana sharira* then undergoes intense transformation through the processes of *ashtanga yoga.* In this integration and annulment of the *koshas,* the experience of Bliss and being One is a natural result. It encourages the practitioner to continue with sincere effort."

Pushya said, "It is also, perhaps, the only way to see oneself in the seedless state of being."

Chandra, who was deep in thought, suddenly said, "Yet how easy it is to slide back into one's old ways." He looked up at the curtain that separated them from *Patanjali.* Others followed his eyes and his thoughts. Silence prevailed again. *Patanjali* watched their thoughts again. Agreeing *Saleta* echoed, "It is so easy to slide back into one's old ingrained, habituated ways."

Chandra moaned again, "Man is propelled and swayed to behave in conformity with the qualities inherent in his causal being. Man's mind is so preoccupied with this tendency that one slides back into old ways." *Patanjali* listened carefully. He never tired of noting why seekers fall off the spiritual path. He knew they must start from the beginning and not from where they'd left off. He repeated to himself and listed the ingredients of *yama*. *Patanjali* voiced their characteristics, "Nonviolence, truth, abstention from stealing, continence, the absence of greed for possessions beyond one's needs, are the five pillars of *yama.*"

Patanjali paused, waiting for the disciples to open a new discussion. The disciples grouped the principles of *yama* as five "don'ts" in human life and daily mundane living.

Pakva began the discussion, "*Ahimsa* is the attitude of noninjury," and clarified, "It includes expelling from the heart, impulses to strike back. This means not causing harm – in word, thought or deed – to any being, creature or the environment. It is an inner attitude of the heart to live harmlessly, in the world of relativity and duality."

"*Satya* is the attitude of avoiding untruthfulness, including the need to distort the truth." said *Ujjaini*.

"What if honesty were to cause another pain?" asked *Chandra*. *Ujjaini* replied, "The alternative would be to remain silent."

Highlighted *Chandra,* "*Satya* includes avoiding self-deception, does it not?" Answered *Ujjaini,* "Yes, it does."

Pushya said, "*Asteya* is renunciation of wish for possessions that were not earned by a particular claim. This is the third ingredient of *yama.*"

"*Brahmacharya* is self-control of every natural appetite for indulgence, including sexual desire," *Menander* said.

Insisted *Bhratahari,* "Spiritual seekers must practice *aparigrahah,* defined as nonacceptance of gifts. They incur a *karmic* debt."

Commented *Saleta,* "But this can be avoided by owning only what one needs, without being greedy."

Pushya noted that *Chandra* was quiet, and instinctively knew his brother was reliving an experience they'd had. Memories are usually best erased for purposes of purity in meditation, *Pushya* knew, but he also realised memory of lessons they had learned then, seemed relevant to this day. *Pushyas* mind, too, traveled back in time...

The *yaksha* had questioned *Chandra* about the five abstentions while obeying self-control. Both *Chandra* and *Pushya* were reminded of universal vows that must be followed, unconditionally, by everyone, especially students of *yoga. Chandra,* who had died under the *yaksha's* spell, was a deep thinker on worldly matters. His speech and outer mannerisms were noble and truthful. He had become a general in King *Pushya's* army and his deep respect for weapons of war was well known, as was his devotion to *Pushya.*

Known to use weapons of war only to defend those who suffered injustice, *Chandra* expected the army's conduct to be without blemish. Both the King and *Chandra* knew society's privileged morals. They knew how rulers of society conducted themselves. They provided all the underpinnings of an honest nation.

Keeping the kingdom's borders free from invading enemies kept *Chandra* away from home for months. His best friend was his wife, *Chandini.* Her ethics and ideals kept them as one – body, mind and soul – whether they were together or separated from each other. Through charity towards one another and those around them, they were able to earn the power of inner purity and divinity. *Chandini,* however, had died prematurely while giving birth to a child. This broke *Chandra's* heart, but he remained in the service of the kingdom. Though childless, *Chandra* had educated and nurtured the crown prince and stayed by *Pushya's* side, until the King abdicated the throne. The widower *Pushya* wished to retire to the caves of the Himalayan forests, where the brothers had spent early childhood among the monks. *Chandra* accompanied *Pushya* into this life of renunciation in *vanprasth.*

The brothers had found *yama* a way of life since childhood. The *yaksha* had predicted they would, someday, meet a great Master under whom they could make the Cosmic Connection. After many years under the tutelage of monks, they were directed to go to *Gonika Amma's ashram,* a hundred miles away. *Malini* greeted them here. They sensed an atmosphere of sadness at the monastery. They were informed *Gonika Amma* had breathed her last a few days earlier, and *Amma's* dispossessed son *Patanjali,* had disappeared into his cave for days.

On the thirteenth day, *Patanjali* appeared from the cavern. He walked towards *Malini's* cottage, reverentially carrying an earthen pot covered with a white cloth. His two hands appeared blanched from hugging the vessel firmly against his chest. As *Patanjali* walked towards the brothers, *Pushya* and *Chandra* knew, instinctively, that he is *Patanjali,* they were foretold would meet. They looked at each other incredulously – *Patanjali* was just a boy!

Pushya and *Chandra* watched *Patanjali* as he gently placed the earthen container in a basket of freshly picked wild flowers. As if transfixed *Malini* waited for *Patanjali.* He stooped his homage at her feet. Both hugged the basket between them and wept silent tears. The brothers understood *Gonika Amma's* funerary rites need completion. As they walked to the river, the brothers followed them. On the sandy banks, *Patanjali* sat down and looked at the river. Her turbulent waters promised the Cosmic Mother would receive *Gonika's* earthly remains into Her ever-generous bosom. Silently, *Patanjali* recited the final rites and committed *Gonika's* ashes to the river. They all watched the earthen pot pass them. It crashed into a rock and emptied its rudimentary contents into the universal elements. Only the flowers now floated on the water's surface. This was the only sign left of *Gonika's* blessed stopover among mortals. Yet, as *Chandra* and *Pushya* knew, those that *Gonika* left behind marveled at the everlasting inscription of her life. Centuries later, Man would talk about *Gonika* through the knowledge she bestowed upon her son *Patanjali.*

Chandra and *Pushya* were still musing over their first meeting with *Patanjali* when they heard him speak. They snapped back to the present. *Patanjali* was saying, "These abandonments or *yama,* are the great universal vows that need to be practiced, regardless of time, place, circumstance or our narrow ideas of duty."

Pushya upheld the thought that one needs intense devotional attitude to empower *niyama. Patanjali* picked up *Pushya's* thoughts and said, "Cleanliness, contentment, religious zeal through self-discipline, self-study and surrendering of the 'self' to an ideal of the Supreme Self are the *niyamas.*" As always, *Patanjali* became silent, prodding his disciples to a discussion. *Pushya* spoke first, "Just as *yama* is the universal code of ethics of Man within society, *niyama* exchanges perfected practices and puts to sleep a seeker's objectionable character." To this, *Chandra* added, "These five observances are the 'dos' for each sheath of the body and for each element in Nature."

Patanjali then invited them to discuss ways to practice *niyama. Pakva* opened the discussion by speaking on *shaucha* of body and heart.

Said *Pakva,* "*Shaucha* addresses cleanliness of Man's *annamaya kosha.* Although bathing the physical body is taken for granted, cleanliness while practicing *asana* and *pranayama* is never carefully thought about. Perfecting these ingredients of *yoga* is also a part of cleanliness. Hygienic organization of Man's posture and breathing is important, if Man decides to delve deeper into himself for long periods of time."

Ujjaini defined *santosha,* saying, "This faculty is complementary to nonavarice and is intended for the *pranamaya kosha.* This form of concentrated effort by using *prana* results in cultivating contentment, compassion, friendliness and indifference, to the imperfections of others and your own."

Chandra decided to tackle and define *tapas.* Said *Chandra,* "Many seekers spend maximum energy in harsh harmful austerity when entering a spiritual search. What is needed is to exercise and silence the mind. It originates from the *manomaya kosha.*" He continued, "It is proper to purge this sheath because unless this is done, emotions embedded in the causal body have a habit of frequent materialization in the *manomaya kosha.* Even advanced seekers can be disturbed by such emotional wandering thought!"

Pushya was a natural reader, who had enjoyed the luxury of a childhood among sages. He spoke of *svadhyaya* and the study of scriptures, for the sake of the *gyanamaya kosha,* "The logic of such reading is futile without the grace of a *guru.*"

Commented *Saleta,* "Not every seeker has the good fortune of meeting the right teacher." *Pushya* countered, "But the right teacher is always available to a receptive seeker. Disciples must ensure that they are with the right teacher by learning of, and witnessing, the successes of the teacher's other reputed seekers."

The kindly *Menander* chose *Ishvara pranidhana,* and said unexpectedly, "*Dhanvantari* is the Lord of my Heart."

"Who is he?" asked *Bhratahari,* "Are you speaking of the celebrated sage of medical science, who was *Bharadwaja's* student of *Ayurveda*?" 'Yes,' replied *Menander* and showed where he felt his dedication. He pointed to his head where he experiences the exalted *chitta* within the *anandamaya kosha.* He continued, "Unless this power is invoked, the seeker is consumed by restlessness and behaves unethically. The seeker must surrender to the Lord-of-the-Heart." Even as he said this, tears welled up in *Menander's* eyes. Said *Bhratahari,* "Only the Lord-of-the-Heart gives each of us patience to await His Will."

Exclaimed *Menander* unexpectedly, "Not mine, not mine!" After *Menander's* reaction, the disciples understood *Ishvara pranidhana* intuitively. Inferred *Bhratahari,* "These are all principles of *Raja Yoga.* Proficiency of *yoga* is impossible without observing *yama* and *niyama.* One has to be prepared to remove **every** fault that hinders one's progress in *sadhana.*"

Said *Pakva,* "Normally, Man is a victim of ingrained desire, anger, greed, infatuation, arrogance and jealousy. These engulf the mind with suffering and misery. Then pain deludes the mind with emotions."

Added *Saleta,* recalling his own fall from grace early in his life, "Seekers in anguish lose their inner balance too. An unstable mind makes for unethical behaviour."

Whenever the practices of a seeker in agony are interrupted by wrong tendencies or rambling theories, it is wise to reexamine all these thoughts and start from the basics. That is the only way to defeat the tendency to do harm. Restart, with *yama* by avoiding negative actions, and *niyama* by performing positive actions."

Patanjali, who had been listening to the discussion, added, "Principles that are contrary to *yama* and *niyama* should be countered with learning and differentiation. Knowledge and discrimination need cultivation."

Saleta was in deep in thought. He said suddenly, "Seekers must be counseled to cultivate a temperament that can resist violence, lying, stealing, nonchastity and venality. To enable *pratipaksha bhavana,* it is important that seekers delve into the what, where, when, why and how, of all negativity. And this should become part of their reflexive reaction to every action."

Saleta knew this from experience. His faultless childhood should have taken him along the path of *dharma*. He had parents who followed cleanliness, contentment, self-study with fervour and surrender to the universal Spirit. They had nurtured these qualities in him as well. These are also the qualities *Patanjali* considered important for students. They empower *pratipaksha bhavana* and cancel immoral tendencies. *Saleta's* father identified with *yama* and *niyama*. *Saleta* could not remember his parents ever having indulged in gossip or unnecessary materialism. Whenever there was disagreement, it was countered with the right knowledge. Through reading or through instruction as stories, keen awareness was nurtured in the children.

But *Saleta* drifted from the path, giving in to desire and indulgence. *Saleta's* experiences with materialism, in fact, often take him back to the days of immoderation. The disciples were aware of this, as also of *Saleta's* experience of death by snakebite. Hearing *Saleta* they were silent, until *Menander* said, "Let us review the eight steps of *Raja Yoga* from a medical point of view."

The disciples agreed to his suggestion, and *Menander* started, "*Ashtanga yoga* is a self-healing technique espoused by *Ayurveda.*"

Bhratahari demanded, "Explain yourself, *Menander.*" But all the disciples, including *Menander,* turned to *Patanjali* instead. *Patanjali* had authored and updated the earliest texts of *Ayurveda*. *Bharadwaja* was the first 'seer' of this science and *Dhanvantari* modernised it for the present time. *Patanjali,* however, explained *Ayurveda* with the logic of combining it with steps that make *Raja Yoga.* The disciples asked *Patanjali* to comment on this combination of science with philosophy. *Patanjali* agreed, but said that he would do so after lunch and a siesta. The sun was at its zenith, wrapping the valley in its inferno, but the gentle mountain breeze made it comfortable.

The disciples agreed, and took leave of *Patanjali*. They walked to the gurgling river to refresh themselves for lunch. They knew *Malini Amma* would have something ready before lunch. When they reached the hut, *Patanjali* was already seated and conversing with *Amma,* who had made a simple meal of plain boiled rice, *dal* and yogurt. After grace, the disciples ate frugally, aware that they had to be fully awake for the second session.

Patanjali invited *Malini* to dine with them, and she did. After lunch, the disciples noted that *Amma* seemed tired. They therefore quickly washed all the pots and pans in the river. By the time they returned, *Patanjali* had withdrawn to his cave. *Amma* was asleep under the shade of the mango tree. The disciples decided to lie down under the tree as well. They agreed to take turns to fan aside the troublesome insects that buzzed around their exhausted *Amma*.

Malini slept a deep and refreshing sleep. Suddenly screaming parrots fighting over the ripening mangoes in the tree awakened her. She looked down and saw the disciples sleeping everywhere around her. And *Chandra* had fallen asleep at the foot of her bed, fan still in his hand. *Malini* smiled to herself. These seven disciples were wonderful and caring seekers.

She crept away and approached *Nani,* the cow, hoping for some milk for *Patanjali* and his disciples. *Nani,* whose calf had died, had much milk to spare. Taking the milk, *Malini* made some *chai*. When the disciples awoke, *chai* was ready. She served the disciples and sent a large tumbler for *Patanjali,* before taking one herself. *Malini* listened to the disciple's chatter. In her wisdom, she knew her 'sons' were making progress under *Patanjali*. She encouraged them to rest awhile with their *chai* before returning to *Patanjali's* cavern.

It was late into the afternoon and the sun had

exhausted most of its heat. The disciples walked up to *Patanjali's* cave. He was squatting outside with *Chandra* sipping his drink. As they all assembled, he greeted them. He finished his refreshment. He suddenly stood up and pulled a flimsy shawl tightly over his shoulders. He then turned to enter the cave. Once inside, he drew the curtain, again separating the teacher from the taught.

He asked *Menander* to continue explaining the medical facts underlining the eight steps of *Raja Yoga*. *Menander* began, "*Asana* is to heal the physical and physiological bodies. All parts of the body are adjusted and strengthened until there is equipoise in every atom. This aids physical calmness." He stopped to clear his throat and then said, "Mental sobriety must be encouraged, as this increases introspection and gradual inner transformation. In the meantime, the intellect develops compassion in both thought and action."

The disciples understood the logic of what *Menander* had said. They also realised this discussion was meant to aid understanding and was not part of their inner realisation and experience. *Menander* continued, "Through *pranayama,* seekers witness the self-propelling control of Man's breathing triggered by the indwelling Soul in the *kutastha.* By gradually adjusting medulla-controlled breathing cycles, the *kumbhaka* between *puraka* and *rechaka* lasts longer. In this state of *kumbhaka,* the Soul supports the physical body with Energy through the inherent power of life force or *prana.* Man suspends himself in a breathless state while supported by *prana* alone. In the silence of this concentrated activity, awareness of bodily and mental stillness is noted and silence realised. Here, in this harbour, transformation takes place."

"What transformation?" asked *Saleta.*

Replied *Menander,* "Gradually, the seeker involuntarily ends, automatic medulla-triggered breathing. Reliance on *prana* as the source of life frees the seeker from the upheavals of *raaga-dvesha*. His mind and intellect experience hope and emotional stability."

Pakva found this logical and reasoned it was helping him understand the scientific truths. He also realised *Patanjali* wanted to ensure that every curve of their thinking saw transformation, until they personally experienced the truth of atomic transformation. The more he thought about it, the more he drifted into deep thought. *Menander* interrupted him, saying, "*Yoga* is, after all, final inner measurement and adjustment of the physical, physiological and psychological processes of the body. And *yoga* works through such transformation."

Exclaimed *Saleta*, "*Asana* is not gymnastics!" And then added, "And *pranayama* is not just *swasayama* or willful deep breathing, as claimed by the sceptic. *Dhyana* is not a self-induced trance. And *yama* and *niyama* are not just rules of conduct!" *Saleta* then let out a sigh of mock relief – the others had been chiding him about his preoccupation with *yoga*. Smiled *Ujjaini*, "Right."

During *Menander's* discussion, *Ujjaini's* mind had raced to make a connection between every atom and the macrocosm. It was possible to transform the mortal body, sheath after sheath, and, at the same time, enshrine these changes in the Cosmic Mind. *Ujjaini* marveled at Nature, finally understanding how She continues to balance, miraculously, the Earth's precarious ecosystem, despite Man's continuous volley of misuse and destruction.

Said *Chandra*, wisely, "Yet Man continues to misjudge and misunderstand Nature's self-corrective mechanisms of earthquakes, hurricanes, storms and mass destruction as incidental." As *Menander* listened to *Chandra*, he was watching *Pushya's* facial expressions. Said *Menander*, "So, *Pushya*, you have understood the cosmic connection between Man and Nature?"

Pakva understood *Chandra's* statement, having realised that Man, the microcosmic image of the macrocosm, lives an unbalanced life. He said, "Man's understanding is veiled by the illusion that he can enjoy health and harmony despite his self-destructive indulgences." Added *Bhratahari,* "The only means Man has, to return to the path, are his body, mind and intellect. Yet, Man feels he is born for the self's whims, fancies and excesses." The discussion had gone off on a tangent, until *Menander* reminded them, "The Master wanted us to discuss how medical knowledge could be put into practice."

As the disciples listened, *Menander* continued, "By accepting *paksha* on *yama, niyama, asana* and *pranayama,* Man is naturally able to erase negative tendencies."

Added *Ujjaini,* "Such activity, as described in *ashṭanga yoga,* balances the flow of energy in the three energy channels of the body – the *ida* or parasympathetic, the *pingala* or sympathetic and *sushumna* or the central path of the spinal cord."

At this, *Pakva* complained, asking *Menander* to simplify his words for the benefit of those who didn't have a medical background.

Continued *Menander,* "By harnessing the flow of *prana* in the *ida* and *pingala* and through the *sushumna,* Man is able to connect to the thalamus [Sun], hypothalamus [Moon] and the self-referring pituitary master gland."

Asked *Saleta,* "So, integrating master glands with spinal cord's *chakra* energy, and peripheral endocrine end organs is the fundamental mechanism for outlying tissue mutation in *yoga?*" *Menander* nodded assent, as *Pushya* asked, "But how is this achieved?"

Menander clarified patiently, "Intense desire by Man, the microcosm, for Oneness with Mother Nature, the macrocosm, releases transformed neurohormones and neurotransmitters from master glands. They target the body for transmutation in keeping with desired reconstruction. When actions and reactions are remade from levels of *yama* and *niyama,* metamorphosed transmitters, over time change every atom, in every cell, in every tissue and organ of the body. And over time, Man integrates with the rhythms of Nature."

There was silence as *Menander* concluded. Behind the curtain, *Patanjali* observed a restructuring taking place in their intellectual perceptions. He wanted these changes based on data from *ashtanga yoga*. He wanted to reemphasise that *yama* and *niyama* are not only foundations of *yoga*, but also a reflection of spiritual success or failure. *Patanjali* understood the dimensions of Man's physical, mental and spiritual misdemeanour. It occurred to him that he repeatedly warned his disciples that even successful *yogis* could invalidate spiritual gains by failing to observe *yama* and *niyama* to the very last word. With this thought, *Patanjali* asked *Menander* and *Ujjaini* to discuss misguided actions and reactions that manifest themselves as disease, pain and distress.

Thus prompted, *Menander* explained, "Disease results from submitting to pressures of desire, lust and pride. Pain comes from reflexive habits and behaviour, due to asymmetry between the senses and life force energies." He paused. He remained watchful that the discussion was absorbing. *Bhratahari* intimately understood the effects of evil tendencies and habit-prompted predisposition. He understood these gave Man the predisposition to lie, steal, indulge himself and covet. *Bhratahari* had enjoyed untold wealth, but found materialism to be the cause of regret and mental upheavals. His father and brother had tried to kill for riches. This caused him untold pain, anguish and fear. Tired of abundance, *Bhratahari* chose a life of spirituality. *Pakva* had suspected a disease takes shelter in a stressed manifestation and becomes enlivened by aggression, anger or delusion. He saw friends with aggressive nature succumb to incurable diseases. Pain whether mild, moderate or extreme, is the result of indulgence and bound by law of cause and effect. To *Pakva*, this discussion was a disclosure.

Menander continued, "Mental fluctuations result from ingrained habits causing psychological distress."

Added *Ujjaini*, "Man must watch out for such reactions. It is possible, through introspection, to escort all thoughts and actions out of negative trends whether physical, mental or intellectual."

"What makes Man vicious?" asked *Pushya*, who had spent years as a king, ruling over his people.

Hearing this question, *Patanjali* decided to conclude the discussion himself. He said, "Questionable knowledge gives rise to violence. This understanding may be acquired directly, indirectly or as an excuse. Furthermore, greed, anger and delusion – in mild, moderate or intense degrees – cause violence. All these cause endless pain and stem from spiritual ignorance. Both of these can be ended through introspection."

Patanjali was advocating nonviolence and passive resistance against evil. He advised use of love, reasoning and spiritual enforcement to negate physical, mental and intellectual misbehaviour. He stressed not to engage in any show of strength. Said *Patanjali*, "When there is desire to harm others, in speech, thought or action, relinquish it. Opponents then abandon hostility also and animosity disappears," *Patanjali* assured disciples the urge to retaliate is an ingrained habit of self-protection. He knew of many true stories of obliteration of harm in those perfected in *ahimsa*. Loathing for Man or beast does not arise unless it is nurtured.

Since war only breeds war, *Patanjali* advised integrating the transformed Soul with the Universal Soul. Peace in word, thought and deed, whether awake or asleep, is a sign of goodwill and love in Man. In the presence of such transformed mortals, *Patanjali* said, even violent men and animals abandon hostility and exhibit friendliness and tolerance. Man must be encouraged to live his own inner Truth.

Truth is causal in origin. This inner voice has the power to implement Man's intentions. Most mortals are taught, from childhood, to think and speak their own 'truths'. If even one cell in the body disagrees with the mind, there cannot be a successful harmonious existence, they were told. Disharmony between cells of mind and body lead to natural downfalls. *Patanjali* therefore explained the potency of 'Truth', "When a seeker is firmly established in Truth, his words become potent. Whatever he says comes to be. That is a realised experience." *Patanjali* paused, and then said, "Once firmly established that theft is unnecessary, Nature assures precious jewels and riches are perceptibly showered, even when unasked for." The disciples were silent as this truth sank in. Then, *Patanjali* continued with the same line of thought, "When the seeker becomes firmly established in continence, knowledge, vigour and valor – all dynamism flows into him."

Bhratahari, the grammarian scholar and commentator of the *Mahabhashya,* was a student of *Patanjali* and wanted to discuss the grammatical essence of the term "continence" as regards chastity. *Bhratahari* was often asked to speak about it but felt most seekers misunderstood the topic. From behind the curtain, *Patanjali* cleared his throat to indicate he approved this discussion. Began *Bhratahari,* "Continence does not contradict sexual pleasure. *Prana* finds natural expression in the warmth of emotion, the passion of intellect and in idealism. These capabilities are the spiritual essence of every Soul." He paused, and then reminded the disciples, "The relationship of *Purusha* and *Prakriti* is based on spontaneous creativity and freedom. Renunciation, therefore, is only a natural disengagement. It is not repulsion or rejection. It is lack of self-mastery that leads to grief, misery and hopelessness."

Patanjali concurred with this opinion. "When Man frees himself from greed of possession of another, knowledge of past and future lives unfold before him. He realises the true meaning of his life's companion," *Patanjali* said. The disciples recognised these as effects of *niyama*. Continued *Patanjali*, "Cleanliness of body and mind help Man develop dispassion. Fascination for contact with others for excessive self-indulgence is then neutralized." He asked *Menander* and *Ujjaini* to guide the discussion.

Menander began with inner cleanliness. "Physical-psychological cleanliness and purity protect the body, making it suitable as residence of "seen-seer", as *chitta-chit*. In addition to keeping the temple of the Soul externally clean, the Master prescribes *asana* and *pranayama*, so the energy of the inner body is bathed in lifeforce-enriched vital fluid, cleansing physiological, psychological and intellectual sheaths."

Patanjali interrupted the discussion, saying Man must detach himself from his sheaths also to make his body fit to pursue spirituality. "Once the body is cleansed, the mind purified and the senses controlled, the joy of Self-realisation fills the temple of awareness. From this, unsurpassable contentment, comes supreme happiness," *Patanjali* said. He sensed the disciples' thoughts were in agreement with his own and continued, "*Tapas* burns away all impurities by transforming the body's atoms and mental energy. It frees *chitta* from past impurities. This, eventually helps Man attain divinity." *Patanjali* then moved on to his "best liked" topics of *yama* and *niyama*. Said the young Master, "*Svadhyaya* leads Man toward the realisation of God, or communication with one's desired deity."

Silence prevailed for many moments. The disciples were in contemplation, for *Patanjali* had said several things. In time, *Pakva* opened the discussion and spoke of *svadhyaya*, "Self-study has the power to lead seekers along one of two paths. The first path takes him by gradual transformation of every atom, through physiological-psychological-intellectual sheaths, and also into the causal core of his being. At the core, *chitta* intellectually acknowledges the individualised self as *Prakriti's* Awareness."

At this, the others applauded loudly, for *Pakva* was beginning to speak like *Menander* and *Ujjaini.*

Patanjali, behind the curtain, cleared his throat in approval and encouragement. Continued *Pakva,* "The second path starts in the causal core of *chitta* by first entering the subtle domains of *kutastha.* Here, Matter and Spirit links. The embracing *Purusha* and *Prakriti* in the pineal gland merge into an experience of Universal Intelligence or *chitta-chit.* The 'seer' and 'seen' are bridged in the *kutastha* or *Krishna/Christ* Centre."

The disciples understood the seriousness and importance of this debate. They sat upright. The valley was becoming cold. They pulled their shawls tightly around them. Continued *Pakva,* very seriously, "This linking and becoming Universal Intelligence in the *kutastha* transforms all sheaths of the body-mind-intellect. Man in conclusion shackles himself into captivity with a single thought, AUM."

This wisdom impacted the disciples like a blow. The more they thought about it, the more overwhelmed they felt. So much so tears welled up in their eyes. They understood *Pakva,* but could they authenticate this mystical truth? Continued *Pakva,* "Man intimately discovers AUM or his chosen deity. But both paths fulfil Man's desire for emancipation."

Pushya was the first to respond, saying, "This state is *samadhi.* It comes from a clearly focused, purified intellect. The "Seer or Knower" of "Knowledge – seen" referred to is *Brahman* or AUM. The Knower is one in whom the division of 'seen', 'seeing', and 'seer' no more exists. The seer and seen cease to mis-perceive 'seeing' experiences. The 'seer' has both intellectual knowledge of Truth and its experience beyond the intellect".

"Your single-pointed concentration and understanding comes from unblemished surrender," said *Chandra,* then as if the brothers were of single mind and intellect. He added, "Total surrender frees the seeker from earthly bonds. Having shed this confinement, the seeker experiences *chitta* and *chit* becoming One. Knowledge of the Absolute Truth and its experience of Knowing is beyond the intellect. It is not caused in Time and Space. Knowing this Knowledge is therefore uncontaminated."

"Total surrender needs determined devotion, which some of us lack," said *Saleta,* speaking effectively for himself. But *Patanjali* interjected, "Surrender to God brings perfect *samadhi,* as both *Chandra* and *Pushya* have realized." Though he confirmed *Saleta's* anguish, *Patanjali* also stressed that through refinement of a stable *asana* it is possible to penetrate the various sheaths of one's body, if endured for long periods of stillness. After a pause, *Patanjali* added, "*Asana* involves the perfect and steady maintenance of body posture, with a steady, single-pointed intellect and in an intense meditative spirit."

Saleta wondered aloud, "Can seekers adjust their bodily positions to suit their need for an unmoving body?" Then as if speaking to himself, he answered, "I can channel my mental and sense energy towards the *kutastha.* I have learned to feel the centres in the brain and spinal cord and back. This back-and-forth transfer of energy has allowed the mind to experience perfect contentment for as long as I want."

Said *Chandra,* "A firmly stabilised *asana* does not need further effort to uphold it. By gradually immersing more into Infinite Awareness, exclusion of finite and merging with the infinite becomes complete. Posture does not disturb one who is deeply immersed in meditation."

Added *Menander,* "Smitten *Prakriti* who is Awareness or Knowledge enters the antechamber of the Knower, who is *Purusha* or Consciousness in the pineal core of the brain to a divine experiencing of Universal Intelligence. Here *Krishna* plays his flute in a symphony of Om. The final destination is the Bliss of *chidakasha.*" *Patanjali* agreed with all three disciples and said, confirming *Menander's* personal experience, "Therefore such perfection in meditation as well as in *asana* is achieved only when effort to 'perform' the posture ends. This happens when immersed in infinite poise. The seeker reaches the core within. From that point, the seeker is not disturbed by thoughts or feelings of duality about the body and mind or the intellect and soul," he added.

Ujjaini wanted to discuss the duality of the individualistic self 'Me' and soul ('I'), versus the Self. He has experienced *chitta* merge into *chit*. Here exists perfect beatitude. Said *Ujjaini* incredulously, "In this exalted state, *chitta*, which is the root cause of *dvandvah*, loses its identity. The self merges with the soul. The senses and organs-of-action retreat into the mind. Man stops to recognise *raaga-dvesha*. All 'opposites' cease to disturb him."

The disciples realised *Ujjaini* was now discussing the effects of perfected *asana* and *dharana*. They wondered what *Patanjali* would say. As if on cue, the Master said, "*Pranayama* is regulating incoming and outgoing breath, as well as the pauses in between. It should be practiced only after perfection is arrived at in *asana*." *Patanjali* was outspoken with his insistence that *asana* be mastered before practicing *pranayama*.

Bhratahari opened the discussion, "Untrained breathing is irregular and varies with conditions of the mind. Through *abhyas*, the mind must be trained to watch the regularity of one's breathing. With a stable posture and regulated mind and breathing, it is possible to experience and channel *prana* through all the sheaths and organ systems of the body. It is also possible to intuitively know that *prana* vibrates to support every atom of every name and form in manifestation, as well as each one of us."

Ujjaini understood that *prana*, the brilliant life-giving luminescence, automatically reenergises everything, giving sentience to life. He said, "Not only does *prana* create a magnetic field of polarities in every name and form, it also lights up the Universe. *Prana* connects the body-mind-intellect to one another, upholds and continues this connection, and then delinks from it. This happens when the need for this palpable connection passes."

Asked *Saleta,* "How long does *prana* support any expression?" "As long as there is a want to live," answered *Pakva.* "Does *prana* have any characteristics?" probed *Saleta.*

Answered *Menander, "Prana* is physically visible in the material body as *ojas.* The uterine secretions in woman and semen in man are the most concentrated physical display of *prana.* Self-restraint and chastity are, therefore, advised to prevent their waste. Just as physiological-psychological sheaths are enlivened by *prana,* so also as the luminescence of the intellectual sheath. *Prana* is obvious here as *tejas.*"

Saleta asked again, "Does this same *prana,* therefore, act as physical energy, spiritual energy and causal energy?"

This time, *Bhratahari* answered, "All that vibrates in the universe is *prana.* Heat, light, gravity, magnetism, power, vigour, vitality, life and spirit are all random vibrations of the same *prana,* functioning from a pre-causal universe. It is the prime mover of all activity and of all Creation."

With all these questions, *Saleta* disappeared into deep thought. Through the practice of *yoga, Saleta* had come to realise that stilling oneself composes the *prana. Chitta* now becomes silent. He had, therefore, trained *pranayama* to stabilise *pranic* energy in the three spinal channels: *tamasic ida, rajasic pingala* and *sattvic sushumna.* By watching *prana* trekking in and out of the body, while listening to *pranava,* he realised the two, meaning subconscious Awareness *[chitta]* and unconscious Consciousness *[chit],* could be merged. And once merged, *Saleta* heard AUM in ever-increasing perimeters from within, until it, too, merged with the Cosmic Whole of Universal Intelligence. *Chandra* was silent. He intuitively sensed *prana* and *chitta* as twins – like the sun and its radiance. When the two were quiet, the core was silenced.

It was *Pakva's* turn to speak. "This churning happens within the *sushumna* which controls the chest and the *kutastha* by fortifying respiration. Why, and how, is this made possible?" he asked.

Answered *Menander,* "The respiratory centre in the medulla *ajna* trigger the *ida* and *pingala* energy channels to control the outgoing and incoming breaths, respectively. The *sushumna* churns five *pranic* subdivisions of life force – for breathing, excretion, circulation, assimilation, and crystallisation. It stores *prana* in the seven chambers, or *chakras* of the spinal cord and provides self-directed, life-giving force created through *pranayama.*

Patanjali waited for *Menander* to finish before discussing *pranayama* in spiritual exercises, "*Pranayama* has three movements – *puraka, rechaka* and *kumbhaka* – in between. All of these need to be regulated precisely, according to duration and place." He then invited *Pushya,* a deep practitioner of *pranayama,* to discuss its uses. "There are two types of *kumbhaka* in *pranayama,*" *Pushya* said, and continued, "Focusing on the control and stabilisation of each unit of breath is also called *pranayama.* Each component can be prolonged, according to ability and potential to lengthen these intervals."

"What benefits have you accrued from years of perfecting *pranayama?*" *Bhratahari* asked.

"My experience of the pauses is potent. This is where one develops the power of intuition," affirmed *Pushya.*

Bhratahari wanted to discuss *pranayama* from a cosmic idea, taking his cue from *mahat* or subtle intelligence, which is the first movement in Cosmic Creation. He knew *chitta* is the first pressure to stir the subdued soul into individualised activity. Said *Bhratahari,* "During inspiration, expiration and the pauses in between, Awareness as *prana* courses through all the five physiological sheaths, starting from within the core of the chest. The knower of these activities and the knowledge of how to keep the body-mind and intellect 'alive' is experienced as a unified act of knowing"

"This is also how evolution takes place!" exclaimed *Saleta. Bhratahari* continued, "During expiration, Awareness also courses through the five sheaths in the reverse order, from the skin to the core of Man's being. During the pause after exhalation, the 'experiencer' as *Purusha* meets to embrace the 'experience' as *Prakriti* once again. This is the path of natural adaptation and unfolding of the self if observed and merged with during meditation."

Pakva exclaimed excitedly that such a transformation could free seekers from the four aims of mortal living or *purusha-arthas-dharma, kama, artha* and *moksha* (duty, want, wealth, liberation). *Patanjali* now re-entered the discussion on *pranayama,* with a description of the fourth breathing that transcends automatic movements of *swasayama* or inspiration, expiration and their pauses. "The fourth *pranayama* transcends the external and internal *pranayama.* It appears effortlessly and is nondeliberate," said *Patanjali,* describing *prana* as breath arrested in an occasional inspiration only.

Said *Menander,* "In this fourth breathing, the seeker experiences effortless breathlessness. In this state, the mind's movements and breathing end together. In this pause, the causal *chitta* awakens to the light-of-intelligence or *chit* in consciousness. In this seedless state in *pranayama,* it is possible to linger beyond the range of movements of mortal breathing." *Patanjali* agreed, and added, "*Pranayama* removes the veils covering the Light of Knowledge and heralds the Dawn of Wisdom." *Patanjali* then stated that through the practice of *pranayama,* all wants, attachments, illusions, habits, ideas, anger, greed, pride, likes-and-dislikes and the veils of ignorance clouding the *chitta* are destroyed. Once these clouds of individual knowledge are blown away, the dawn of personally experienced supreme intelligence removes all veils of Man's ignorance. "*Pranayama* is not only an instrument to steady the mind, but also the gateway to concentration or *dharana*," *Patanjali* said.

But before lingering on *dharana, Patanjali* wanted the disciples to discuss the aim and uses of *pratyahara*. "Withdrawing the senses, mind and awareness from contact with external objects and, then, drawing them inwards to the soul, is *pratyahara*," said *Patanjali*. The disciples were silent for some time. They wanted to end the discussion. Much ground had been covered. They were reluctant to revisit the subject. Also, *Chandra* was exhausted from having taken down all the notes. *Patanjali* added, hoping to prod them into discussion, "*Pratyahara* results in control of the sense organs."

When the disciples did not utter a word, he smiled behind the curtain and brought the session to a close. It was nearly dusk, the sun-drenched afternoon a fast-fading memory. The disciples had another reason to end the session, besides being tired and hungry. *Malini Amma* had promised to tell them how she came to stay in *Gonika Amma's ashram*. They wanted to spend this evening with her.

Also, the villagers had sent fresh fruit and vegetables, sacks of wheat, millet, rice, corn and different types of lentils, and butter. The disciples had promised *Malini* they would help her store the grain in bins for the winter. When *Patanjali* heard this, he agreed to join them and help out too. The next session was scheduled for the following morning.

As they toiled in the *ashram*, the exercise kept them warm. It had become chilly in the valley, for winter was near.

The leaves on the deciduous trees were beginning to change colour. The snow line was sliding towards them, as if by the hour. At twilight, their task complete, the disciples walked to the river for a refreshing dip. They then retreated to their own meditation seats. So engrossed were they with this day's discussions that it inspired them to look even deeper into themselves. They were oblivious of the time. They became stimulated only when they heard *Malini* hammer her *thali* with the wooden spatula.

Amma had prepared an elaborate meal. The disciples arrived with *Patanjali.* They all decided to attend to *Amma* first. *Malini* felt embarrassed by this attention, and laughed nervously. After dinner, they helped clean up the pots and plates. During dinner, they realised that *Amma* was exhausted. They did not press *Amma* to tell her story. After the chores were complete, they tucked her into bed. They thanked her for the feast and retired for the night.

The next morning, the disciples were awake at the crack of dawn. After a dip in the river, greetings to the rising sun and a light breakfast, they were ready for another day of weighty discussions. As they approached the cave, they realized *Patanjali* wasn't in his grotto yet, but they took to their usual seats. They pulled their shawls tighter, and decided to review yesterday's discussions till the Master arrives. *Pakva* reminded them they left off at *pratyahara* but it was *Menander* who said, "The mind is able to rise to the inner core of the brain. *Dharana* effortlessly moves towards Awareness. The outgoing five senses, mediated through the cranial and spinal nerves have been drawn away from objects, emotions and thoughts. *Pranayama* if done correctly secures this."

Added *Pushya,* "*Pranayama* fosters *vairagya,* but the movement is that of Awareness. The mind and the senses are Nature's *prana.* From the skin to the core of brain and spinal cord, and back, perfected *pranayama* with resulting *pratyahara* result in breathlessness. These have the power to transform every atom in their path."

Said *Ujjaini,* "*Prana* coursing through the body's *nadis* nourish as well as retract into the divine cave of the brain and spinal cord. This to me is *pratyahara.* One can travel deeper on the two wings of perfected *yama-niyama* and *pranayama.*" He explained all this on how he sees the process.

Saleta's experience and understanding of *pratyahara* were also personal. He said, "The seeker, first, enters the core of his awareness as *chitta.* He must shed his mind-intellect-ego, so he can penetrate pure *chitta* or Awareness. He enters Awareness through the *kutastha chaitanya,* found between the eyebrows. While resting in the *kutastha* and listening to the Cosmic Sound of AUM, he sees the microcosmic brilliant Cosmic Being. The experience of merging with Consciousness needs patience, faith and endurance. Within *chit* he is allowed to witness the photoplay of Creation echo on an underpinning of AUM. In this vision of Infinity, it is possible for a seeker to become combined *chitta-chit.*"

Bhratahari agreed with both *Ujjaini* and *Saleta.* He also defined *pratyahara* as "the withdrawal of the mind from the senses". But he had a slightly different, though relevant, experience. Said *Bhratahari,* "In the causal centre in the thalamus, *pratyahara* allows the seeker to witness the unenlightened *chitta* becoming the enlightened *chitta.* From here, it has the freedom to move towards *chit.* And finally, one needs to enter being One with *Paramatma,* the Universal Soul, where there is an experience of *chidakasha.* Then, *Brahman* becomes a personal experience."

Chandra groaned. When he saw others looking at him quizzically, he said, "Despite this inner movement, the past, recorded within the causal centre, ensnares the *yogi.* He can, again, be trapped in the world. Everyone needs to know that *pratyahara* is the means to erase the footprints of previous births. If the practice is continuous and intense, there is transformation at all four levels of expression – physical, mental, intellectual and spiritual."

Menander discussed the changes and transformation from a medical point of view. "All four lobes of the brain must be stilled and silenced. The frontal lobe of analysis and understanding, the occipital lobe of investigative reasoning and personal realisation, the temporal-lingular lobes for experiencing inner joy and the parietal lobe for individuality, must merge. The *chitta* becomes a single experience. Through transformation, *pratyahara* allows for this singular attention. All works of the brain are arrested at Will. This single thought is the seed of the soul. With intense meditation, the seed-soul can enter the depths of "no thought"."

The disciples were so deep in discussion they did not see *Patanjali* quietly standing behind them. As *Patanjali* stood listening, *Menander* began to define *pratyahara,* "Withdrawing energy from the senses and the organs of action is physical *pratyahara*. Quieting the four lobes of the brain is mental *pratyahara*. Drawing the intellect into the brain stem is intellectual *pratyahara*. And taking the intellect in Awareness to the seat of Consciousness is spiritual *pratyahara*."

Patanjali cleared his throat. The disciples turned around and saw him. As they prepared to move back to their usual seats, he gestured to stop them. This time while standing behind them he said, "*Pratyahara* results in control of sense organs." The disciples remembered that he had said the same at the previous session. They now understood, the effects of *pratyahara* are felt at many levels, when senses are mastered and the mind is ready for its spiritual search. They saw the self as it unfolded and they understood. The next step was for them to experience Self-realisation.

Book Three – On Powers

Vibhuti Pada

Patanjali entered the cave and pulled the curtain. As he settled into his seat, he knew this session was of special importance. He would not only discuss *yoga* but also the art of integration in meditation or *samyama.* He intended to take his disciples through *dharana, dhyana* and *samadhi* [concentration-contemplation-meditation] – the remaining limbs of *ashtanga yoga,* that still need much explaining and discussion. It was equally important that *Patanjali* warn his disciples about *vibhutis* and *siddhis.* These are naturally picked up when engaged in such types of intense meditation. He pondered how to discuss the "fallout effects" of an intense spiritual life. At some stage in the innermost search of the Self or *atma,* gaining particular powers is natural. When a *yogi* succeeds in integrating his body, mind and intellect, the changing soul is in danger of being seduced by psychic powers. Many seekers get shuttled away from *sadhana.* Their effort at true emancipation, through *kaivalya,* is then lost.

In the second discussion on *Sadhana, Patanjali* spent many hours schooling the disciples to earn physical and mental poise under all types of external stress. Now, he must walk them through *vibhutis* and *siddhis.* Taking them into an intense inner search towards *samyama, Patanjali* must carry them deeper by linking and integrating their efforts during *dharana, dhyana* and *samadhi.* They must aim to become a unified whole. He warned the disciples that at each stage of transformation, there always exists the possibility of regression. And most of the time, retrogression is caused by failure to follow basic building blocks of *yoga* – *yama* and *niyama.*

Patanjali reiterated that *yama* involved restraint and observations of moral injunctions. The seeker, said *Patanjali,* should have the courage to make right judgments when exposed to temptations of lying and harming. He stressed *niyama,* are moral and religious observances. They help seekers adhere to actions favorable for a spiritual journey. Unless these restraints are adhered to, no spiritual gains can be made.

Patanjali warned the disciples, repeatedly, that invoking *siddhis* takes ignorant seekers down a path of indulgence and unimaginable fantasy. He highlighted that whenever a seeker struggles vigorously for a goal, it is natural to receive incidental bounty along the path. But the seeker shouldn't become enamored with this fortuitously earned strength. Nor must they mistake them for the Goal.

The seeker must not allow being sidetracked by "spiritual materialism". These are merely bricks-and-mortar of temple's walls, no matter how beautiful and ornate. The seeker must strive to enter the temple's sanctum sanctorum, and ignore the temple walls. *Patanjali,* then, outlined the *ashta siddhis* that came, unasked, to seeker of concentrated spiritual practice – *Anima, Mahima, Laghima, Garima, Praapti, Prakamya, Ishatva* and *Vashitva.* Though these *siddhis* are indicators that a seeker's *sadhana* is on the right path, they need ignoring. The seeker must always preserve his goal of freedom and beatitude. Pride in the power of *siddhis* cause distractions. They trigger a new set of attachments and afflictions. *Patanjali* advised the seekers to dismiss *siddhis.* He urged his disciples to devote their complete energy to self-unfoldment and Self-realisation.

After an introduction to the subject of divine powers, *Patanjali* first tackled *dharana,* saying, "Fixing the attention of Awareness at one point is *dharana.*" He then invited the disciples to discuss the subject. *Pakva* introduced the discussion, "The eight units of *ashtanga yoga* are interwoven. They are subdivided into the external journey or *bahiranga sadhana,* the internal search or *antaranga sadhana,* and the innermost crusade or *antaratma sadhana.*"

After a short pause, *Pakva* continued, "Through the practice of *yama* and *niyama,* the seeker develops emotional stability. Through *asana,* he keeps his body free of disease because he recognises the body as the temple of his soul. Through *pranayama,* he learns to recognise *Brahman's* power as it upholds the soul's existence as a mortal. Through breath control, he identifies this powerful Occupant who regulates the flow of breath in and out of the body. He recognises Life Force or *prana* enlivening the creature. He sees the *nadis* supplying life through the six energy *chakras* to every part of the body – from the skin to the core of his being. He learns to rest on negligible amounts of breath in the core, as if in hibernation. Through *pratyahara* and a harnessed Will, he detaches himself from senses and organs of action. He enters his essence through the four layers – anatomical, physiological, mental-intellectual and spiritual. Being there in the causal core, gives clarity of thought."

Saleta requires reassurance. He interrupted, and asked mournfully, "Have I now reached my objective? Have I reached freedom from mortal oppression?"

Replied *Pakva,* "This is only the beginning of brain culturing. As a seeker becomes indifferent to worldly matters, he is readying for an inner search. By reaching maturity and refinement, the mind withdraws from the senses. In *dharana,* attention must be on a selected particular, within or outside the body."

Asked *Chandra,* his brow furrowing, "What is the best place for a seeker to unite his concentration?"

"The navel, the tip of nose, the midpoint of the eyebrows or the centre of the chest are traditional points of attentiveness," replied *Pakva,* adding, "Through *dharana,* the mind is controlled and brought to a single focal point. This act tolerates penetration by innermost thoughts and feelings."

When *Pakva* finished, the disciples had drifted into deep thought. In the otherwise silent valley, the rhythmic cooing of ring-necked doves in the *peepal* tree has a hypnotic effect. There was a long, pregnant pause, until *Ujjaini* broke the silence. He said, "While performing *asana, dharana* and *pranayama,* the seeker watches and feels the breath being drawn up by a mystical power in the *kutastha*. The inspired air expands the chest. *Kutastha* inserts oxygen and life force to all parts of the body and enlivens it. All the way through inspiration and expiration, *prana* clutches to all of Man's physical expressions."

Added *Chandra*, "Through such intense absorption, the seeker succeeds in withdrawing senses, organs of action and mind into the divine cave of the spinal cord and brain."

"What absorption?" asked *Saleta*.

Replied *Chandra*, "Absorption happens when and while watching and looking at the Cosmic Vision in the *kutastha* and hearing the Cosmic Sound. Having the tongue rolled back in the *kechri mudra* ensures perfect concentration in *dharana*."

"But that is *pratyahara*," said *Saleta*, voicing his own grasp on absorption. Continued *Chandra*, "In this inward movement, all external *sadhana* becomes internalised. From *sthula sharira*, the seeker enters the halls of the *sukshma sharira*. As he changes, the seeker penetrates, in sequence, the *pranamaya kosha*, *manomaya kosha* and *gyanamaya kosha*."

"Intense *sadhana* takes him into the *gyanamaya kosha*," said *Bhratahari*, adding, "He can, then, link the energy of the body-mind-intellect with the ideational *karana sharira*. This is awareness of the enlightening *chitta* and once it is linked with *prana*, there is mysterious fusion within innermost *sadhana*."

All the disciples were practicing *yogis*, and *Pushya* sought to watch and outline their inner voyages. Said *Pushya*, "Through *yama*, *niyama*, *asana*, *pranayama* and *pratyahara*, the seeker's commitment to *kama* for 'exteriorised' living is dislodged. And through *dharana*, concentration ascends to absorption in the Self. This journey leads to inner humility, necessary to penetrate the subtlest layers of one's personality. The seeker, through this path, gradually cancels disturbances of the mind and senses."

There was a long pause as the disciples delved into their own journeys. *Menander,* himself in deep thought, broke the silence "The eternal witness or *Purusha* is the *chit,* who 'watches' all changes in the essence of an altering *chitta.* All these changes are recorded in the seeker's causal being – the essence of individualised *Prakriti* – who 'looks' at these changes. As individualised Nature, the Soul or Self awaits its Goal. It aspires to become One with the Cosmic Whole. Once the seeker has reached this ability, he has progressed to integration or *samyama* and is ready in the future to experience the ecstasy of oneness or *samadhi.*"

As *Menander* finished, *Patanjali* realised the discussion needed further dissection and expansion. Though the debate was mature, *Patanjali* was aware each disciple is at different level of understanding and practice. He decided to trigger a new discussion, on meditation or *dhyana* and the different levels of absorption in *samadhi.* Said *Patanjali,* "A steady flow of attention directed to a single point is *dhyana.*"

Saleta began this discussion, by trying to narrow down the definition of *dhyana.* "Although commonly translated as 'meditation', there is no overt or seeming activity noted by the onlooker. Should it not, then, be called contemplation or *dharana,* given that its main characteristic is keeping uninterrupted flow of attention at one point?"

Answered *Ujjaini,* "In *dharana,* the seeker is absorbed in methods to still the mind's fluctuations. He sinks into the symphony of Om. Through *pranayama* he discovers life force called *prana.* With this personal Knowledge he seeks detachment. Time now stops as Mind watches its own behaviour. Intensity moves from 'single-pointed attention' to 'no-point attentiveness'. That is when the seeker has moved from *dharana* to *dhyana.* He has gained Detachment and Tranquility and therefore Happiness born of Renunciation and Steadfastness."

Agreed *Chandra,* "During this period, a seeker converges his entire attention into the Infinity behind his eyebrows. He adjusts hearing on the *antardhvani* of *pranava.* He decontaminates feelings by watching and feeling his breath striding in and out of the divine cave. The deeper he penetrates, the less frequent becomes his breathing. The heartbeat and bodily works corroborate suchlike retraction. With a single thought, he experiences the beatitude of such effort. This is *dharana.*"

The difference between *dharana* and *dhyana* is clear.

"In *dharana,* Man succeeds in erasing fluctuations of thought. In *dhyana,* his emphasis is on steady contemplative observation," interjected *Bhratahari. Chandra* reminded the disciples that *dhyana* was the seventh ingredient of *Raja Yoga.* At this, *Bhratahari* said, "In discussing the units of *Raja Yoga,* we must realise the implications in the previous six phases are conquered. In the practice of *yoga,* Master *Patanjali* has stated that some degree of success in *dhyana* is attained at all stages of *sadhana.*" *Menander* reanalysed the processes of *ashtanga yoga,* saying, "Awareness moves from the physical body to the astral body and, then, to the causal body, until one achieves a single focus of attentiveness." *Menander* had outlined the progress made through the eight steps. *Pushya,* like the others, felt *pranayama* alone measures the sensitivity with which to change the *chitta.*

"As *chitta* changes with each breath, Awareness embraces Consciousness. In the end, *chitta* and *chit* rest as the Self. In this fashion, *dharana* grows and changes into *dhyana,*" said *Menander.*

Patanjali responded, agreeing with *Menander's* observation, "When the attention of Awareness merges with Consciousness, the object and the subject merge into One. Self-awareness is lost, and only Consciousness remains – this is *samadhi.*" As he heard *Patanjali, Pakva* who had temporarily drifted into his own meditative experience, quickly added, "For the *yogi,* the enlightened *chitta* is a changing ego. His awareness, once an object, now has no form or physical expression. In *dhyana,* this condition takes the shape of formless Awareness and merges with *chit.* This absorption is devoid of 'Me'. And 'I' merges with its core. This is intense serenity, beyond time and space."

The young Master drifted into thought and became quiet. He began to assess the progress of each of his seven disciples. Those who reached Awareness in the *kutastha* were starting to see the Cosmic Whole. They saw Nature's Will, Wisdom, Intuition, and Love. They understood Her Volatility and demand for Selfless Service. Now, they must expand from *chitta* to *chit.* They must see themselves in every atom in space. They must recognise the Cosmic Whole in their own physical expression. *Patanjali* found that *Pakva* prevailed as the most changed. Having reached advanced stages of development he could easily converse with Mother Nature. *Patanjali* noted *Pakva's* distaste for material pleasure, despite tasting royal pleasures. *Patanjali* noted *Pakva* avoids actions that disturb surroundings – his own and of those around him. *Pakva* was, by nature, gentle and thoughtful. Having matured through *yama* and *niyama* at a young age, it was easier to mature through the remaining steps of *yoga.*

At first, *Patanjali* was dissatisfied with *Saleta's* development. *Saleta,* who had childhood virtues, had led a life of indulgence, provoked by scars of past lives. A persistent lingering for material pleasures hunted his peace. However, his experience with death had chastened *Saleta.* Although shocked at the force of his own, often uncontrollable, restive thoughts and mental opposition, he made progress. Now, his awareness seemed redirected and organized. He was able to concentrate on the path of self-unfoldment. By turning repeatedly towards his intuitive soul, he was faithful to the goal. *Patanjali* was sure *Saleta* would reach emancipation with concerted effort.

Bhratahari is *Patanjali's* own student. His devotion to

Shiva was well-known. His earlier lives of anguish, pain and poverty left him unblemished. Though gifted with untold wealth in this life, it caused him outrageous pain. He yearned for *Shiva's* love and became a renunciate. Under the guidance of *Patanjali, Bhratahari* nurtured intellectual wealth. He was enriched with a legacy of the *Mahabhashya. Bhratahari* went through stages of evolution. *Patanjali* viewed *Bhratahar's* journey a steady inner movement towards clear-sighted perception. *Bhratahari* traced his psychological battles to sense attachment and restless thoughts. He matured as a deep thinking scholar who preferred a life of renunciation and devotion. *Patanjali* was sure both *Saleta* and *Bhratahari* had grown. *Patanjali* felt happy to see these two disciples will eventually surrender to the Cosmic Self.

The *Pushya* and *Chandra* brothers had won the battles of flesh early in their lives. Their time spent in forest hermitages gave them early lessons of life. *Dharma* reigned supreme in their lives. Having been tutored by sages and a *yaksha,* the brothers were already in the halls of Self-discovery, even before meeting with *Patanjali*. Under *Patanjali,* they felt sublime peace and bliss of as yet unverified Self. While in deep meditation *Patanjali* would make sure they arrive at being One. But he also knew the brothers still questioned whether they experience Self-realisation at all.

Ujjaini and *Menander* had practical minds. *Patanjali* harnessed this tendency by allowing them to speak. Their platform of discussion sprang from selected knowledge and logic. These two disciples would, by nature, arrive at correct conclusions about the subtle, thought *Patanjali. Menander* viewed *dharana* as bringing the mind to a single point of stability. He thought *dhyana* brought maturity to the intellect, and that *samadhi* was about diffusing the ego. *Patanjali* was comfortable with *Menander's* conclusions. It came from a mingling of mind, intellect and awareness or *samyama* of the three. *Patanjali* was satisfied with *Menander's* progress in spirituality. *Ujjaini,* as everyone knew, was devoted to the Cosmic Mother. His scientific mind was not different from *Menander's,* even though his ideal was the Cosmic Mother. While *Menander* lodged his discussions in the divine cave, *Ujjaini* focused on the Universe. Both practiced *ashtanga yoga* and both were advanced *yogis.*

Yet, *Patanjali's* concern swirled around a goal of successful *yogic* practice and experience of Consciousness. *Patanjali* was comfortable starting the subject of deepening meditation.

Patanjali smiled, grateful that his disciples were learned seekers themselves and pleased with their intelligent interaction. *Patanjali* had started by defining *samyama* as integration of *dharana, dhyana* and *samadhi. Pakva* and *Pushya* had successfully grouped these three into a single effort of uninterrupted attention, even before *Patanjali* had brought up the subject. With long-drawn-out support from these three, *Pakva* and *Pushya* had reached a partial state of *samyama. Patanjali* had often watched them as they drifted in and out of intense immobility. They temporarily succeeded in subduing their passions, individuality and ideas of comparisons. *Patanjali* also noted each of his disciples are able to narrow the dissociation between Awareness and Consciousness.

It suddenly struck him he must show them to merge the two, until 'Knower' and 'Knowledge' lose their separate identities in 'Knowing'. After this tortuous assessment *Patanjali* said, "These three together "*dharana, dhyana* and *samadhi,*" work as integrated *samyama.* By mastering *samyama,* the lustre of wisdom and insight becomes brilliant. *Samyama* may be employed in different realms to spin its usefulness."

The curtain swayed in the gentle mountain breeze. The disciples remained silent. There were no questions. They remained immersed in their own thoughts. *Patanjali* retreated into his feelings too. Despite the fact the day had just started, *Patanjali* reminisced about his origin. The "*Shesha* personality" in him wished to return to his Master, *Vishnu*. *Patanjali* understood when reawakened into reincarnation, Man identifies with ego. He is burdened with past tendencies and habits, and suffers them as *samskaras*. *Patanjali* was glad he didn't carry a weight from past births and their effects into his present life. He realized only the inner-directed Man can remain neutral to the pull of the senses. However, if he prefers meditation to sleep, such an introspective Man will naturally travel towards dispassion and renunciation. He realised he'd have to teach how disciples can eradicate an introspective still mind off worldly compulsions.

Inherent negative *tamasic* and *rajasic* tendencies need sublimation. He must reveal to them *Prakriti* carries both tendencies. He must discuss this duality in Awareness, which gives birth to good and evil. *Patanjali* encouraged disciples to use thoughtfulness, to unravel painful predicaments they face, on the path of spirituality. For now, they must be taught to trust the Cosmic Self.

With this, *Patanjali* awakened to the present, realising he had started a new subject. To make sense of the subject, he would have to clarify 'meditation' and *samyama*. *Patanjali* suddenly said, "These three aspects of *yoga* are internal, compared to the former five."

The disciples returned to the present with a startle. Whispered *Saleta*, "What is the Master talking about?" *Pakva* requested *Patanjali* for a moment to respond to *Saleta*. "Compared with the previous five aspects of *yoga* – *yama, niyama, asana, pranayama, pratyahara*, the three paths we are going to discuss – *dharana, dhyana* and *samadhi* – are subtle, intimate and subjective in nature," said *Pakva*.

As *Pakva* finished, *Patanjali* invited the disciples to discuss the purpose of *ashtanga yoga*, the eight steps of *Raja Yoga*. With vigour, *Saleta* rattled off, "The first five steps clean the five outer sheaths of the body. As I understand,

Yama purifies the organs of action. *Niyama* purifies the organs of perception. *Asana* stabilises the body. *Pranayama* negates waste of energy and increases stamina. *Pratyahara* withdraws the sense-mind to its source. *Dharana* develops and sharpens the intellect. *Dhyana* purifies Awareness. And *samadhi* leads Awareness to Consciousness, the inner search." As his voice trailed off, *Saleta* asked, in a softer voice, "Now, what is this *samyama*?"

Answered *Patanjali*, "*Samyama* is external when compared with the seedless state of *samadhi*."

"But despite more integrity, the unity arrived at in *samyama* is not the 'incomparable' unity Man experiences. *Chitta* may become One with *chit*, but it is, still, *sabija samadhi*. It still depends on a substratum of form and seed. Only when the Self crosses the causal seed does Man enter the seedless state *of nirbija samadhi*. And that must be how it is." There was a pause, as *Pushya* mulled over what he had just said. Then, almost meekly, *Pushya* asked, "Am I right?"

Answered *Pakva*, "Merging *chitta* with *chit* is the aim and the purpose of this *sadhana*. We have all understood that." He looked towards the curtain, appealing the Master for more information. *Patanjali* elaborated, "Study of the silent moments between the rising and restraining of disturbances leaves impressions in Awareness – the transformation happens only while restraining awareness or *nirodha parinama*."

The central theme of teaching in *Patanjali's yoga* is to master the characteristics of Spirit and Matter. Next it is to unravel the relationship between the *Purusha* and *Prakriti*, within the body and outside it. Through *sadhana* of eight steps of *ashtanga yoga*, Man learns to free himself from Nature, by surpassing Her qualities. Man must experience – as the disciples personally have – that sense involvement with indulgence is what leads to desire, anger, greed, attachment, pride and jealousy. Resultant disoriented thought leads to bodily and intellectual decay. Over the course of these sessions, *Patanjali* had repeatedly advised the combined use of *yama, niyama, asana, pranayama* and *pratyahara* to restrain the "wrenching" by *samskaras.* The disciples had continued to experience holiness but had also shifted back to their old ways, now and again. They wanted a permanent shift beyond this seesaw. They realised that persistence in the principles of *ashtanga yoga* was the way 'inwards'.

Said *Pushya,* "Even after the mind has advanced into *samyama* to cancel its tendency to desire, the causal inclination for emancipation must also be eliminated. Even the desire to become 'desireless' must be disposed. Transformation of a changing *chitta* is achieved by studying and prolonging silent moments, occurring between rising thoughts, as Master *Patanjali* just said."

Added *Ujjaini,* "The Master also advises the use of *pranayama* as a means to reverse the outward flow of awareness. He enlists *pranayama* for successful *pratyahara,* a means to withdraw *prana* from sense perceptions and the organs of action."

Interjected *Chandra,* "But these are preparatory efforts to align *Prakriti* with *Purusha.*" As he said this, *Chandra* stood up to stretch his legs. The realisation this discussion would take them to a need for a desirable body-culture and harmonious development seemed obvious. Suddenly, as he stretched out, he estimated the science of meditation made sense. The technique of *ashtanga yoga* outlined a homogenous mixture of techniques to decrease problems of a human birth.

It seemed as though hours had passed. *Chandra* finally sat down beside his older brother, *Pushya.* He could read *Chandra's* mind, which was now preoccupied. *Pakva* continued with *Chandra's* thoughts, "This effort results in limitless growth from within. They gradually shorten distances between polarities of negative or *tamasic* and positive or *rajasic* tendencies. Then, as harmony or *sattva* prevails, the *chitta* becomes quiet. Awareness intermittently moves up into the embrace of Consciousness." *Bhratahari* smiled knowingly, and said, "In this embrace, the seeker is able to identify the subtle qualities of *Prakriti,* within a respectful distance from *Purusha.*"

"And in the silent intervals of *pranayama* and while in *pratyahara,* the seeker discovers that Nature's *gunas* lie within the stress lines and swings of time. He realises *yoga* of meditation uses life force or *prana* for tissue renewal and better health. He recognises the eternalness of *chitta* and *chit* beyond time," added *Menander.*

"Hasn't the Master already stated that *dharana, dhyana* and *samadhi* are three ingredients in the practice of *ashtanga yoga*?" asked *Saleta.*

Menander explained, patiently, "Right, but each part takes a seeker to better understanding born of personal experience. These three are synonymous with perfect health. Willfully increasing inner strength allows Man to provoke transformation and integration in every cell in the body."

"Each ingredient of *ashtanga yoga* takes seekers towards uniform performance of all three bodies – gross, astral and causal. The experience is a harmonious merging of Man's sheaths and body parts. The Energy in Awareness, then, naturally embraces the Life force or Light of Consciousness," added *Ujjaini,* and asked, "The *chitta* is, the soul... is it not?"

As *Saleta* listened, he seemed disturbed. Finally, he asked, "Where does the subject of 'Energy' and "Life force" come from? How does one come to the conclusion self and soul are one and the same?"

Answered *Chandra,* "Just as moonlight is a reflection of the sun, the *chitta* reflects the Energy of Awareness and Light of Consciousness in *chit* or Universal Intelligence."

"Transformation of *chitta* occurs as a continuous flux,

in deeper states of concentration and meditation. Awareness eventually loses all outgoing tendencies. It comes to rest in the embrace of Consciousness. Here, Nature is pensive, not restless. The body and senses are withdrawn into the divine cave. The seeker experiences the dawn of discrimination or *dharma parinama.*"

"With concerted effort, he develops innate *chitta* transformation or *lakshana parinama.* With even deeper practice and maintenance of this picked up condition, he reaches the zenith of perfection or *avastha parinama,*" said *Bhratahari,* who seemed to be speaking from personal experience. As he finished, the disciples drifted into silence. The chirping of birds overhead stopped. The soft breeze stalled. It seemed as if the elements, the creatures, even the leaves awaited, with baited breath, to hear what *Bhratahari* would have to say next. *Bhratahari* took a deep breath, and said, "The seeker is, then, fit for higher meditation and entry into single-pointedness or *samadhi parinama.*"

A gust of wind blew through the valley as *Bhratahari* finished, as though marking his words with a collective sigh. The other disciples, still silent, braced themselves for a chilly onslaught of a cold wind howling down from the mountain peaks. They pulled their shawls close, immediately.

A true hurricane of wisdom had come through. Walls of doubt came crumbling down around them. Indeed, it had blown away the curtain of *Maya.* In their hearts, love for Him and His knowledge had flourished. It was growing stronger by the day. Now, yearning to break free, each disciple sought *Patanjali's* help to go beyond the rough spiritual path. They silently asked, individually and in unison, "Just tell me about my Love. When will He meet me, when can I finally be known to Him?"

Even as he heard the disciples' unspoken plea, *Patanjali* remained attentive but silent. He saw the disciples retract from the world. *Patanjali* followed their attention move, from swings of thoughts and wants, to periods of calmness. As he witnessed their periods of peacefulness or *nirodha parinama, Patanjali* asked the disciples to lengthen these intervals. He assured them these prolonged periods of silence would erase past impressions emanating from the *chitta* personality.

Sensing the Master, *Pakva* decided to walk with the others into meditation. Said *Pakva,* "Each of us is on a revolving wheel of transformation. In this silence, let us practice *pranayama,* and watch breath make its four movements. After inspiration, there is a pause and, after expiration, there is another pause. By prolonging *kumbhaka* at the end of *puraka* and *rechaka, chitta* becomes untroubled and thought formation is hesitant. In this void of restraint, the *chitta* personality gradually transforms. This is single-pointedness or the "no-pointed" attention of *samadhi parinama.*" With this, *Pakva* drifted into silence. As the disciples advanced into deeper meditation, they practiced enduring in breathlessness during *kumbhaka.*

A few moments later, *Pakva* said suddenly, "When a beginner-seeker passes the early stages and arrives at the middle stages of meditation, he is able to make out intuitively both polarities of Nature, which are born of the ego. The intuitive acceptance of these polarities is born of a spiritual ego." He was referring to the need to develop distaste for materialism, to reach single-pointedness.

He knew that ingrained tendencies of restlessness and fickle thought countered the willful rejection of sense tendencies, likes-and-dislikes and habits. As a beginner seeker, *Pakva* convinced himself he would gain nothing by destroying sense indulgences. He faced doubts and difficulties. But one day, in deep contemplation, *Pakva* experienced being One with the Cosmic Self. The haunting memory of this perfect Bliss drew him back to reassess his convictions. He realised that unenlightened *chitta* does indeed wander, but is restrained and silenced also.

Pakva understood silent intervals need lengthening to ensure progressive transformation. A change towards purifying experiences of Awareness as single-pointed attentiveness come from retraining. Endurance in stillness is directed against embedded impressions in the subconscious and unconscious minds. Over time, *Pakva* learned that every effort at self-restraint reinstates restfulness. When tranquillity is sustained for long periods, *dharana* and *dhyana* merge into *samadhi*. Here one experiences unbroken equanimity.

Silence, as usual, Commands circumstances for some time. The disciples processed their experiences while in *kumbhaka*. *Patanjali* carefully watched *Pakva* when the latter was speaking. *Patanjali* willed his own mind to reach out and come together with the seven disciples. He realised they already understood the purpose of *kumbhaka*. Said *Patanjali*, interrupting their thoughts, "By restraining all rising impressions and wants, the mind becomes permanently tranquil and undisturbed." The disciples immediately emerged from deep rumination.

Saleta spoke and broke the silence. "By restraining thought in the intervals between breaths, awareness endorses perfect stillness. One effortlessly confines even past impressions. Stillness now turns into inner silence. There are no ripples in the springtime of awareness, but rather, a stream of tranquility that flows unhindered. Repetitive efforts transform awareness into a refined, cultured *chitta*, undisturbed by swings of thought. This causes steadfastness in meditation for a genesis of knowledge."

Saleta had just voiced his experience of *kumbhaka*. The other disciples seemed engrossed in what he had just said. *Chandra* added, "Awareness need not wield its presence through such constant practice or *abhyas*."

Bhratahari said, "Freedom from disturbance escorts renunciation or *vairagya*. The seeker and the sought become One. There is proficiency in meditation. The seeker discovers tranquility. The experience of the 'seer' and 'seen' become One." Added *Chandra,* "We make excuses for not slaying past habits and tendencies. Irrational thoughts arise from such past tendencies. Discrimination is blinded by inaccurate opinions. The seeker can of course counter these, if tried, by *pranayama.*"

Said *Patanjali,* after he had heard the discussion, "The weakening of shifting attention and strengthening of steady attention is the *chitta* transforming itself and moving towards *samadhi.*" *Patanjali* had chosen to interrupt the disciples' thought flow. While they discussed the benefits of silencing the *chitta* for longer and more prolonged intervals during *kumbhaka, Patanjali* as an alternative wanted to introduce the subject of a three-stage transformation of *chitta.*

Patanjali threw the floor open for discussion. *Menander* began the discussion, "Awareness see-saws between inclinations for multifaceted concentration and single pointed alertness. When single-pointed attention becomes fixed, multifaceted mindfulness fades away, and vice versa. The seeker as *chitta* makes certain observations. He learns to focus his watchfulness at a single point. This leads to transformation of the *chitta.* This, eventually, results in *samadhi.*"

"*Chitta* has only two characteristics. It can either be multifaceted or become single-pointed. When multifaceted, the *chitta's* attention is externalised. When *chitta* is single pointed, its attention is internalised. But when these two facets merge, their combined alertness escorts the *chitta* to spiritual absorption," noted *Bhratahari.*

Saleta commented, "*Chitta* has the ability to take on any appearance it desires. It cannot be destroyed. Its restlessness can, however, be subdued. And it can also be transformed by thoughtful single-pointed attention."

Ujjaini said, "The restless stream of attention can be transformed to become a habit of restful single-pointed attention." *Pushya* agreed, and said, "This transformed *chitta* is ready for *samadhi*. This is the stillness that heads to silence."

"Silence is the fragrance of the Self, of *chit*," *Chandra* asserted. After a flurry of this discussion, the disciples became silent. Like any seeker on the inward and upward path of meditation, they looked into themselves and wondered why their progress in reaching emancipation was so slow. Unconvinced *Saleta* was more restless than the rest. From behind the curtain, *Patanjali* read *Saleta's* mind. He cleared his throat. Mentally taking his Master's cue, *Saleta* said, "My thoughts wander to my old ways. Sometimes, I feel remorse over separating myself from old friends, my natural habits and tendencies. My sense sympathetic mind is still exposed to past habits that are embedded in my nature. I still allow them to squabble with the spiritual mind. It's important to be at war with the demands of my past indulgences."

Pushya's face reflected sympathy, for he knew seekers sometimes felt disconnected from acts of worship. It was impossible to 'presuppose' the prescription used by different worshippers at different times and in different places. He also knew a single endeavor to perfect and remove past tendencies is not sufficient. What proves to be even more difficult, *Pushya* reasoned, is those seekers do not take responsibility for their flaws and deficiencies. It also struck *Pushya* that no individual should imagine he has reached a moral level higher or lower than the group to which he belongs.

Saleta was, therefore, an evolved disciple who suffered the natural remorse of separation from the Cosmic Whole. *Pushya* addressed *Saleta*, "You are here with us because you were unhappy with past sense tendencies. It is natural to not gain or perceive happiness from early meditative practices. The mind and intellect are more familiar with the five sense pleasures and will intermittently make their demands felt. Yet, the sixth – the sense of intuition – is gradually rousing through meditation. *Saleta*, like the rest of us, you feel and have experienced inner calmness. You too have surrendered yourself to it." *Pushya* looked around compassionately and continued, "The voice of intuition has revealed to each one of us the imposing task that lies ahead. Intuition must unfold the challenges you must address."

Added *Pakva,* "Until *chitta* is enlightened and absorbed in *chit,* do not count on the mind to giving up its demands. Remember that *chitta* although naturally externalised, can be internalised and synthesised. When externalised, it is multifaceted and plagued by wandering thoughts. When internalised, it is single-pointed in purity. When synthesised, it becomes *chit.*"

Patanjali agreed and said, "When fluctuating and single-pointed thoughts are balanced, only single-pointedness emerges. Sustaining Awareness from single-pointedness to no-pointedness is *ekagrata parinama.*" With *Patanjali's* pronouncement that *chitta* could either be fluctuating or single-pointed, the disciples were silent again. They were familiar with the difficulties and passions of the wayward mind. Said *Pakva,* "Bringing Awareness to a controlled state of balance takes time and effort. Stillness can only be brought about through constant practice and endurance. Silence, on the other hand, makes its appearance, at first, in snatches. But silence will, finally permeate the whole *chitta.* And once *chitta* is both still and silent, the past and future are wiped out."

Speechless from this discussion, *Saleta* and *Chandra* felt encouraged to persist with their efforts. Their eyes filled with tears. It was a sign of anguish, but also a symbol of devotion. *Patanjali* recognised these emotions. He silently assured his disciples that all of them would gain timelessness of existence. When stillness and silence consummates in the mind, they would change into *ekagrata parinama.*

Thus bolstered, *Pakva* continued, "*Chitta* and *chit* are

two sides of one coin. While building results through three levels of single-pointedness or *ekagrata samskara,* the knowledge and the knower become known in a single experience. After that, there is neither a subject 'I' nor an object 'Me'. When depth of stillness and silence is lasting through perpetuation, the seeker reaches the final stages of transformation. It is usual to experience doubt and despondency at even such critical moments. Be assured realised Masters have always rescued evolved seekers who painstakingly challenge sense battles. Prophets, who appeared in every cycle of creation or *Yuga* as Messiahs of Universal Intelligence, repeatedly voice the same Truth. True devotees of transcendental meditation received universal guidance since Time began." *Pakva's* words gave all a renewed enthusiasm even after *Patanjali's* silent assurance.

After the disciples had absorbed what *Pakva* had summarized, *Menander* asked *Pakva* to describe the three stages of *ekagrata samskara* of *chitta*. *Pakva* answered, "*Nirodha* or restraint is the first stage of transformation. Control of multifaceted thought is achieved through concentration or *dharana.* This, being the path to *stillness,* allows the seeker to experience *silence* in snatches at this stage. *Samadhi* or absorption is the second stage of *chitta's* transformation. When silence is prolonged and filled with awareness, the mind is single-pointed. *Ekagrata* or single-pointedness happens in the third stage of *chitta's* transformation. When externalised attention moves inwards, it becomes seedless Awareness."

His companion disciples regarded *Pakva,* as did *Patanjali,* an established *yogi.* They all knew that he had offered his past as oblation to the consecrated fires of self-purification. He asked to become purified by the Supreme Light of Consciousness. But *Patanjali* recognised that *Pakva* had matured with the help of his seer and preceptor. Naturally gifted with both knowledge and wisdom, his teacher initiated *Pakva* as a gifted disciple.

Freed of impeding transgressions, *Pakva's* thoughts were pure and free of passion. The disciples always took his words seriously. *Pakva* continued, "The benevolent Light of Consciousness comes to the rescue of all faltering devotees. Universal Intelligence knows Man's life is a riddle. Although Man knows true Happiness is arrived at through divine preference, yet, in the battle with sense tendencies, he must make real choices through discrimination. Transformation of *chitta* is only the beginning." The others were silent but attentive.

"I am convinced there is more to mutation. Indeed, transforming *chitta* is only the beginning," said *Pushya*. Behind the curtain, *Patanjali* agreed too, and said, "Through these three stages, cultured Awareness is transformed from its potential-state of cosmic discipline or *dharma* to the refined state of *lakshana*. *Chitta* reaches its perfection or *avastha parinama* in the third stage. Transformation of mind and senses, as well as the formational elements, comes about."

Exclaimed *Menander*, "So, the three stages of transformation – **restraint, tranquil stillness and single-pointed silence – influence one's entire manifest being**!" Then he asked, "The organs of action, of perception, the body and the mind, are they all balanced into stillness?"

"It all makes sense," *Bhratahari* commented, and then added, "*Prakriti* is now in balance. When Her qualities of inertia or *tamas* and creativity or *rajas* stop swinging, a state of harmonious stilled Awareness in *sattva* emerges. So, naturally, Man's link with time is severed. His Awareness remains in its own intrinsic silence." *Chandra,* the silent, observant seeker, known for his intense discipline in study and effort, spoke next. These discussions had led him to realise that Man's awareness has to undergo three processes to evolve completely. "When *avidya* is prominent, thoughts in the *chitta* wander. But when discrimination dawns, *chitta* gains the ability to restrain thought. The capacity for transformation is inherent in the dawn of *dharma parinama.*" There was a thoughtful pause. *Chandra* then continued, "The effect of such restraint is that *chitta* moves towards tranquility. But that is its quality or *lakshana.* This tendency to serenity has the ability to prolong silence. This mutation into tranquil silence or *prashanta vahita samskara* is an inherent quality transformation of *chitta.*"

The disciples listened closely, following *Chandra's* logic. They understood the next step in concentration and absorption was to prolong the silent intervals to reach perfection or *avastha parinama.* Here Awareness reaches the final attribute of unfolding. As his thoughts emerged, *Pushya* felt he had to warn and at the same time, reassure others. "Remember that *Purusha* is forever changeless. But *Prakriti* is forever changing, because of Her inherent *gunas.* When Awareness in Man, as *Prakriti,* loses all its tendencies that link it to the past, present, or future, She comes to rest in the Spirit. She merges with Consciousness, as if in pensive Awareness. As this happens, Man undergoes further transformation – in tranquil awareness, changed *chitta* flows peacefully into its own 'Selfhood' as the intelligence of *chit,*" *Pushya* said.

Patanjali was happy with the progress of this discussion. He knew how ordinary mortals live and identify themselves in their possessive hearts and egoistic brains. Emotions and flawed logic drive the ignorant Man's activities. For Man to be directed to Self-consciousness he must be taught to reach some degree of Awareness. Every atom and cell of his body needs awakening. He also must dwell on the Universe, until he finds himself in every atom of its expression. Man must abandon ambivalence and bartering with a proneness of a double life. By remaining anchored in 'changelessness', all states of awareness become disciplined. As these thoughts went through his mind, *Patanjali* was overcome by a sense of urgency. He must finish instructions on *ashtanga yoga.* His disciples were ready to move to the next step, he knew. And deep inside, his heart repeatedly jerked him inward bound towards his last expression, as *Shesha.*

Patanjali had already illustrated the power and inherent quality-characteristics of *Prakriti*. For those who searched for Her, She was to be found in Her calm expressions where She is in a latent state [*shanta, udita avyapadesha*]. She becomes visible to Man as a special or an indistinct entity, depending on the depth of the seeker's identification with the Cosmic Mother. *Patanjali* knew what he said grasps each disciple depending on their instinctive, individual intellectual understanding and development.

"The substratum that supports all states of being – conscious, subconscious and latent or unconscious – exists continuously and helps preserve the characteristics of each state. The sequential and successive changes in these various phases cause distinctive changes in *chitta*," *Patanjali* said. The disciples understood that in the practice of *yoga*, there is an advancing sequence or *krama* of distinct changes or *anyatvam*, which takes place in *chitta*.

They knew they should first increase restraint to reach awareness, which helps secure experiences of intermittent stillness of thought. After that, they can experience tranquil awareness and persistent stillness. Once absorbed in Awareness, they can expect to experience *chit* in the fulfillment of pure Consciousness. Here stillness of *chitta*, and silence of *chit*, are One.

Patanjali allowed the disciples to assimilate what he had said. But he also wanted to explain the properties of *yoga* triggering *siddhis*. Every *yogi* earns *siddhis* that amass through transformation of *chitta*, from unenlightened to an enlightened state. He outlined a *yogi's* accomplishments, acquired through intense *yogic* discipline. They occur in sequence. *Patanjali* knew he'd have to list and review each of these stages.

He decided first to speak about Time and its ranking in the mind of a *yogi* during the process of evolution. *Patanjali* saw Time, whether past or future, as a disturbance Man experiences in his awareness. He, therefore, knew he must shed light on Time first. To achieve undisturbed awareness, all awareness of Time needs quiescence because the final Reality is without the disturbing idea of 'Time'. *Patanjali* said, "You must reflect upon the three changes in Nature. Its predisposition or *dharma,* its quality or *lakshana* and its circumstance or *avastha* need integrating. Through restraint, absorption and single-pointedness or *nirodha, samadhi* and *ekagrata, a yogi* is able to do that. He then gains knowledge of past and future which is not constrained by Time," *Patanjali* concluded.

The disciples listened with interest. Each had experienced modicums of psychic powers or *siddhis.* They were warned by preceptors to ignore *siddhis,* because being enamoured by powers could sidetrack them from the Real Search. *Saleta* asked *Patanjali,* "Master, please outline "intuitive knowledge" and the way it is recorded and experienced in the mind. If the intellect is perfected, can a *yogi* penetrate the depth of all "word experiences"? Would a *yogi* instinctively understand exactly what is being suggested by a sound? Can he intuitively make out, and precisely distinguish, the meaning and feeling of every word and every sound uttered?"

As if justifying this flurry of questions, *Saleta* added, "They say a perfect *yogi* gifted with *siddhis* has instinctive and accurate knowledge of the meaning and feeling of any word uttered in any language of the world." The others looked towards the curtain, but most already knew the answer. They were not surprised when *Patanjali* said, "Words, objects and ideas are overlaid upon each other to create confusion in awareness. By integrating of Awareness with Consciousness, one gains knowledge of language of all beings."

Asked *Bhratahari,* "What, then, of insight? How does a *yogi* go about arriving at such knowledge?"

"Through direct perception of previous impressions from past incarnations, the *yogi* gains knowledge of previous lives," answered *Patanjali.*

"Is insight a function of memory? I understand that memory belongs to the subconscious mind. Does it exist as subliminal impressions? Or is memory an instinct, born of the fruits of desires that one experienced in one's previous lives?" asked *Menander.* This time, it was *Pakva* who answered, "Unfulfilled desires belong to the domain of the unconscious or the causal body. When the *yogi's chitta* is free of instincts and desires, his memory is submerged. His unblemished mirror-like awareness sees another's directly. Through the power of intuition, he reads insights into a person's lineage, future status and also the lives of others."

"What, then, of telepathy?" *Ujjaini* asked, "That too is a *siddhi* born of intense *yoga,* is it not?"

Answered *Patanjali,* "By practicing integration or *samyama* confidently, the seeker earns the ability to understand the minds of others." With this, he had cleverly defined telepathy and went on to outline how a *yogi* could develop clairvoyance and read minds of others. "First, the *yogi* must master his own mind and intellect," explained *Patanjali* and then said, "Through purity of Awareness, the *yogi* realises the nature of his own mind and the minds of others. He can read other's minds in general and, if necessary, precisely, to identify that which is beyond the reach of the ordinary mind."

Pushya had been listening quietly, but interjected, "A *yogi* who controls the gifts of general and specific insight is unlikely to waste his time looking into other's minds. He risks losing the grace of *yoga* by delving into such 'pastimes', except if he seeks out a person's exact motives."

Added *Chandra,* "At this altitude of evolution no seeker wants entrapment with *sidhis.* The seeker is drawn towards those who are free of desire. For instance, he is attracted to his *guru.* He now takes on the graceful disposition of his teacher and guide."

Saleta had more questions anyway, and asked, "It is said that a *yogi* can become invisible both in shape and in form. How does this *anima* happen?"

Behind the curtain, *Patanjali* smiled and replied, "By having power over his physical body, the *yogi* can suspend, at will, the rays of energy originating from matter, so he becomes invisible to onlookers. He can make himself visible again by bringing back, the gross power of perceptibility. In the same way, he can arrest and release sound, smell, taste, form and touch."

Asked *Pakva*, "What about the Law of *Karma?* Does a *yogi* understand he has to deal with the effects of such actions?"

"He knows effects of such action may be immediate or delayed. Through *samyama* of actions, a *yogi* gains foreknowledge of the final fruits of such actions. He, in this fashion, also knows the exact time of his death,' *Patanjali* replied. *Pakva* understood the answer. Since the fruits of action and the Law of *Karma* are linked to Time, a *yogi* who has regulated Time can infer reactions to all action, either immediately or later.

He can intuitively gauge death by watching environmental disturbances or by hearing the Divine Voice. He knows that he wouldn't amass 'consequences' of his actions so long as he remains with the Self.

Patanjali then moved to discussing the value of friendliness, goodwill, gladness, compassion and benevolence. He warned the disciples that they must nurture all virtues with indifference and without personal involvement. They must keep *chitta* free of desire, anger, greed, lust, pride and jealousy. Said *Patanjali,* outlining the benefits of fostering such virtues, "The seeker gains moral and emotional strength by perfecting friendliness towards everyone, as well as other virtues" *Patanjali* said.

Pakva, shy and reticent by nature, was often mistaken as arrogant and unfriendly. He could recognise *Patanjali's* words of encouragement. *Pushya* understood such statements. He used this technique when he ruled as a king. By attacking weaknesses, a *yogi's* single-pointed awareness can spread around much happiness. The seeker's equipoise ensures the heart has a gracious disposition towards all of Mankind – young or old, rich or poor. As if continuing with *Pushya's* thoughts, *Patanjali* said, "By *samyama* or integrating strength with friendliness, the *yogi* develops physical strength, grace and the power of endurance."

In the valley, a cool breeze took away the harshness of the sun, which was at its zenith. The disciples sat under the shade of the *peepal* tree. Apart from the gentle sound of gushing of the river and the occasional chirp or flutter of birds, the valley basked in sunlight and in silence. After finishing his last sentence, *Patanjali* became quiet. Although he sat behind the curtain, the disciples felt the Master was becoming more and more distant of late. The thought of breaking for lunch did not strike them. Despite a feeling of uneasiness, they launched another discussion. They recognised many other *siddhis* and wanted *Patanjali* to continue the discussion. *Menander* asked *Patanjali,* "And what of the Secrets, Master?"

"Cloaked things, near or far, are revealed to a *yogi,*" answered *Patanjali*. But *Menander* persisted, "As I understand, integrating with Inner Light helps a *yogi* gather insight. But what of Cosmic Secrets, embedded within the Total Mind of the Cosmic Mother?"

Patanjali answered, "It is by integrating in *samyama* in the *kutastha,* the *yogi* earns knowledge of the seven outer worlds and the seven cosmic centres of the brain and spinal cord." With that, *Patanjali* had launched into a new subject. The disciples looked at one another and tried to assimilate and analyse what the Master had just said. After a few moments of deliberate silence, *Chandra* started the discussion, "Just as the Sun illumines the world with its rays, *prana* concentrated in the heart and medulla spreads to illumine all spiritual *chakras,* from the brain to the spinal cord." Then, *Chandra* asked the others, "What of these seven outer worlds?"

Said *Bhratahari,* "According to Hindu Philosophy, the Universe is divided into fourteen worlds, seven above and seven below. The above-regions are *bhuloka, bhuvaloka, suvaloka, mahaloka, janaloka, tapaloka* and *satyaloka.* The below-regions or nether-regions are *atala, vitala, sutala, rasatala, talatala, mahatala* and *patala.*"

The physician in *Menander* said, "As the macrocosm, so is the microcosm. Man's body epitomises the structure of the Universe. *Bhuloka* matches with the pelvic region, *bhuvaloka* with the navel, *suvaloka* with the diaphragm, *mahaloka* with the heart, *janaloka* with the neck, *tapaloka* with the eyebrows, and *satyaloka* with the crown of the head."

After a thoughtful pause, *Menander* continued. "The netherworlds are also represented. The hips for *atala,* the thighs for *vitala,* the knees for *sutala,* the calves for *rasatala,* the ankles for *talatala,* the metatarsal for *mahatala,* and the soles of the feet for *patala.*"

Pushya added, "According to *yogis,* within the above-regions of the body are seven major psycho-physiological astral energy centres, or *pranic chakras. Muladhara* or coccygeal, *svadhistana* or sacral, and *manipura* on the level of the navel in the spinal cord are worldly foci. *Anhaata* at the heart level and *vishuddha* at the throat level are creative centres. The harmonious *ajna,* within the medulla, reflects in the *kutastha.*"

"The *sahasrahara,* in the crown of the head, is found in the parietal lobes of the brain," *Menander* interjected.

Added *Ujjaini,* "In the brain are many centres that conform with the planetary system of the Universe." As he said this, *Menander's* ears perked and he leaned closer. *Chandra* said, "Please clarify, *Ujjaini.*" The environmentalist in *Ujjaini* had worked it all out. He began, "The *Surya* in the microcosmic brain is the thalamus, at the *kutastha.* It is through the medulla that *prana* breathes life into the body through nerve centres. The *ajna chakra* reflects off the occipital lobe and then onto the thalamus, to appear like the Sun. Individual Man connects with the Energy of the Universe through *prana*."

"And it is the *Surya* that connects through sun channels, represented by *pingala* of the sympathetic nervous system," exclaimed *Menander*.

Added *Ujjaini*, "And the hypothalamus is the planetary *Chandra* in Man, which connects past lives through memory. The moon channels are represented by *ida* of the parasympathetic nervous system."

"The *manas*, therefore, must be represented as the limbic system of the brain?" Said *Menander*, a statement posed as a question.

Interjected *Pakva*, "In the *Bhagavad Gita*, *Krishna* speaks of the Universe as the eternal tree. The Wise have embodied it to the everlasting *ashwatha tree*, with its 'roots' reaching out above and its 'branches' fanning out below. The leaves are *Vedic* hymns, and he who understands this Tree of Life is a Knower of the *Vedas*. This metaphor is as found in the *Gita*."

Said *Pushya*, "The Tree represents the Cosmos, to depict size and longevity. It also refers to the transitory nature of beings and creatures. While products don't endure, the creative Principle, the life force and seed of the *ashwatha* tree are eternal."

Added *Bhratahari*, "The inverted or upside-down tree corresponds to the brain above, and the spinal cord with its cranial and spinal nerves below. A seeker understands and sees this Tree of Life as a means to emancipation. Only its Knower understands the Knowledge."

"The true nature of this Tree, its origin, its end in a resting-place, its continuation, an extrovert Man understands none of these. Having destroyed the firmly rooted *ashwatha* tree with the powerful axe of nonattachment, Man should seek refuge in the Original *Purusha*. From Spirit and from Him alone, has Man come through the many processes of creation in time, with involvement of energy and activity. Once Man seeks and finds the Supreme Self, he need not return to this processing."

Behind the curtain, *Patanjali* was pleased with the discussion. Just as *Surya* is referred to as the core of Man's Awareness, *Chandra* is referred to Man's mind and memory, as also the *chitta* personality. *Patanjali* was pleased the disciples identified the *pingala* on the right side and the *ida* on the left side of the spine. They connected them to the hypothalamus – as memory – at the base of brain. *Patanjali* knew he can now describe integration of the autonomic nervous system. This fact will allow *yogis to* gain more knowledge of the past. Said *Patanjali,* "By *samyama* on the moon, the *yogi* can know the position of the stars."

"If I recall correctly, these paths have also been referred to in the *Bhagavad Gita*", asked *Pushya.*

Pakva replied, "Yes, *Krishna* described the path of evolution, by transformation. The sympathetic and motor nervous systems are the whitish paths, which are open to conscious awareness. The parasympathetic autonomic nervous system or black path, is closed and hidden within the subconscious system or the hypothalamus."

Said *Menander,* repeating himself, "The somatic modalities are channeled and controlled by the thalamus, which corresponds to the *Surya.* Somatic inputs are consciously experienced as sound, sight, taste, smell, heat and cold, the pain of pricks and burns, touch, pressure and vibrations on the skin or hair. A second group of somatic perceptions detects Man's position in space through balance, joint and limb pressures, with reference to the body's midline."

Said *Saleta,* who had been silent for a while, "*Krishna*

refers to the somatic nervous system. He tells *Arjuna* that an exiting *yogi* who knows to travel by this route, goes with the knowledge of fire, light and day, and may choose to die in the *Shukla* half of the month and year. A *yogi* who knows this path understands *Brahman* and, therefore, goes to *Brahman*."

Interjected *Pakva*, "But the *Gita* also refers to the autonomic nervous system as smoke and night. Dying during the *Krishna* half of the month signifies leaving along this path. This allows the *yogi* to gain the light of the moon, and to return through processes of reincarnation."

"Placed below the thalamus or *Surya* is the hypothalamus. It corresponds with *Chandra*. The hypothalamus is the expert processor, capable of orchestrating the visceral and autonomic nervous system," said *Menander* wisely.

Throughout this discussion, the disciples who didn't have a medical background could not understand *Menander*, but all of them recognised the part of the *Gita* that was being referred to. Each of them acknowledged as much information as needed. *Menander*, *Bhratahari* and *Ujjaini* understood the scientific explanations that were being explored. *Pakva*, *Pushya*, *Chandra* and *Saleta* were convinced that *Krishna's* statements in the *Gita* are based in science. *Patanjali* was both physician and philosopher and his terse statements were understood in varying degrees of clarity, by each disciple.

Said *Saleta*, "Input of sense-centres in the nervous system do not influence Awareness unless there is wakefulness. In the sleep state, Awareness is blind to all sensory input. This also happens in *pratyahara*".

Ujjaini added thoughtfully, "Wakefulness and sleep are controlled by the brainstem stars or *nakshatras*. Twin meditating *ashwins* control the reticular activating system, in particular during sleep-awake cycles. The blind mind or *kanwa* is prepared and integrated by the thalamus, with

Surya's stimulating light."

"This unveiling removes the shroud of *avidya* that covers perception," said *Pakva,* looking from one disciple to the next.

"The *Gita* asserts these anatomical and physiological facts. These two paths, *shukla* and *krishna,* are considered the world's Eternal paths. And the *ashwins* remove the blindness of *kanwa,*" *Pushya* summed it all up. Planetary arrangement as transcribed in Man's brain outlines how each nucleus or planet has a specific influence on *chitta. Patanjali* described how these centres could be used in meditation, "By *samyama* and integrating with *dhruva* the polestar between the eyebrow area, the *yogi* knows the course of destiny."

Confirmed *Bhratahari,* "True. A *yogi* can identify the movements of stars and their effect on world events."

"By integration or *samyama* at the navel, the *yogi* can earn perfect knowledge of the body's constitution and can, eventually, become its master," *Patanjali* continued. At this, *Menander* explained, "The root of all nerves is in the navel area. Some 72,000 sympathetic nerve roots swivel out of the *manipura chakra.* The hypothalamus is the control centre of the sympathetic and parasympathetic nervous systems. Through this *samyama,* the *yogi* makes out the various sheaths of the body and how these are controlled by different nerves." There was a pause. The disciples realized they were being told how to heal the body.

Continued *Patanjali,* "By *samyama* at the pit of the throat, the *yogi* overcomes hunger and thirst." The disciples understood *Patanjali* was referring to the *kechri mudra.* They were being told to conquer hunger and thirst. Even as they were processing this statement, *Patanjali* went on, without a pause, "By *samyama* on *kurma nadi,* found at the pit of the abdomen, the *yogi* can make the body and mind fixed, similar to a tortoise."

Pushya asked Menander, "Where is *kurma nadi* found, precisely?

Menander answered the physician-*yogi*, "*Kurma nadi* is found in the epigastric area of the body and does not correspond with any *chakra*. The influence of this *nadi* is magnified in emotional upheavals. Since mental works revolves around desire, anger, greed, attachments, pride and jealousy, they are considered indulgences of a tormented mind. By integration or *samyama* with this centre, the *yogi* hibernates, mentally immobilizing bodily and intellectual functions."

"What is the purpose of such concentration?" asked *Saleta*.

"The *gunas* of Nature are directly able to influence tormented mental functions. Fluctuations of *rajas* and *tamas* must be stilled, until *sattva* gains dominance," answered *Pakva*. Though this answer satisfied *Saleta*, he wanted to know how he could change his demanding nature, which forces him to respond to discomfort with displeasure. *Pushya* answered this query, "This can be done by converting and sublimating the expressions of pain and pleasure, likes and dislikes and other such opposites into synchronised harmony. Once transformed to *sattvic* energy in the astral body, the physical body is stilled by perfect integration. The emotional centre is, then, stilled and the seeker gains emotional stability."

Patanjali waited until *Saleta* had no further questions. When there was silence at the other end, *Patanjali* said, "By practicing *samyama* on the light of the *ajna chakra*, between and behind eyebrows, the *yogi* sees images of perfected beings. By *samyama* on the effulgent light, the *yogi* becomes a Knower of all Knowledge. He intuitively senses anything and everything." *Patanjali* implied that a *yogi* with a balanced mind and poised heart can gain intuitive guidance from perfected masters, whom he inwardly sees. Once impulsiveness is replaced by transformed intuitive thought, a *yogi* can gain universal knowledge by conquering Nature and Her qualitative-quantitative impositions on Man and creature. At this moment, *Patanjali* stirred a discussion on the fifth spiritual centre of intuition, the *vishuddha chakra* or cervical centre.

He first started speaking about the fourth energy centre in the spinal cord, the *anhaata chakra.* "By *samyama* in the region of the heart, which is the seat of pure knowledge, the *yogi* realises that it is the Seat of Awareness," said *Patanjali.*

There was silence. The valley was still, as though gently swaying in the early evening breeze. The sounds of the world seemed to have paused. Even the elements were listening to *Patanjali. Pakva* asked, "Master, what are the results of such integration and concentration? One needs to be successful at *samyama* obviously. But what happens here after successful integration through meditation?"

Replied *Patanjali,* "Because of effort at *samyama,* the *yogi* can easily distinguish between intellect in Awareness and intelligence in Consciousness. The *yogi* is able to identify the Real from the Unreal. Pure intelligence, which serves both Nature and Spirit, allows him to detect the distinctness of each."

"What is the difference between intellect and intelligence?" asked the ubiquitous *Saleta. Patanjali* mentally commanded *Pakva* to answer the question. Almost immediately, *Pakva* said, "*Sattva buddhi,* which is free of ego, sees itself as different from intelligence. By knowing one, a *yogi* can enter the other. By using pure intellect, a *yogi* enters the gates of the Soul." *Saleta* thought he understood, but did not seem satisfied with *Pakva's* answer. *Patanjali* now turned to *Pushya* to explain, and said, "Although refined intellect is the peak of Nature's perfection, it is still nothing but Matter and is subject to the changeable experiences of *chitta.*"

Saleta nodded. He now understood. *Pushya* added,

"Intelligence is the Soul. It is the immutable luminescent *Purusha*. By *samyama,* the *yogi* gradually disentangles intellect of the self from intelligence the Self. He develops intuitive perception." *Patanjali* coughed approvingly and said, 'Through the dawn of the self-luminous light of intuitive view, the *yogi* also gains divine faculties of hearing, touching, seeing, tasting and smelling. He can cause this emergence by his own will."

Pushya added, 'This is possible only because the restraining effects of the mind have been erased and the *yogi* is able to contact the core of his being." Pleased with this discussion, *Patanjali* warned the disciples that *siddhis* are the natural fallout effects of integration and meditation. They are not to be used to gain *praapti* or powers over others. "These attainments are a hindrance to a *yogi* on the path to Self-realisation. These *siddhis* are accomplishments but they still fall in the domain of Nature's inherent *gunas.* Using them leads the seeker to forgetting his goal of *samadhi,*" *Patanjali* said.

Chandra, entrusted with the task of taking down notes, had been silent for some time. *Patanjali* knew this disciple to be a deeply intellectual thinker. Practical by nature, *Chandra* was preoccupied by the Law of Cause and Effect. He had come to the conclusion that nondedicated action would always be the Cause of Bondage, no matter how evolved the *yogi. Chandra* reasoned with the Master and asked, "A *yogi* has to pay debts of his past actions. How does he resolve this problem?"

Patanjali replied, "The *yogi* can enter the body of another and, also, leave the body at will. To free him from the bondage of *karma,* he enters other bodies as well, until all *karma* has been exhausted." The answer confused *Chandra,* so *Patanjali* again turned to *Pakva,* who understood his unspoken message. "The *yogi's chitta* enters newborn in suitable environments, where the reborn *yogi* will exhaust the bondage of past *karma.* If he is an evolved *yogi,* he is able to move from body to body. He continues until he exhausts bondage and rebirth. Having earned a personal experience of bondage-causing issues, as also of ignorance, egoism, desire, malice and the fear of death, he neutralizes them for purposes of Self-realisation,"*Pakva* finished. There was absolute silence among the disciples. This new information had great significance for each of them. The message that evolved *yogis* can enter wombs and environments for exhaustion of nondedicated actions was of immeasurable importance.

After a long pause, *Chandra* started the discussion, "Can someone explain the difference between dedicated and self-dedicated action?"

Pakva answered, "Activity dedicated to the service of the Cosmic Mother, and undertaken for the love of the Universe and Mankind is dedicated action. Their results are renounced and relinquished. Such acts leave no stain of effect on the acting person. All other deeds are self-benefiting and, therefore, subject to the Law of Cause and Effect." *Chandra* nodded, letting what *Pakva* had said sink in. Then he asked, this time turning to *Patanjali,* "How does a *yogi* enter and leave bodies at will, Master?"

The others followed *Chandra's* eyes towards the curtain. The valley strained under the silence. Even the birds and leaves paused to hear *Patanjali's* answer. After a few moments, *Patanjali* said, "By mastering brainward travelling of *prana* also called *udana vayu* and through integration or *samyama,* the *yogi* can make his body weightless. He can walk on water, mud and thorns, without them 'touching' him or him 'feeling' them. He can make *prana* move up, through the spine to the brain, so he is able to levitate, float, enter another or even die, at will."

The subject under discussion – physiological works of body supported by *prana* – was of intense interest to all the disciples. Those with a medical or scientific background understood that *prana* was the Cosmic Mother's life giving air, which breathed life into every creature, thing and Man.

They also understood that energy in matter is rejuvenated with life force to support works performed by the anatomical, physiological, psychological, intellectual and causal layers of all expression. *Menander,* in particular, knew that *prana vayu* was functionally subdivided into five vital energies within creatures. He told the disciples that *prana vayu* supported respiration, excretion, digestion, circulation and psychic expansion as *prana, apana, samana, vyana* and *udana* respectively.

Ayurveda, as taught by *Patanjali,* recognised that *prana vayu* activates inspiration, and *apana vayu* activates expiration and expulsion. *Vyana* coordinates works of *apana* and *prana* and is involved in the transfer of energy to every cell and molecule in the body. *Udana* raises energetic excellence from the base of the spine to the brain, while *apana* exhausts the same energy, as *prana,* through elimination and indulgence. Asked *Saleta,* "How does one use the divine cave to channel *prana* towards the altar in the brain?"

Menander answered, "When a *yogi* masters *udana,* he raises his energy away from *apana.* He raises *prana* in the central river of *brahmanadi* going upward through the spine and into the brain." *Pushya* added, "This spiritual river is, symbolically, the Jordan of Christians and the Ganges of Hindus." Interjected *Pakva,* "Awareness merges with Consciousness, first in the *kutastha* and then in the *sahasrahara* before lodging in the centre of Universal intelligence in the pineal gland. This movement is supreme baptism, washed by spiritual waters already flowing in the divine cave."

Menander asked *Patanjali,* "Master, what are the effects of such intense inner integration?"

"By *samyama,* the *yogi* conquers *samana vayu* and gains control over the fire of digestion. This is the conquest of fire," *Patanjali* said.

"Where is the *prana* for digestion found?" asked *Pushya. Ujjaini* chose to answer, "The epigastric area is the region of *samana*. It stokes the fire of digestion and preserves harmonious functioning of all the digestive organs. It also controls functioning of the heart, through which *prana* permeates the body." At this, *Bhratahari* just had to ask *Patanjali,* "Please speak to us about sound, Master."

"By integration or *samyama* of sound and space, the *yogi* earns the power to hear divine sounds. The ear grasps every sound in space. That is the conquest of air," said *Patanjali*.

"You speak of conquest of the element of space. Is that not one of the *siddhis* gained through intense *yoga*?" *Bhratahari* asked.

"That is called becoming light as air or *laghima*. What is the use of this power?" *Ujjaini* posed another question.

"By knowing the relationship between the body and space, the *yogi* transforms his body and mind so he becomes as light as a cotton fibre. He can then levitate in space. That is the conquest of space," *Patanjali* replied, moving along his chain of thought.

Quoting the *Ramayana, Saleta* said, "*Hanuman,* son of *Pavan,* the Wind God, used this ability to reach the sun as a youngster. He used it again to reach the *Himalayas* to fetch *sanjivani* to save *Lakshman's* life. Also, *Narada,* the heavenly son of *Brahma,* the Creator, has the ability to crisscross the three worlds with this integration." *Saleta* then addressed *Patanjali,* "Master, speak to us of invisibility or *anima.*"

"By *samyama* on becoming disembodied is *mahavideha.* Here *chitta* exists without a body. The seven veils that cover the light of *chit* are destroyed," *Patanjali* answered, and drifted into silence. The disciples could see his unmoving form behind the curtain and knew that he'd drifted into meditation. The subject under discussion led *Patanjali* to revel in the ecstasy of being One, beyond the bodies and sheaths that had made him *Gonika's* mortal son. The disciples did not want to disturb the Master. They decided to discuss this subject among themselves.

"A *yogi* who is trained to exist without veils first discards the gross body or *sthula sharira* and, of course, the food sheath or *annamaya kosha.* He, then, goes on to cancel the subtle body or *sukshma sharira* in layers. He cancels *chitta* by first cutting out the mental sheath or *manomaya kosha,* then the intellectual sheath or *gyanamaya kosha* and physiological sheath or *pranamaya kosha.* Finally the causal body or *karana sharira* is cancelled," *Chandra* said.

Added *Pakva,* "He, then, lives in a pure state of *chitta.* He can exist for hours in the body of pure Awareness in *chittamaya kosha.*"

Pushya warned, "Although he is a true *yogi,* he can still slip back into the grip of Matter because he remains under the influence of Mother Nature!"

"The *yogi* must enter the body of Consciousness or *chitmaya kosha,*" said *Bhratahari.*

Ujjaini added, choosing his words carefully, "Only then is the yogi beyond the compulsory influence of Nature's *gunas.* The *yogi* intuitively understands that he and *Prakriti* are One. He learns to love and serve Her. The afflictions of Matter interrupt their influence on him only when he learns to serve Her."

"He is now free from the Laws of Cause and Effect and does not feel the compulsions of the Matter's *gunas.* He is also free from the Laws of Relativity, and accepts good and bad, hot and cold, pain and pleasure as expressions of Her glory," said *Chandra.*

"After that, a *yogi* becomes pure *Consciousness,*" *Menander* muttered under his breath.

"But to become universal and divine by merging *chitta* with *chit* is what I want more than anything," sighed *Ujjaini.*

Decided *Bhratahari,* "At that point, the *yogi* can allow himself to be absorbed into *chidakasha* at will."

Patanjali was mindful of the discussion even as he drifted in and out of meditation. As *Bhratahari* finished, *Patanjali* cleared his throat. The disciples' wistful discussion came to an abrupt end, as they waited for him to speak. "By *samyama,* the *yogi* gains control over the gross and subtle elements of Nature. He transcends Her *gunas.* He identifies the purpose elements are in the life of a mortal," said *Patanjali,* and drifted into silence again, a cue to the disciples to discuss Matter's *gunas. Saleta* started the discussion, by addressing the others with, "Please explain the relevance of this statement."

Ujjaini said, "The ingredients of the Universe are five Elements of Nature: earth, water, fire, air and space. Each element, in turn, has five attributes – mass, subtlety, form, pervasiveness and purpose. The characteristics of the gross elements are solidity, fluidity, heat, mobility and volume. The subtle counterparts of the gross elements are smell, taste, sight, touch and sound."

"What has that got to do with the purpose of life of a mortal, *Ujjaini*?" demanded *Saleta.*

Replied *Ujjaini,* patiently, "Every element has properties. Earth has five properties – smell, taste, sight, touch and sound. Water has four properties – taste, sight, touch and sound. The third element, fire, has three – sight, touch, and sound. Air has the properties of touch and sound. The fifth element, space, has the property of sound alone, and it rings with the hum of *pranava AUM.*" As he said this, *Ujjaini* drifted into his own *antardhvani.*

Complained *Saleta,* "But you have still not answered my question, *Ujjaini.* In what way do the *gunas* offer a seeking Man his solace?"

"The purpose of the *gunas* is either worldly enjoyment or to attain freedom," *Ujjaini* replied absentmindedly. *Pakva* knew that *Ujjaini* was reveling in the hum of *AUM,* and decided to enter the discussion. Said *Pakva,* "Through restraint, the *yogi* gains control over the gross, as well as the subtle elements, their qualities and their purpose."

Behind the curtain, *Patanjali* was making a great effort to end this discussion. He therefore moved to the next topic. *Patanjali* said, "By *samyama* on the elements, the *yogi* can reduce himself to the size of an atom *[anima],* or expand magnificently *[mahima].* He can become light *[laghima]* or heavy *[garima].* He can have domination over *[praapti],* or have access to everything *[prakamya]* or master anything *[ishatva]. Yogis* are able to subdue or *vashitva]* also."

"What, then, are the real benefits of mastering the elements in Mother Nature?" *Saleta* asked.

"By *samyama,* the *yogi* earns the eight *siddhis* that are measured as the supreme abundances of the body. The *yogi* gains perfection in the art of living and gains freedom from all Nature's limitations. He gains proficiency in three fields and earns many *siddhis,*" said *Menander.*

"What are they?" *Saleta* asked.

"Perfection of body," *Menander* replied.

"And how does this express itself?" probed *Saleta.*

"Perfection of body means nothing contaminates, dampens or burns the physical body. His immunity and health suffers no ill-effects of compulsions of Nature," *Menander* replied.

Added *Patanjali,* "By *samyama,* perfection of the body is reached in form, grace, strength, compactness, hardness and brilliance – like a diamond." He paused for a moment and then continued, "By *samyama* of senses, their role and receptivity is increased with or without unification with Nature. The *yogi* recognises the objective of Nature, interacting with senses and a particular individual self. He wins competence over all of them." With this statement, *Patanjali* introduced sense perception. He wanted the disciples to discuss this topic. As the session advanced, *Patanjali* was displaying a different tutoring style. He would become quiet before embarking on a new subject. He moved to sense perception after discussing the resources of senses, with qualities of natural elements.

The disciples understood *Patanjali* wanted them to discuss the five movements and compliance of sense in retrospection. *Chandra* started the discussion, "The properties of senses are first judged by knowing their natural state. Next there is recognising external objects of desire and reasoning 'why' the contact is made. Involving the individualistic self with perception and then changing objective comes next. Knowing by subjective understanding comes last."

Bhratahari asked, "To sum up, we experience the universe through a sense of 'Me' and transform it to 'I' awareness?"

"The senses are attracted to objects and earthly bonds for the sake of pleasure," said *Ujjaini.*

"And pleasures create the desire for more of the same, which results in human entanglement with sense forests and loss of purpose,"*Pakva* interjected.

Added *Pushya,* "But appeasement of such yearnings for pleasure produces only transient tranquility. And that too only until one sees the next object of want."

"It obviously takes a cultured *yogi* of chastened intellect to turn inwards and explore sense perception, mind and ego," said *Saleta.*

Menander was the last to comment, "Only when a *yogi* abides and endures within Awareness can he befriend the individualistic self, also known as the unenlightened *chitta.* He must take the enlightened *chitta* personality of mind-intellect-ego to touch the depths of Consciousness. Here the ego is in self-awareness. It recognises the light of consciousness."

Patanjali agreed and added, "By proficiency over senses of perception, a *yogi* conquers the properties of Nature in the body, senses and the mind. He picks up speed and subtlety of *chitta,* independent of Nature's *gunas.* Unaided by awareness, his consciousness subdues principles of Nature."

Asked *Saleta,* "When the properties of Nature have been conquered, are the body and *chitta* purified?"

"Yes, but temporarily" *Pakva* replied, and then added, "The *chitta* independently sees Nature as itself. *Chitta* drinks its own sweetness. The Self or soul transforms itself. In this state, *chitta* loses interest in satisfaction of its senses."

"And every cell in the body reflects the light of pure Self. It drinks the nectar of soul," *Pushya* added.

Patanjali was pleased his disciple *yogis* had developed an ability to distinguish Matter and Spirit. They understood Awareness or *Prakriti* to be the enlightened *chitta* displaying as the Knowledge that merely looks and records Man playacting in the world. And Consciousness or *Purusha* as *chit* who is the Knower and witnesses the Knowing of shenanigans by the senses.

Prana enlivens the whole life-drama and energy of matter. *Patanjali* knew the disciples would eventually gain knowledge over all states of expression. They had shown signs of seeing their Oneness with the 'seer' and the 'seen' when in deep meditation. They stilled mind, intellect, senses and organs of action.

Smiling behind the curtain, *Patanjali* said, "Only one who personally experiences the difference between lit up intellect and Consciousness arrives at Supreme Knowledge. It is described falteringly in the *Vedas.* Only he can know all that 'exists' and all that is 'manifest'." As *Patanjali* shifted from one topic to the next, it was obvious he was nearing ascension towards emancipation.

There was thoughtful silence until *Pakva* started the

discussion, "The experience of a released mind is so superior that it can get attached to its own perfected state."

"The final liberation of the soul comes when the enlightened *chitta* gives up its attachment to its changed state with *chit,*" *Pushya* added.

"When enlightened *chitta* realises that its condition depends on Awareness inherent in Nature, it is nearly freed. It is still in its seed state of Matter," said *Bhratahari*.

Said *Patanjali,* "By destroying the seeds of bondage and by renouncing the powers that come from such emancipation, a *yogi* is freed from sorrow and grief. He can live in complete emancipation in Spirit – in his own Self."

"If the *yogi* does not spurn these psychic and spiritual experiences, they become seeds of sorrow. He gets entangled in the subtle afflictions of being attached to them. And, of course, there is pride," *Saleta* mused, almost to himself.

Insisted *Chandra,* "The Master is clear that involvement with *siddhis* leads to pride, which immediately swallows up the *yogi*. But renunciation of these *siddhis* leads the *yogi* to everlasting emancipation. He can, then, rest in his own eternal nature as pure Awareness."

"And when approached by heavenly beings, there should be neither attachment nor surprise. This also allows undesirable attachments to be born again," added *Patanjali*. The disciples were aware celestial beings often try to seduce a *yogi* away from the grace of *yoga*. The *yogi* must guard his freedom. He must not succumb to temptation. He might end up losing his hard-won spirituality.

Patanjali had no personal experience of temptations that hound sincere seekers. *Pakva,* on the other hand, had experienced these enticing traps. *Patanjali* asked *Pakva* to discuss this important subject. Began *Pakva,* "There are four types of *yogis*. First, there are *prathama kalpika yogis,* who have worked hard at meditation. For them powers of progress or *siddhis* are just rudimentary basics. Then, there are *mahabhumika yogis,* who make out *chitta* from *chit* and are trying hard gaining proficiency over themselves."

Pakva became silent, pondering over what he had said and allowing the rest to absorb his words. Suddenly, a gust of wind blew his shawl off his shoulders. As *Pakva* stood up to capture it, he saw it get caught on a thorny bush a few paces away. *Pakva* walked to the bush to bring back his shawl, still deep in thought. When he reached the bush, he saw a rabbit struggling to free itself from the thorny bush. The rabbit was after a patch of luscious grass near the bush.

Pakva immediately asked *Ujjaini* to help him lift the thorny bush. The rabbit did the rest. Out from his temporary, self-inflicted confinement, it leaped to freedom. Commented *Ujjaini,* "This is how mortals too ambush themselves with sense objects." As *Pakva* and *Ujjaini* walked back towards the *peepal* tree, *Pakva* said, "The biggest hurdle Man faces is himself. Once he crosses this hurdle, Man can master himself and his environment."

When they joined the others, the breeze had died down, but *Pakva* secured his shawl. He twisted two corners around each wrist.

Chandra asked, "What are the other two types of *yogis*?" Said *Pakva,* "The third type are *prajnajyoti yogis,* who subdue the environmental elements, senses and organs of action. Having overcome the mind, they realize through personal experience, the inwardly looking *chitta* is Awareness of Matter."

Pakva paused to plan his next few words, "And, finally, there are *antikranta bhavaniya yogis,* who have reached the highest knowledge. They have merged the light of *chit* with the energy of *chitta.* They experience the ecstasy of Universal Intelligence in a seedless state. But such enjoyment cannot exist by itself. He knows the difference between seeking this bliss and timeless freedom." *Patanjali* coughed in approval. He had coached other students about these four types of *yogis*. Falling into such angelic traps, even if they are divine temptations, are binding on the soul.

Patanjali decided he wanted to describe a different method to reach Oneness. He wanted the disciples to recognise a moment in time. By getting an idea of *samyama* of timelessness, they would understand a continuous flow of moments. This would give a *yogi* an understanding of Time and its relativity. *Patanjali* knew they would come to realise timelessness as eternal and real. By understanding movement of moments, within past and future, they could become free of time. The disciples would understand *samadhi,* the moment itself – an everlasting, changeless and sacred moment. *Patanjali* had to provide evidence of this unconditional reality. He said, "By *samyama* on a moment and understanding the continuous flow of moments, the *yogi* can gain knowledge that is exempt of limits of time and space."

His silence prompted the disciples to discuss the topic. *Menander* started, "In such a timeless moment, there is no awareness of physiological or psychological time. There are no rising or falling moments, no impressions and no restraints. There is only that moment of quiet within pure Awareness. This Awareness needs to be stabilised, prolonged and expanded into Consciousness. When Awareness and Consciousness are One, the seeker becomes the whole. But this is only a gateway to liberation or *kaivalya.*"

"When a *yogi* supports his *chitta* in the moment, he has conquered Time. Having lost the time, his *chitta* loses its significance. He catches a glimpse of *chit,*" *Chandra* said and became pensive. But he added, excitedly, "This magnificent glimpse is into Universal Intelligence, the Supreme Secret and Sacred Knowledge."

Pushya said, knowingly, "All spiritual cultures and masters have advised seekers to live in the moment. A moment is all we have. This is to be able to live in it as it is, and not as it might be. This is to live in reality. Reality can only be in the present. It too dies if we have not lived it, especially if the secret is not understood. That is the Secret of Living."

"For those who are constantly running away from the present, experiencing the today can be exhausting. But for a seeker who experiences even a moment in *asana,* that moment is exhilarating," *Saleta* added.

Said *Bhratahari,* "If we can live in the moment – whether good, bad or indifferent – we can be free of the body and its many veils."

"*Samyama* with a moment allows Man to see the distinction between a perfect Intelligence *[chit]* and a freed soul *[chitta],*" said *Pakva* thoughtfully.

"An insight into the difference between pure Consciousness and pure Soul is a realisation of the moment, beyond time. Even this final likeness, and distinction, disappears in *sâmyama,*" said *Ujjaini.*

Patanjali agreed and said, "Intuition that results from such discriminative insight yields emancipation – complete, utter and instantaneous. The *yogi* distinguishes, unerringly, between similar objects – which cannot otherwise be distinguished."

"This is exalted intellect of the Soul. The *yogi* sees all distinctly and faultlessly. And this 'quality' of intelligence is impossible, unless the seeker is connected to divine spiritual knowledge and an able Master," *Pakva* said.

Patanjali added, "When pure intellect and the soul have been purified equally, the moment the two merge is the perfect and exalted state of Oneness."

"Exalted in understanding and clear in action, the seeker dominates and transcends Nature and reaches the Light of the Soul through *yogic* practice," commented *Pakva.*

In the cave, *Patanjali* coughed his agreement and said, "When the purity of intelligence of *chit* equals the purity of the soul or *chitta,* the *yogi* has reached freedom or *kaivalya.* He is perfect." After a brief pause, *Patanjali* added, "When the distinction between *Purusha,* as intelligence, and *Prakriti,* as intellect, ends, both dissolve in *chidakasha,* the source of all Universal Intelligence or combined Light and Energy. The seeds of affliction are finally burned. *Chit* now exists in its outstanding form as *chidakasha.* It is indivisible and in truth, existence and knowledge. It is *sat-chit-anand.*"

With that, *Patanjali* closed this session. He fell silent and started to stand up from the slab. Evening had set in, and a misty blanket of gray covered the valley. There was again a chill in the breeze. Only the creatures of the night uncovered the valley with their sounds. The disciples were hungry, having eaten nothing all day. They readied themselves for their evening dip in the river.

No sooner had they emerged from the river that *Malini* called them for dinner. They assembled and walked to *Malini Amma's* hut. They saw *Patanjali* approach the hut too. The disciples readied to dine with the Master. As always, *Amma's* meal was hot, tasty and plentiful. It filled them with devotion. After dinner, they helped clean up and decided to retire early, knowing the next day would again see exhaustive, thought-provoking discussions.

Book Four – On Emancipation

Kaivalya Pada

He who seeks to realise his spiritual Reality must have complete understanding over his physical needs and inclinations. *Patanjali* highlighted that Man is fit for inquiry only when he becomes discriminating, dispassionate and calm. He must have self-control, faith and concentration. He encouraged the disciples to promote patience. He taught them the importance of accepting pain and misery without grief, anxiety or evasion. In many ways, *Patanjali* stated, that longing for Self-realisation and cultivating bodily enjoyment at the same time, is like trying to cross the sea hanging on a shark's fin. This combined with the fact that each disciple has already declared celibacy, made oblations to deities of hunger and thirst ludicrous. Each disciple adhered to the path of spirituality.

For the final days, *Patanjali* introduced *Kaivalya,* the fourth and final commentary on *ashtanga yoga.* He began the next session. *Patanjali* told the disciples he would describe renunciation and freedom, through detachment from worldly wants and objects. He had emptied their Awareness face-to-face through Consciousness. He planned to explain how *chitta* is purified and freed from entanglements of Nature and Her enchanting power of *Maya.* He believed firmly the seven disciples will become exalted *yogis.* They will proclaim *Raja Yoga* for years to come. *Patanjali* must now show them how to take care of enlightenment. They had earned it consecutively, over so many births.

When mind and intellect reaches a point in maturity, ego gradually loses its strength and retreats. *Chitta* becomes chastised to pure intellect. *Patanjali* had already described how enlightened *chitta,* with pure intellect approaches the Spirit of Consciousness and becomes Universal Intelligence or *chit.* By losing individual identities of Matter and Spirit or *Prakriti* and *Purusha* they merge as One. This is emancipation or *kaivalya,* where intellect and intelligence become One. *Patanjali* declared emphatically Awareness and Consciousness can, and do, become One. This is the final accomplishment of a spiritual journey. But there are levels and methods of involvement for such an accomplishment. *Patanjali* said, "This state can be reached at a premium by spiritual practice of self-discipline or *samadhi* or by using herbs and incantations," *Patanjali* then asked the disciples to talk about the subject. He asked them to use the knowledge gained while under their own individual preceptors. He wanted to facilitate a collective deliberation amalgamated with his own account. He told them their preceptors would visit with him later in the day.

Started *Pakva,* "There are five types of *siddhayah* who practice the *yoga* of meditation. First, there are those that have already succeeded in *janma* or *birth.* They are manifest with ambitions to become faultless. Second are those who gain spiritual experiences from drugs and herbs or *aushadha.* The third group gains spiritual experiences by incantation of *mantras.* The fourth have performed austerities or *tapas.* And, the fifth group, arrives at a state in which self and Self become One through *samadhi.*"

"The first three methods cause pride and lead to a fall from grace. The last two are ways to reach the inner core of one's being. This happens gradually, through continued practice of *yoga.* Is the exercise for pride or purity? That is the supreme choice," said *Pushya.*

"Just as water is transformed into ice or vapour, so too can variations of thought are controlled and transformed, by removing *avidya. Yama* and *niyama* help Man make right choices," *Chandra* exclaimed, echoing his brother's thoughts. Said *Ujjaini,* "An adept seeker can tap the plentiful energy of *Prakriti* through devotion and service. She transforms it to awareness. He can, then, exist in a pure state of being. I think the choice is clear."

"*Prakriti,* in that case, is the dreamboat for spiritual journeys and evolution," *Menander* said.

"It is by immersing in *Prakriti's* awareness that seekers are led to *Purusha's* consciousness!" *Saleta* exclaimed.

In the cave behind the curtain, *Patanjali* agreed. He had settled into his seat and said, "It is the generous flow of Nature's energy as *prana* that brings about a transformation in one's birth. If used correctly it aids in reckoning growth and change. Nature's efficient motive does not compel *gunas* to act. But it does help to remove the obstacles to evolution, just as farmers build channels to irrigate fields."

The disciples had made certain conclusions. Cultivating a stirring awareness is important in *yoga,* and an evolved *yogi* channels *Prakriti's* rich energy to free oneself from the bondage of action. He uses this same energy to develop spiritual insight. Just as Matter and Spirit reabsorb into the Universe – the dream world of God or *Brahman,* He attracts all things and creatures to engage in the dream. So, even if *sadhana* fails to bring about complete transformation in one lifetime, it serves to remove obstacles from paths through progressive evolution. Good actions in past lives are instrumental in speeding up natural tendencies towards Nature's Awareness, and eventually to Consciousness.

A disciplined *yogi* can intensify Nature's energy spontaneously. He removes changes and afflictions hindering spiritual growth. He gains insight into his own being, first as enlightening *chitta* and then as *chit.*

Seekers assemble and concentrate energy through *asana* and *pranayama.* Proper channeling of *prana* regulates senses through *pratyahara.* It infuses the mind and intellect of the *chitta.* Prudent use of this energy builds strength, courage, wisdom, freedom and even latent genius. The seeker now becomes a delegate of the Cosmic Mother's beauty, prosperity, charm, nobility of character and other graces. These may agreeably correct the *yogi* but even they cause an intense feeling of individuality.

Warned *Patanjali,* "Creation of a cultured mind springs from egoism or *asmita.*" He was referring to understanding values and contradictions. Beauty is stacked against ugliness, night with day and gods with demons who equally churned the milky ocean for ambrosia. This tendency for flawed discrimination is individualistic and stems from *avidya* or ignorance – that all is relevant in the Cosmic Whole.

"The seat of individualistic blind mind is within the temporal-limbic cortex in the brain, where past memories and old habits are etched. It creates swings of desire, anger, prejudice, greed, ego and infatuation. These are a source of pain and need restraining," *Menander* said wisely.

"The Master has stressed that Man should uproot all devaluating tendencies," noted *Bhratahari*.

Chandra sighed and said, "Cultivation of such innate beauty, prosperity and virtue happens only through the grace of God and *guru*."

Commented *Bhratahari*, "But Intelligence is the single rootstock of Awareness. It is the core and seat of the spiritual heart. *Chitta* must rid itself of egoistic individuality. As pure intellect it naturally earns the radiance of intelligence."

"Right," said *Saleta*, and added, "Even a cultured intellect sprouts self-conscious individuality and the soul goes astray. This can branch out to become the unenlightened *chitta* once more. This *chitta* then displays worldly thought waves. Such swings in unenlightened *chitta* are, and have always been, a source of pain and affliction."

Ujjaini said, "There is hope, of course. By *yoga*, the seeker can penetrate the unenlightened *chitta* by restarting with *yama* and *niyama*. By transcending senses through *pranayama*, the *yogi* channels *prana* to rediscover its source." Added *Chandra*, "This is the only way a seeker persuades mundane awareness to a righteously cultured Awareness."

Saleta interjected, "As far as can be seen, it is the only way to retrace oneself to the source."

"To become positively pure, *chitta* must seek

enlightenment through deep concentration, contemplation and absorption through meditation," said *Pakva.*

Patanjali agreed, and said, "Awareness is one, but it branches into many different types of activity and many thought waves."

"This awareness is of multiple depths. As a seeker intensifies his inward journey, he may make advances. But sometimes it causes dissimilarity between one's words and deeds. It becomes a source of want, engrossed in attempted fulfillment," noted *Pushya.*

Pakva said, "But that is not all. The Master wants us to channel our multiple thoughts in an authorised direction. There must be no distortions or disparities between our words, thoughts and actions. Lack of understanding causes swings in thought. These confusions are doubts, desires or greed, all of which create afflictions that disturb the mind. Only through discrimination are such weeds pulled out as unwanted thoughts. Once that is done, *chitta* is speechless and open to further cleaning. Nature becomes a seeker's best friend. An abundance of conserved energy is amassed through *yoga.* It purifies *chitta.* Once fully purified, it becomes enlightened *chitta.* It looks for its other half, the *chit.* Coming together is a true marriage of two halves, separated by Ego. Awareness and Consciousness are experienced as One Being, the Saviour and Messiah of Universal Intelligence."

Pushya reiterated that a stirring mind-intellect needs culturing by stilling body, mind and intellect through deepening deliberation. He reminded the disciples, meditation not only frees *chitta* from past impressions, but also removes obstacles from progressive evolution towards Awareness.

Chandra agreed and explained how emotions, impressions and attachments from past births afflict and torment a seeker. Despite meditative effort, swings created by persistence of lust, anger, greed, infatuation, pride and jealousy led to defeat. Only persistent meditation, said *Chandra,* helps in subduing such afflictions, entrenched as they are at the centre of emotion. *Bhratahari* joined in, and commented that such victories lead to self-expansion and spiritual growth. The *chitta* personality can, in time, be cultured and awareness chastised.

Patanjali smiled to himself behind the curtain, and said, "With reference to Awareness in perfected beings, only those that gain sharpness from meditation, are free of latent impressions and influences."

"Does this mean that actions of a *yogi,* who is burdened with past births, impede his growth?" *Saleta* asked.

Answered *Patanjali,* "A *yogi's* actions are neither white nor black. Actions generally are of three kinds – white, black or gray". With that, *Patanjali* emerged from behind the curtain, and walked slowly towards the river. He was now ready to meet the six preceptors, who had gathered by the river. *Patanjali* was nearing completion of discourses on *ashtanga yoga.* The seven disciples would return to their respective monasteries. Seated with the sages, *Patanjali* described the progress made by the disciples over these many days. He assured them discussions were profound and intense.

The seven disciples watched the sages from afar. They felt a sprinkling of apprehension. They then witnessed smiles around the assemblage. They felt accredited. Pleased that Master *Patanjali* was perhaps not disappointed with them, they turned away and restarted their discussion. Said *Pakva,* "*Karma* of a *yogi* is neither pure nor dark."

"But the Master said *karma* is of three kinds – pure, shadowy or a mixture of the two," *Pushya* added.

"Murky actions must originate from an evil Man, since they bind him to their disastrous effects," said *Ujjaini* knowingly, for he had seen greed destroy creatures, beasts, plants and forests. He had committed his life to conserving his beloved Cosmic Mother.

"Actions of a worldly Man are a mixture of the shadowy and the pure and are, therefore, described as gray," noted *Chandra*.

"Then actions of a *yogi* are pure white," commented *Saleta*. *Bhratahari* agreed and said, "If his actions are dedicated to the Cosmic Whole, they do not bind him. And nobody knows this as well as *Bhratahari*. His love and devotion for *Shiva* over many reincarnations gives him materialistic and spiritual wealth. He dedicates everything to the Cosmic Whole."

"How is that possible?" *Saleta* asked.

"Master *Patanjali* described three kinds of actions and reactions, motivated and impelled by Nature's *gunas* – *tamasic* or dark, *rajasic* or gray, and *sattvic* or white. Their reactions are their natural munificence. There is a fourth action that does not trigger reaction. It is not motivated by Nature's *gunas*," said *Menander*.

Reasoned *Pushya*, "Action cannot be evaded, because inaction is an 'operation' also. All of us practice *yoga*. But there are entanglements even with this act, surely?"

Answered *Pakva*, "It is selfish action, and attachment to their fruits, that lead Man to entanglements."

"How does a free man act, then?" *Saleta* probed deeper.

"By action that does not trigger the cause-effect cycle. A *yogi's* action must be unselfish, without motive or desire," said *Pakva*. "Such acts are dedicated to the Mother of Nature and therefore renounced. Their fruits are relinquished."

"Who earns the fruits of such actions?" asked *Saleta*.

"Mother Earth magnifies its effects for the benefit of the Universe," replied *Pakva*.

The disciples saw *Patanjali* walk towards them, but he entered his cave without a word. *Patanjali* drew the curtain, and settled down. He had silently overheard most of the ongoing discussion. He wanted to describe the effects of three types of actions. Said *Patanjali,* "These three types of actions leave impressions and become obvious when conditions are favourable."

"Of the four types of actions, Master, do the first three leave impressions in the causal memory?" *Saleta* asked.

Patanjali invited the disciples to discuss *Saleta's* question. He also connected with them by speaking out aloud. He agreed desire is the motivating force behind Man's actions seeking fulfillment. They decided, together, that desire and memory of past births compel Man to act for self-gratification. Fruition takes place either in a future birth or in the present span of life.

"What then of meditative actions and of spiritual efforts?" asked *Saleta.* As far as such actions go, *Patanjali* agreed even this person who is given to his senses, abandons them when the unenlightened *chitta* works for enlightenment. They all decided that meditative actions left no reactionary impressions.

Patanjali then moved to discussing *vasanas.* He pointed out they implied the Law of *Karma.* Successive lifetimes, with previous life impressions and behavioural patterns are stored in the causal memory. The seeds of future lives planted in present lifetime implant themselves for future germination in new life spans.

Patanjali then urged the disciples to inspire children and students to penetrate their current life with noble movements. This would give them the competence to perform 'desireless' action in the future. Reasoned *Patanjali,* "Life is a continuous process, even though it is demarcated by race, place and time. Because of uninterrupted, close relationship between memory and subliminal impressions, the fruits of action remain intact. They stay from one life to the next – as if there is no separation between births."

Patanjali knew intuitively that some of the disciples

would go on to become teachers of *Vedic* living, and said, "These impressions of memory and desire exist eternally. Just as the desire to live eternally." He paused, and petitioned audibly for grace for the ignorant Man lacking True Knowledge.

He continued, "Lack of understanding causes wants. Past impressions and wants are bound by their dependence on each other, as cause and effect. Without desires, impressions stop to exist. Therefore, desires also cease to work." The disciples concurred. A Man normally lacks true understanding of motivation of actions. He also does not understand the 'movement' of moments. He instead measures entities of finite Nature as infinite. *Patanjali* asserted, repeatedly the Knowledge he has specified can release the disciple *yogis*. It will surely free them from the web of bondage and reincarnation. But they also understood this was possible only when a *yogi* remains in the moment and stays away from 'movement' of moments. The *yogi* can, then, rest in the moment of eternity and keep desires suspended.

As they were discussing this, *Patanjali* urged them to educate the worldly Man. Not all men are receptive to culturing, he said. He advised the disciples to spur parents and teachers to train children and youth in *Vedic* culture, so they become receptive to *yoga*. Said *Patanjali*, "The existence of a past and a future is as real as the present. As moments roll into movements to appear yet into the future, the quality of knowledge in Man's awareness and intellect is also affected. The three phases of time – present, past and future – mingle rhythmically. They intertwine with Nature's *gunas*. They change the composition of Nature's properties from gross to subtle."

Patanjali invited the disciples to discuss change and 'changelessness'. He once more reiterated for those yearning real knowledge and happiness, to be wary of becoming entangled in the illusive power of *gunas*. He said, "Changes in time caused by Nature's *gunas* have the power to modify objects. But their unique essence or reality does not change." *Patanjali* asked the disciples to voice their thoughts. Said *Bhratahari*, "There is a harmonious transformation between *sattva, rajas* and *tamas,* both in Nature and in Man. But there is a difference in the way Man views objects of our wants."

"Man understands objects according to the predominating *guna* of his intellect. An object can be perceived in various ways, even though the essence of the object remains the same," *Ujjaini* said.

"But if the ego in *chitta* is filtered and refined through correct knowledge and meditation, Awareness can reflect on the real essence of any object," said the scholarly *Bhratahari*.

Added *Chandra,* "The Master says such dualities disappear when *yama, niyama* and *asana* are practiced correctly. Similarly, *pranayama* helps lift the veil that covers *chitta*. Awareness then recognises its true essence as Consciousness."

"As soon as Awareness is purified, there are no more fluctuations in the mind," said *Pushya*.

Patanjali, who had been listening quietly, approved of the chain of thought and noted, "Because of variance in the quality of the mind's content, each individual may view the same object differently, coloured by his own particular way of thinking."

Insisted *Pakva,* "The essence of an object does not depend only on the person's mind or awareness. If the mind and its awareness do not see or recognise an object, all it means is the "seer-seen" are not aroused by it. It does not mean the object does not exist!"

Patanjali was puzzled with *Pakva's* statement and probed him further, "An object exists, independent of any person's awareness and impressions. What happens to the object when there is no one to give it an impression by seeing it?"

"*Prakriti* as Awareness and *Purusha* as Consciousness are both real as Matter and Spirit. Each individual gives it realism according to his own intellectual position. The essence of a subject does not change," replied *Pakva*.

Intervened *Pushya,* "Awareness is purified *chitta* and an instrument of Spirit's expression."

Behind the curtain, *Patanjali* smiled and asked, "So, this object remains known or unknown in accordance with the conditioning or expectations of awareness?"

Replied *Pushya,* "Conditioned *chitta* can never make out anything rightly. But enlightened *chitta* is without expectation or desire, so it is free. It reflects the essence of the "seer-seen". As the purified 'seen' it is already enlightened. *Chitta* then, sees the world without conditioning, bias or prejudice."

Patanjali agreed, but wanted the discussion to move forward. He said, "*Purusha* is ever lit up and changeless. Being constant and the master of *chitta,* it always witnesses the moods and modes of *Prakriti.*"

When the disciples heard this, they became silent. After a pause, *Pushya* opened the discussion, "In deep sleep, Awareness is 'conditioned awareness' because *chitta* forgets itself. It is the *Purusha,* the eternal witness, who watches over Man and reminds *chitta* to wake up."

Added *Chandra,* "*Purusha* also reminds *Prakriti* of the astonishing peace of sleep She experiences. *Purusha* however endures as the ever conscious, alert and existent awareness. *Prakriti,* although existent and aware, is asleep until awakened."

"As the 'seeker' becomes the 'sought' while 'seeking', he realises that an oblivious Awareness has consequences conditioned by impressions and memories of previous births. He realises that unenlightened *chitta* is the seed and root of the 'Me' site and enlightened *chitta* is Awareness. When the seed germinates into 'I', unfoldment begins." said *Ujjaini*. The disciples listened to *Ujjaini* in silence, till *Pakva* added, "The tree-trunk in the 'I' position is also the ego or *asmita*. It is 'I' the ego that branches into the mind, intellect to becomes the unenlightened *chitta*."

"Then, it goes without saying that unconditioned *chitta* is a continuation of the 'Me' from previous lives," *Bhratahari* said. The others nodded in agreement, and *Menander* added, thoughtfully, "The intelligent Awareness in *chitta* 'looks' and records all changes and transformations taking place, birth after birth. It registers all actions and reactions. *Chit* is the eternal witness who just 'watches' the changes being recorded in *chitta*. *Chit* freshens up physical existence with energy and life for all expressions, without being personally involved."

Patanjali agreed and said, "Awareness cannot illumine itself as it is a knowable object." The disciples listened, and *Pushya* felt the need to clarify, "If Awareness, the object, is a seedling of the subject – Consciousness, then its growth and luminosity depend on the light of Consciousness. This is like the light of the Moon, which has no light of its own but reflects the luminosity of the Sun."

Noted *Pakva*, "But the 'seer' or Consciousness can become the object – Awareness, and the subject Consciousness, at the same time – that is, Awareness and Consciousness can become One."

"Awareness cannot stand on its own, without Consciousness," said *Menander*, and added, "It is like the sun and sunlight. Sunlight cannot be without the sun, but sunlight, in the eyes of the beholder, represents the sun."

Patanjali was pleased with this exchange. "Well said!" *Patanjali* exclaimed, and added, "Awareness cannot understand both the 'seer' and the 'seen' at the same time." He asked the disciples to think over his statement before they entered into any discussion.

The disciples stood up, and suddenly realised they were sitting all morning. As they stretched, they pondered over the incisive and fathomless discussion. They were now challenged to make intuitive conclusions. They walked away in seven different directions. After walking a few paces, they returned towards the *peepal* tree outside the cave. The rising sun had taken away some of the sting of today's cold morning. Light outlined every object in the valley.

The disciples watched day turning to midday. *Menander* watched the horizon with renewed interest. He exclaimed suddenly, "Just as day and night cannot exist at the same time, restless fluctuations and restfulness cannot coexist!" As the others sat down, he added, "Unless there is a meeting point – as are dawn or dusk – the secret flow between them is not perceptible. The dawn of enlightenment occurs when there is a secret surge of *chitta* into *chit.*"

Menander could not contain his excitement. He turned to face his companion disciples. From their expressions, he knew they had heard every word. He also knew and realised they'd been given a technique to meditate on the Cosmic Vision. *Patanjali* waited for a few moments. He asked *Menander* to sit down and continue. *Menander* took his seat, and said, "For a *yogi,* dawn is the pause between two states – night and day. When two thought-states are linked by a pause, he sees the seat of Awareness." *Patanjali* coughed his agreement, but felt *Menander* had more to say. *Patanjali* said, "You have more to say. Go on, *Menander.*"

Thus encouraged, *Menander* continued, "At this point, the *yogi* gets a glimpse of the *chitta* being shored up, but still some distance away, from *chit.* What we are seeing during the pause is the substratum energy of Awareness reflecting off Consciousness. It is like the moon reflecting the light of the sun. It waxes and wanes, because that is its inherent nature." As he said this, *Menander's* eyes were almost closed. He was trembling with this revelation. *Patanjali* waited for *Menander* to put this experience into words. "Ingoing Energy into the Light merges Awareness with Consciousness. This is the supreme experience of being complete as Universal Intelligence. The experience is unanimous. It is reveals itself as the Cosmic Being in the *kutastha* – as the Messiah who can be Krishna, Ram or Christ!" *Menander* spluttered suddenly. Consumed by the experience, he broke into tears, unconscious of his own reaction.

The others looked at *Menander* silently. Each intuitively understood what he had said. After a long pause, *Saleta* broke the silence, "There is no plurality in Awareness and Consciousness." *Saleta's* statement snapped the disciples to the present. *Saleta* continued, "Plurality stems from a lack of understanding in individualised souls. It leads to utter bewilderment."

A gust of wind blew across the valley. *Saleta* and *Menander's* utterance seemed to whisper across the valley for everything to understand. *Patanjali* smiled and agreed. The disciples speculated there is more to *Menander's* experience. *Patanjali* asked, "If Awareness is many in different beings, Consciousness also must be many? Will projections of Awareness be varied, with each having its own memory?"

Asked *Saleta,* impatiently, "What, then, is the deduction?"

It was *Pakva* who answered. He said, "Awareness and Consciousness are one, and cannot be many. In other words, *Prakriti* and *Purusha* are one. Just as the light of the moon and the light of the sun are one." *Saleta* was not satisfied, and demanded, "Give me another example."

Said *Pakva,* "Just as the branches of a tree are connected to a single trunk, thoughts are linked to a single source – the pure and divine spiritual heart of Awareness. From one moment to another, individualised awareness, as *chitta,* makes contact with external objects of desire and indulgence, and becomes seemingly tainted. This triggers thought waves. These fluctuations create moods and the five types of afflictions. These moods should not be mistaken for plurality in Awareness. *Chitta* remains the same, but moods create an illusion of several *chitta* personalities."

"But *yoga* disciplines the *chitta* personality and cultures individualised awareness through analysis, precise judgment, the experience of bliss, progress towards mature awareness and intelligence," *Pushya* said. He paused, waiting for the disciples to digest what he had just said. Then, once they are ready, he added, "Finally, there is the dawn of wisdom. The *yogi* becomes the 'seen' and is able to make out the 'seer'. Purified Awareness realises it is a reflection of Consciousness. But the *yogi* also realises that he has a long way still to go."

Patanjali was delighted with *Pushya's* commentary. He echoed it, by saying, "Awareness distinguishes its own awareness and intelligence when it can finally reflect and identify its source of Consciousness, the changeless 'seer' – and assumes its form."

Saleta looked askance at the curtain and *Patanjali* understood that *Saleta* wanted further explanation. The Master directed the disciples to start a discussion, which he would join. *Pushya* said, "One needs to remove the ego from the *chitta*. Let us remind ourselves the *chitta* is the complex of mind-intellect-ego. It is the individualistic soul. Through the practice of *yoga, chitta* becomes a purified mind and intellect but still with the ego. When *chitta* has reached the peak of meditative accomplishment, the *yogi* is nearly pure Awareness. His intuitive Knowledge knows She is the one and only reflection of the unchangeable Knower, Consciousness. Awareness sees Her reflection mirrored in Consciousness. He must work harder still to become one with it."

Asked *Saleta,* "So, when there are no fluctuations in *chitta,* is it purified as unalloyed awareness? Does it know itself?"

Answered *Menander,* "Individualistic Awareness is changeable, exhibitory and transient *Prakriti.* Unharnessed, it is subjected to the influence of *gunas.* Man is buffeted around, until Awareness and Consciousness face each other. Awareness and Consciousness must now merge as two sides of one coin. The coin is Universal Intelligence."

Decided *Saleta,* "So the realisation is immediate. It is always pure, divine, immutable, and obvious as knowledge, existence and bliss. Is that right?"

"Yes, but because of ignorance of this fact, the extrovert unenlightened *chitta,* or 'Me', impersonates the enlightened *chitta,* or 'I'. When Awareness withdraws from contact with the external world it no longer wants, *Chitta* stops to gather impressions and memories. Only then do Awareness and Consciousness face each other. Only then does Man see himself as the Soul. The individualistic self comes face-to-face with the Self. Unfoldment and eventual Self-realisation is the result," ended *Pushya.*

Patanjali was pleased. The disciples understood that fulfillment comes from *chitta* identifying with *chit.* They understood this needed intuitive understanding. The inner voice of Awareness would speak to them. *Patanjali* wanted to go a step further, and said, "Consciousness reflected by the *chit,* as 'seer', and *chitta* as 'seen' appears to be all-knowing."

Patanjali then declared the discussion on *chitta* concluded. The disciples had trekked that path. They must now move to examining the *chit.* Awareness had been the object of their discussions. Now the subject of Consciousness needs integration with each other. *Patanjali* explained that he would break new ground. By merging Awareness with Consciousness they will discover the Self. He planned to discuss how the impersonating *chitta* can be made to change into the pure 'egoless' Awareness. Said *Patanjali,* "Though the fabric of *chitta* is interwoven with many desires, as well as unconscious and subconscious impressions, Awareness exists because of its close proximity with Consciousness. Awareness is also in close proximity with the objective world of things and beings."

Patanjali had often stated the aim of Man's life is liberation or *kaivalya* from his own mortality. Though impressions and memories cloud *chitta* throughout eternity, the aim of life is not to satisfy sense desires for indulgence nor for self-gratification. Rather, it is to use the body, mind and intellect to emancipate the *chitta.* The object of a human existence is to use the human body, mind and intellect to achieve Self-realisation through meditation. *Yogic* practices hasten processes of emancipation. It starts with conquest of the body and ends in the vision of the Soul. *Patanjali* reiterated that *kaivalya* can be hastened only through meditation. He insisted, "One who realises the distinction between the *chitta* and *chit* can see the sense of separation disappear,"*Patanjali* reasoned.

Asked *Menander,* "When one recognises the difference between *chitta,* as seen Knowledge, and *chit* as the Knower and seer of this Knowledge, the search of seeing and Knowing Self-realisation ends, does it not?"

Said *Pushya,* "The inquiry into unenlightened *chitta* ends as ego-less *chitta* emerges. The seeker then masters being both the Energy of Matter and Life force and Light of the Spirit – the Soul or Self."

Behind the curtain, *Patanjali* was deep in thought. He instinctively knew that his classes with the disciples will soon end. His person wept to return to *Vishnu. Patanjali* withdrew his thoughts into himself, and said, "Then, Awareness is drawn towards the 'seer' with force, because of the gravitational force of an exalted intellect." It seemed as if *Patanjali* was talking about his own Self. His voice was imprinted with a palpable urgency. *Patanjali* had already outlined the difference between intellect and intelligence. The disciples understood that when exalted awareness becomes intelligence, it is ablaze with illumination. *Chitta* is free and caressed by the divine light of *chit*. Exalted intellect is, then, drawn towards its own source of Light. The disciples knew they must gradually merge one with the other.

Patanjali told the disciples that this experience of being One makes the *yogi* a king among men. He also warned them, the strength of past impersonation, memories and desires can create cracks in a transparent *chitta*. These fractures, said *Patanjali*, might take the form of pride. The *yogi's* own success can induce varying moods and modes of thought. Breaching the newfound tranquility of a chastened *chitta* is not difficult. It leads to disturbances in harmony. There is loss of serenity that comes from being One. Loss of this vision of Universal Intelligence, which he strived so hard to achieve, is simple. He stressed this point, which the disciples already knew.

What *Patanjali* said next did not surprise the disciples, "If there is carelessness during continued *sadhana*, past impressions and desires reappear through fissures in the *chitta*. This results in re-separation of the 'seen' from the 'seer'."

"Why this repetition?" *Saleta* asked the disciples, impatiently. Replied *Pushya*, "What the Master is saying is that subconscious and unconscious minds have enormous potency. They have the ability to resurface and sway the awakened state of being. He advises the need for constant vigilance to overcome old habits and impressions."

Pakva said, "He also asserts that uninterrupted practice of *yoga* is effective in closing these fissures of doubt and prejudice."

Patanjali sensed *Saleta's* petulance and said, "Just as a seeker strives to free himself from the afflictions of thought, a *yogi* must deal with these latent impressions and judiciously stifle them." *Saleta* realised, as did the others, that they would have to commit themselves to their studies with greater sincerity, if they are to maintain continued *kaivalya*.

Patanjali repeatedly spelled out the techniques of salvation as an eightfold practice. Emancipation is arrived at only by strict adherence to the rules of conduct – *yama* and *niyama*. By progressing through the various stages of *yoga – asana, pranayama, pratyahara, dharana, dhyana,* and *samadhi* there is gradual unveiling of the *chitta*. The *yogi* discovers and becomes AUM. The essence of *Patanjali's* approach is that he who knows AUM, becomes AUM.

As the disciples sum up what the Master had said, *Patanjali* suddenly emerged from behind his curtain. He asked the disciples to discuss the topic of AUM. With that, he turned to walk to *Malini Amma's* cottage. He wished permission to go to the next hermitage and wanted her sanction. As if by instinct, *Malini* knew she would be alone at the *Gonika's ashram* once the students leave. She understood *Patanjali* would leave too.

She greeted *Patanjali* with a proud smile. She hastened to give him a sip of water. The two sat together, and reminisced about their years with *Gonika Amma*. They talked about the good times, and the sad times. Much life and experiences had come their way. They laughed about *Patanjali's* impatience with his motor immaturity as he was growing. *Malini* thought to herself that *Patajali's* sophistication and growth from a childhood to youth was astounding and most unusual. She admitted that to him.

Meanwhile, back at *Patanjali's* cave, the disciples were deep in discussion. The topic was AUM. Said *Chandra*, eloquently, "Sage *Vyasa*, the father of the *Bhagavad Gita*, asserts through *Krishna* that a devotee who listens to the *pranava* – AUM forgets the limits of his physical body. He detects AUM vibrating as an intuitive perception through all bodies and sheaths within and without. Deep meditation allows entry into the Cosmic Whole. Once he touches these shores, he admits AUM in a Cosmic Connection. He is aware of *pranava* entering and leaving the body with each breath. Until this happens Man remains unaware of his or her true identity. He accepts his own body as an atom in the Cosmic Body of AUM."

Saleta never tired of his thirst for knowledge asked, "What, then, is AUM?"

"AUM is TAT," *Bhratahari* said.

"*Yogis* realise and understand TAT as THAT or Knower, and Knowledge experienced by Knowing that which comes with emerging and merging with AUM," answered *Chandra.*

"A *yogi* who engages his *chitta* with THAT, exists in the Cosmic Vibration of *chit.* He realises THAT holds together the tapestry of Creation with Cosmic Intelligence," *Ujjaini* reflected, rather absent-mindedly.

Said *Chandra,* addressing *Bhratahari* in particular, "Since you have introduced TAT, let me remind you that *Vyasa* also stated that all human endeavour has its origin and existence in *SAT,* the source."

Pakva responded knowingly, "Once the *yogi* has made a way into AUM towards That or TAT, he is within the domains of "Beyond Creation". He, now, merges with Cosmic Consciousness."

"But the disparity between *chitta* and *chit* has the ability to cause disturbances," *Pushya* intervened. But *Chandra* said, responding to his brother *Pushya's* concern, "Master *Patanjali* advises that a *yogi* can uproot every affliction and disturbance by re-entering *yogic* practice with vigour and faith."

It was *Menander's* turn to speak. He listened to the others with deep attention and realized as before they are all very learned. It dawned on him that they, like him, still had a long way to go before emancipation. He knew entering AUM and becoming AUM is possible and very close to them, but penetrating TAT and SAT needs intense spiritual practice. Said *Menander,* "Subconscious and unconscious impressions can resurface as ego born of knowledge – it is *gyana ahamkar.* This hinders spiritual progress. The fire of wisdom or *vigyana* alone destroys the seeds of past impressions and habits. Only then can the 'seen' uphold its connection with the 'seer'. This individualised self must outgrow ego to become AUM TAT SAT, or realise that AUM alone is Existence and Truth."

The disciples were listening to *Menander* with such concentration that they almost did not see *Patanjali* walk back into the cave with *Malini Amma* leaning forcefully on his arm. *Malini* wanted to spend as much time as possible near *Patanjali.* She felt a need to be close to him. She was, however, also thinking about how much longer she would have to wait to meet *Shesha,* since she will soon be alone once *Patanjali* and the disciples leave the valley.

As they approached the cave, *Malini Amma* settled down on a flat rock near the *peepal* tree, and joined the disciples. *Patanjali,* who had overheard what *Menander* had said, returned to the cave and closed the curtain. With a flourish, he began exactly where *Menander* had left off, "A *yogi* who has no interest left in even the highest intellection, but preserves supreme attentiveness, reaches *dharma-megha samadhi.* He reflects on the fragrance, virtues and justice that come from meditation."

"What are these, Master?" asked *Menander.*

"When currents of virtue and justice unleash their torrents on the Awareness of a *yogi,* his Awareness is washed clean of all bias, ambition, desire and prejudice. The light of the Soul dawns on him. This is *dharma megha samadhi,* the fruit of the practice of *yoga,*" *Patanjali* replied. There was dead silence.

The disciples battled with the idea that ego has so many faces. They also came to a single realisation – that education and intellection must be experienced as Wisdom. Said *Pakva,* "If the *yogi* thinks this highest form of awareness and intellection is a hindrance he withdraws. His need for taintlessness eventually overpowers him. He erases individuality. His only 'desire' is to uphold his spiritual gains and health. He gains purity and clarity. His spiritual personality is transformed. He becomes more humane and universally divine."

There was a moment of silence. *Patanjali* spoke again. In response to *Pakva,* he said, "Then comes the end of afflictions and the effects of action. This is the end of *karma.*"

As she sat with the disciples, *Malini* wondered how much longer she must suffer the effects of her past actions. More than seventy years had passed since the misdeed came to pass when she was a young bride, She is now eighty-nine. And she waits patiently for the healing touch of *Shesha,* who will release her.

Her thoughts were interrupted by *Pakva's* excited voice. "The effect of *dharma megha samadhi* is freedom – freedom from the five afflictions and fluctuations of thought in the *chitta* personality. The blend of acquired knowledge, illusion, delusion, sleep and memory is erased. This is real freedom from bondage of *karma.* The *yogi* is freed from the grips of Matter."

Continued *Patanjali,* "When the veil of impurities is removed, the *yogi* reaches the highest subjective knowledge. Then, both the trivial and the definable appear foolish."

"If virtues uproot the veil of impurities, the *yogi* is left without doubt, prejudice or misconception. The Infinite Light of Consciousness illumines him continuously. His Awareness and Consciousness have become One. He realises the wisdom he gained from Soul is superior to any knowledge he had ever gained through his organs of perception and the *chitta,*" *Pushya* added.

Patanjali coughed in approval. Once more he urged the disciples to unwaveringly educate the intellect in awareness through *yoga.* He cautioned them also. Once awareness reaches maturity, the *yogi* must prevent fissure-formation in the *chitta.* Any afflictions within *chitta* will influence them instantaneously, and not just in future lives.

Said *Patanjali,* "When *dharmamegha samadhi* is reached, Nature's *gunas* end. Having fulfilled their purpose, their sequence and successive mutations halt as well."

Once *dharmamegha samadhi* is reached, the essence of intellect in the enlightened *chitta* retires into intelligence of Consciousness. The *chit,* therefore, is independent and has no further use for the *gunas.* Thus, Nature serves the Soul without any authority. Continued *Patanjali,* "When mutating *gunas* cease to be, the 'movement' of moments or Time, also ends. But this dissolution of Flow of Time is understandable only at the final stages of emancipation." With this, he invited the disciples to comment on his words.

Bhratahari started the discussion, "As long as the two, Time and *guna* of Matter, are moving and causing fluctuations, there is affliction in the *chitta.* When a *yogi* finally evaluates movement of Time and the *gunas,* his *chitta* undergoes transformation."

"But the average person is not aware of a moment. He is only aware of Time as it moves from the present, into the past or to the future," commented *Saleta.*

"This is an affliction caused by memory. It exerts its influence on awareness as well," *Chandra* said.

Pakva added, "For a *yogi* who lives in the moment itself, there is no 'movement' of moments. Therefore, there is no time. In the moment, the *yogi* sees the 'seer'. That is evolution. It is instantaneous."

Patanjali agreed and added, "Liberation comes when a *yogi* has fulfilled his *purusha-arthas* and transcended the *gunas* of purity, creativity and inactivity. Wants, aims in life and the *gunas* return to their source. Awareness, as *Prakriti,* is then settled in its own natural purity." He asked the disciples to discuss the fourfold aims of an accomplished *yogi.*

"A *yogi* controls a stream of virtuous knowledge, which

is free from aims of life and also free from Nature's *gunas.* All these leave the *chitta.* He merges into Nature. *Chitta* is, then, free to merge in *chit,* is it not?" asked *Saleta* impatiently. *Patanjali* and the disciples heard *Saleta.* For answer he was greeted with silence. *Saleta* turned to the disciples, "Why has the Master brought about the subject of *purusha-arthas* again?"

Chandra said, "Perhaps to understand the purpose of expression and to open a discussion from a different understanding. Anyway, the fourfold aims of life are *dharma, artha, kama* and *moksha.*"

Began *Menander,* "*Dharma* is the careful observation of Man's ethical, social, intellectual and religious duties of everyday life. It is learned in the first quarter of Man's lifespan, as a student. It is the foundation on which improvements are made in the remaining three-quarters of human life."

Added *Chandra,* "*Artha* is the purpose of life, including earning wealth. Wealth is needed to advance towards the higher pursuits of life, which is the main reason Man is reborn as a mortal. Lack of effort to become self-sufficient leads Man to a parasitic existence. Greed to hoard creates the urge for indulgence. It invokes the unrighteous living ethics for pleasure. The life of householder paves the way for Man to love the world family."

"*Kama* is levelheaded enjoyment of pleasures of life, by a physical expression that is gifted with health and harmony of body and mind. For those involved in *yoga,* the paths *of asana, pranayama* and *dhyana* lead to further evolution. Through these efforts, Man learns to purify the mind, stabilise the senses and gain intellectual clarity. Man sets his goal to reach the Soul by stabilising *chitta* at this stage," commented *Ujjaini,* after deep thought.

Decided *Pushya,* "*Moksha* is the final liberation of Man, when he is freed of all physical, physiological, psychological, intellectual and environmental obstacles through intense *yoga.* Man is fixed in the Soul. In his spiritual heart there is no 'Me' and no 'I'. The purified *chitta* has surrendered to the Seed of All Seers. He becomes seedless in *Paramatma.*"

Behind the curtain, *Patanjali* sat quietly. The disciples were perplexed. This last discussion seemed irrelevant in the context of the whole session. Also, they were concerned there was complete silence behind the curtain in the cave. They tried to decode the Master's command. *Malini* alone understood the relevance of *Patanjali's* assertion. As the disciples tried to work out the significance of this last discussion, *Pakva* reviewed the recent sessions with *Patanjali.* He realised the four-*purusha-arthas* were the basis upon which *Patanjali* based his discussions over the last five days.

Pakva cleared the minds of his fellow disciples, "In the first section or *pada,* the Master dealt with *dharma.* He dealt with the science of disciplining the fluctuations of the mind, body, intellect and ego. He also introduced us to *chitta.*"

As they heard *Pakva,* the disciples sat up straighter. There was a slight noise from behind the curtain. *Patanjali* was also listening attentively to *Pakva. Malini Amma* was thankful she was getting a summary of what she had learned as a renunciate, over the last sixty years. Continued *Pakva,* "The second *pada* is about *artha.* The Master gave us a detailed description of the practice and purpose of *yoga.* The purpose was clearly, to seek good physical health and contentment, so one can enjoy the pleasures of the world or seek emancipation."

The disciples' minds were racing. *Chandra's* quill moved furiously as he made every effort to complete his notes. *Pakva* went on, "The third *pada* is about *kama,* or desire. The Master described the extraordinary wealth of hidden powers a *yogi,* who undertakes *yogic* discipline, can earn. He also warned us *yogis* shouldn't succumb to *siddhic* temptations, especially to gain worldly wealth. The Master asserted that *yogis* who ignore *siddhis* make advances in spiritual gains."

Without a pause, *Pakva* continued, "The fourth *pada* is about *moksha*. Master *Patanjali* spoke of actions that did not stir reactions. He highlighted that a *yogi,* after gaining spiritual wealth, must reject *siddhis* and take his Awareness to the Soul. Here he can dissolve into Consciousness of his spiritual heart." As *Pakva* spoke, the disciples became excited. It struck them they were discussing the 'what' and 'why' of *Patanjali's* teachings. They also realised although the intellect was educated, but Wisdom had not as yet dawned.

Pushya was the first to enter the discussion. He said, "That is not all the Master made us discuss. He described characteristics of a changing seeker as he progressed through the four *padas*. A beginner undergoes a struggle to grasp ideas described by the Master. He, therefore, asked that a seeker labour manually through *yama* and *niyama*." *Pushya* paused to watch the others. He continued, "In the second stage of evolution, the Master stressed a seeker must make conscious effort. Gathering experiences of gains made through spiritual efforts is for the sake of reaching both wisdom and virtue. He also urged the seeker to teach others to follow the path of both material and spiritual wealth."

Interrupted *Saleta,* "What is material and spiritual wealth you speak of, *Pushya*?

Bhratahari said, "Let me answer that. The characteristics of a changing seeker include heroism, vigour, firmness, resourcefulness, generosity and upholding of justice and truth." Then added *Pushya,* "The highest *yogi* is serene, austere and pure. He has the characteristics of self-restraint and tolerance. He will perfect his knowledge by leading a pure and divine life."

As *Pushya* finished, it occurred to the disciples that *Patanjali's* teachings and discussions are tersely condensed into 196 sentences. Since it was *Chandra's* job to record these discussions, he had succeeded in penning down statements of distilled wisdom. The disciples unanimously decided to call these aphorisms "*The Yoga Sutras* of *Patanjali*". In their completeness, these aphorisms boasted a universal philosophy. Its creed preserves a practical method. The practice and its application unravel *Vedic* philosophy. The discovery is of Truth.

All the disciples, except *Saleta,* understood that *Patanjali* described and defined various stages of intellectual evolution. Each disciple experienced and recognised his own level of awareness. Each knew how much harder he would have to work to reach emancipation. Each disciple understood which level he would have to transcend to reach the core of his being. The goal was clear – to reach the pure *chitta* and its identity with *chit.* It is the state where Nature's awareness becomes consciousness of Spirit. Here there is no division and no separation.

As this realisation dawned on the disciples, silence also enveloped the valley. There was neither a flutter of leaves, nor chirping of birds. Even the mighty river below held back its babbling. The valley entered into oblivion. It dawned on the disciples they had come to the end of the road. Their spiritual education under the young master was over. They each must return to their former particular preceptors. These wonderful days of interaction with a realised Master of Meditation had drawn to a close. As they came to terms with an imminent separation, their hearts filled with sadness. They had grown close to *Patanjali* and *Malini Amma.* It would be difficult to leave, they thought. Time stood still for the seven disciples.

The curtain continued to separate the Master from his disciples. They waited for *Patanjali* to emerge. Many moments passed but *Patanjali* did not come out. *Saleta* became impatient and stood up as if to stretch. After a few moments, he slowly walked to the edge of curtain. The valley was still silent and the other disciples were absentmindedly watching the slow, silent scene as if it was a dream. All eyes moved with *Saleta*. The curtain that separated them from the Master was billowing gently in the breeze. Abruptly, *Saleta,* unable to wait any longer, pulled the curtain aside. As the light of the setting sun filtered into the cave, the scene that met the disciples forced a loud collective gasp.

On the ledge, where *Patanjali* was supposed to be sitting, sat *Adishesha-Ananta,* the Lord of the Serpents. His thousand heads, adorned with a thousand gems to illumine all fourteen Regions of Creation sparkled brightly. The noblest of *nagas* looked at *Saleta* in dismay. As the disciples stood transfixed, *Malini* walked past them and fell at *Shesha's* feet. As soon as she touched the ground, she breathed her last, as an oblation to *Shesha*. Her life had, finally, been fulfilled. *Shesha* looked at the disciples who stood gaping. He returned to the familiar form of *Patanjali*. He lifted *Malini Amma* into his lap and cradled her. Tears welled up in his eyes. Then, as the seven disciples watched in disbelief, *Patanjali* dematerialized and disappeared. His earthly duty complete, he had retreated from the world of mortals.

AUM TAT SAT

For the enlightened, the world is unfamiliar but ready!

For the seeker, the angels promise to quench his spiritual thirst!

To Him, the perfect teacher, I prostrate myself!

Bibliography

The Mahabharata translated by Kisari Mohan Ganguli

Sources & Resources by Erna M Hoch

Light on the Yoga Sutras by B K S Iyengar

Patanjali's Yoga Sutras: With a Commentary of Vyasa and Vashaspati translated by Rama Prasada

A Reappraisal of Patanjali's Yoga Sutras in the Light of the Buddha's Teachings by S N Tandon

God Talks With Arjuna: The Bhagavad Gita by Paramahansa Yogananda

Glossary of Sanskrit Terms

A

ABHAYA: Fearless

ABHIMANA: Egoism, identification with the body

ABHINIVESHA: 1. A prolonged life, living 2. Self-preservation

ABHYAS: Constant, repetitive meditative practice

ADHIBHAUTIKE: Imbalance of the body's elements

ADHIDEVIKA: Problems brought on by fate or genetics

ADHIMATRA: Intense

ADHISHTHANA: Substratum, support.

ADHYATMIKA: 1. Self-inflicted problems 2. Spiritual calling

ADI: First, meaning original

AGNI: 1. Fire, one of the elements 2. The Fire God

AHAMKAR: Pride or Egoism, the 'I'-stance. It can be gross, subtle or somewhere in between

AHIMSA: Non-violence or 'non-damage', in thought, word and deed

AJAP MANTRA: 'HAMSA', a chant that goes with the flow of breath

AJNA CHAKRA: The medullary centre, also called the Third Eye

AMMA: Mother

AMRITA: The nectar of immortality

ANANDA: Bliss of Self-discovery, happiness, joy

ANANDAMAYA KOSHA: The Bliss sheath

ANHAATA CHAKRA: The thoracic centre

ANIMA: To becoming tiny as the atom

ANJALI: An oblation or offering

ANJALI MUDRA: Hands folded in prayer, a palm salutation at the heart.

ANNAMAYA KOSHA: The physical-anatomical sheath of Man

ANTARDHVANI: Inner reverberation of the sound

AUM ANTARANGA SADHANA: The internal quest

ANTARATMA SADHANA: The innermost quest

ANU: Atom

ANYATVAM: Of different and distinct changes

APANA: Excretion

APANAYA: Outward negative tendencies

APARIGRAHAH: Non-acceptance of gifts, unless one incurs

KARMIC debt

APATSANYASA: To take up the life of a renunciant if one is threatened by the danger of death

ARTHA: Wealth in the pursuit of life

ASANA: Correct meditative posture, to be in one position

ASHAYA: Desire

ASHRAM: A monastery or hermitage, the sanctuary of a sage

ASHTA: Eight, in number

ASHTANGA YOGA: Eight-limbed yoga, the eight-fold part to spirituality

ASHTA SIDDHIS: The eight psychic powers

ASHWATHA: The Upside-down Tree of Eternity

ASHWIN: Meditating deeply while awake

ASMITA: The "I" state, experience of individuality or that 'I Exist'

ASMITARUPA: The 'pure Soul' state of the mind, where Man dwells in divine knowledge

ASTRA: Weapon

ATMA: Soul

ATMA SAMYAMA: Integration of CHIT with CHIDAKASHA

AUM: The Lord, God, the Universe, the Supreme Soul or Spirit

AUSHADHA: A medicinal herb

AVASTHA: 1. The final refinement 2. Condition

AVASTHA PARINAMA: Acquired perfection, the zenith of transformation

AVIDYA: 1. Ignorance of true spiritual knowledge 2. Sleep

AVYAPADESHA: Nature's latent state

AYUR: The gift of a larger life

AYURVEDA: The natural science of Healing, the Science of Long Life

B

BAHIRANGA SADHANA: The external quest

BER: An edible berry, native to India

BHAKTI: Devotion

BHAKTI YOGA: The path of devotion

BHOGA: The enjoyments of living

BRAHMA: The Lord of Creation, the Creator

BRAHMACHARYA: Childhood study, to maintain celibacy or both

BRAHMAN: The Cosmic Universe, the Divine Cosmos

BRAHMANADI: Spiritual River

BRAHMARANDHRA: Ascend from the spine to the brain

BRAHMIN: 1. A religious man 2. Righteous birth in a learned family

BUDDHI: Intellect

BUDDHI SAMYAMA: Integration of the intellect

BUDDHI VRITTI: Wavering intellect

C

CHAKRAS: Spinal centres of energy

CHANDRA: Moon [represented as the hypothalamus]

CHARPAI: Four-legged string bed

CHIDAKASHA: All-pervading limitless unbounded Consciousness, the Supreme Cosmic Self or Soul

CHIT: Universal Consciousness as Intelligence

CHITMAYA KOSHA: The sheath of Intelligence and Consciousness

CHITTA: 1. Mind-stuff, made up of the mind-intellect-ego complex 2. Awareness, individualised self or personality

CHITTAMAYA KOSHA: The sheath of Pure Awareness

CHITTA SAMYAMA: Integration with CHITTA

D

DAHI: Yoghurt

DAL: A light lentil curry

DEVAS: Celestial angels

DHARMA: Cosmic disciplines or duty, Codes of righteousness

DHARMAMEGHA SAMADHI: The outpouring of the fruits of meditation

DHARMA PARINAMA: The dawn of discrimination

DHARANA: 1. Concentration in contemplation 2. Concentration in silence

DHRUVA: The Pole Star

DHYANA: Single-pointed attention or absorption in meditation

DHYANA SAMADHI: Complete absorption in meditation

DUKHA: An element of unhappiness

DVANDVAH: Duality, a state of dualism

DVESHA: Aversions or dislikes

E

EKAGRATA: One-pointed attention

EKAGRATA PARINAMA: The result of sustaining Awareness from single-pointedness to no-pointedness

EKAGRATA SAMSKARA: The three stages of transformation to EKAGRATA

G

GAJAR HALWA: A dessert made of carrots, candied in butter and sugar

GANGA-SNAN: The ultimate baptism, through the spiritual water medium

GARIMA: Becoming heavy

GUNAS: 1. Nature's three qualities of Matter 2. Inherent compulsions

GURU: Teacher, a learned one

GYANA: Correct knowledge or intellectual input

GYANA AHAMKAR: Intellectual pride

GYANAMAYA KOSHA: The intellectual sheath

GYANA YOGA: The path of knowledge

H

HATHA YOGA: The path of physical exercise

HIRANYAGARBHA: The Cosmic Egg or Golden Womb

I

IDA: The parasympathetic nerve channel, the lunar-powered plexus

INDRIYA SAMYAMA: Integration of all the energies of all the senses

ISHATVA: Supremacy over everyone and everything

ISHTAPURTA: Acts of charity

ISHVARA: Universal Being, Cosmic Person, God

ISHVARA PRANIDHANA: To surrender the egoistic self to the Self or God

J

JAGRAN: Wakefulness, or in the conscious state

JAGRATA: The conscious state

JANMA: Birth

K

KARTIKA VRATA: The Kartika Fast, a fast to ward off accidental death, a celebration of celibacy from earthly enjoyment

KADHI: Sour buttermilk, thickened with chickpea flour and flavoured with tamarind and other spices

KAIVALYA: Emancipation, Absolute freedom

KAMA: 1. Wanton abandon, lust 2. Desire or a passion

KANWA: The blind mind

KARANA SHARIRA: The Causal body or ego

KARMA: 1. Law of Cause & Effect 2. An action

[KARMAS: actions]

KARMA YOGA: The path of dedicated action, serving the Cosmic Mother

KECHRI MUDRA: A position in which the tongue is rolled back and touches the roof of the mouth, usually used in PRANAYAMA

KHEER: A milk pudding with rice and nuts

KHICHRI: A mix of lentils and rice, flavoured with spices

KLESHA: 1. Causal hindrance 2. Affliction or obstacle

KOSHA: Sheath

KRAMA: An advancing sequence

KRISHNA: 1. The Hindu God, an incarnation of Vishnu 2. Dark colour

KSHETRAM: A breeding-ground

KUMBHAKA: The pauses or retention between inspiration and expiration, inter-breath intervals essentially in PRANAYAMA

KUTASTHA: 1. The Centre of Awareness or centre of Universal Intelligence, in the glabella, behind and between the eyebrows 2. Thalamus

KUTASTHA CHAITANYA: Consciousness that knows itself and others

L

LAGHIMA: To become light as air or cottonwool

LAKSHANA: 1. A refined state 2. A tendency or quality

LAKSHANA PARINAMA: Inherent quality transformation of the CHITTA LAKSHMI: The Goddess of Wealth

LOBHA: Greed

M

MADHYA: Medium

MAHABHASHYA: Great Commentary on Ṣanskrit grammar

MAHAT: The subtlest state of inherent intelligence

MAHAVIDEHA: A disembodied state

MAHIMA: Waxing, or becoming larger, more potent, in magnitude

MANIPURA CHAKRA: The navel or lumbar centre

MANAS: The blind BUDDHI or CHITTA

MANOLAYA: A transitory state of quietude

MANOMAYA KOSHA: The psychological or mind sheath

MANO SAMYAMA: Integration of the mind's energy

MANTRA: A sacred chant or symbol with dormant potency

MAYA:1. The delusory powers of Nature 2. Delusion

MOHA: Possessiveness or lust

MOKSHA: Liberation from the body, mind and intellect

MRDU: Mild

N

NADI: A channel or river

NAGA: Serpent

NAKSHATRAS: Nuclei

NAVIKALPA SAMADHI: Seedless state in the experience of void

NIDRA: The unconsciousness deep-sleep state

NIRBIJA: Seedless

NIRBIJA SAMADHI: The seedless state of being One with the Spirit

NIRODHA: Moving to restraint

NIRODHA PARINAMA: 1. Transformation in Awareness towards restraint 2. Periods of calmness from fluctuations of thoughts and desires

NIRODHA SAMSKARA: The ability to restrain thought

NIRUKTA: Self-referring, used to describe the pituitary gland

NIRVICHARA: Absence of investigation and examination

NIRVICHARA SAMAPATTIH: The ceasing of being non-intuition

NIRVITARKA: Absence of analysis

NIRVITARKA SAMAPATTIH: Superconscious state, with no intellectualism

NIYAMA: Moral observance, adherence to restraints

P

PAAP: De-meritorious action and attitude

PADA: Section or path

PAKSHA: Unsolicited advice

PAKSHA BHAVANA: To espouse the position of the advice given

PARAMATMA: The Universal or Cosmic Self

PAVAN: 1. Wind 2. The Wind God

PEEPAL: Ficus religiosa, the sacred tree of Hindus and Buddhists

PINGALA: The sympathetic nerve channels, the solar-empowered plexus

PRAAPTI: The power to dominate and obtain whatever you want

PRAKAMYA: The attainment of wishes

PRAKRITI: Mother Nature, Manifest Matter

PRALAYA: Dissolution of Matter

PRANA: 1. Life-breath or life-force 2. Life 3. Breath or respiration

PRANAMAYA KOSHA: The physiological sheath

PRANA SAMYAMA: Integration of the five physiological energy elements

PRANA VAYU: Life-force that the Mother breathes into every creature

PRANAVA: Cosmic sound of AUM

PRANAYAMA: The art of breath-control, or breath-stabilisation

PRANIDHANA: To surrender one's being to God

PRASHANTA VAHITA SAMSKARA: The tranquil silence of transformation

PRASUPTA: Dormant

PRATIPAKSHA: Negative tendencies

PRATIPAKSHA BHAVANA: To espouse opposite views

PRATYAHARA: Deliberate withdrawal from sensory pleasures or extroversion, sense and mind abstraction and withdrawal

PUNYA: Meritorious action

PURAKA: Slow and prolonged inspiration

PURUSHA: The Supreme Spirit or God

PURUSHA-ARTHAS: The fourfold aims or stages of mortal living

PURUSHOTAMMA: The Universal Cosmic Soul

R

RAAGA: Attachments or likes

RAAGA-DVESHA: 1. Law of Relativity or dualism 2. Like and dislikes

RAJAS: 1. Nature's Quality of creativity or positive polarity 2. Activity

RAJASIC: Active or hyperactive, of RAJAS quality

RAJOGUNA: The upper positive polarities

RECHAKA: Expiration

RISHIS: Venerable sages

S

SABIJA: In seed, the state of superior awareness

SABIJA SAMADHI: Seed-state personality,

SAMADHI with seed

SADHANA: Spiritual self-effort or practice, endeavour, spiritual path

SADHUS: Monks

SAMAPATTIH: The final stage, conclusion

SAHASRAHARA: The fontanel or brain apex, the topmost spiritual CHAKRA

SAMADHI: Being One with the Spirit, profound spiritual absorption

SAMADHI PARINAMA: Ascent into the state of superconsciousness or single-pointedness or no-pointed attention

SAMADHI YOGA: The yoga of being One with the Spirit

SAMANA: Digestion

SAMANA VAYU: The energy used for digestion

SAMPATTIS: 1. Virtues 2. Ownership or functions

SAMPRAJNATA SAMADHI: The stage towards the void of being One

SAMSKARAS: Residual merits, prenatal tendencies, subliminal impressions

SAMYAMA: The art of integration in meditation, to become a unified whole, fusion through concentrated practice and extreme restraint

SANJIVANI: Herb that was used to save the life of Lakshman, Rama's brother, in the epic Ramayana

SANTOSHA: Contentment, to be in this state

SANYASA: Renunciation

SARASVATI: The Goddess of Knowledge

SATSANG: A meeting with the Wise

SATTVA: Nature's inherent quality of Harmony, the neutral field where TAMAS and RAJAS meet

SATTVA BUDDHI: Refined, harmonious intellect

SATTVAGUNA: A state or promised tendency of harmony

SATYA: Universal Truth

SAVICHARA: Investigation and examination

SAVICHARA SAMAPATTIH: Closure through deliberation and reasoning

SAVIKALPA SAMADHI: Being One within the triad of Knower, Knowledge, and Known, a seed-state in the experience of void

SAVITARKA SAMAPATTIH: The logical conclusion

SHANKHA: The conch, which embodies the Energy of Sound

SHANTA: Calm, a sense of ease

SHARIRA: 1. The mortal body 2. A body-like form

SHARIRA SAMYAMA: Integration of bodily energy during yoga

SHAUCHA: Cleanliness, the quality of being clean

SHIVOHAM!: "I am Shiva", a state of blessedness

SHUKLA: Bright

SIDDHAYAH: Accomplished YOGIS

SIDDHI: Psychic power, a side effect of yoga

SMRITI: Memory, the function of being memorable

STHULA SHARIRA: The gross physical or anatomical body

SUKHA: Happiness

SUKSHMA SHARIRA: The Subtle Astral body

SURYA: Sun [represented in the microcosmic brain as the thalamus]

SUSHUMNA: The spinal cord, the central path of the spinal cord

SUTRAS: Terse, concise aphorisms

SVADHYAYA: 1. Wisdom 2. Self-study of the Ideals and scriptures

SVAPNA: The subconscious dream state

SVAYAMBHU: To be born of one's own Will, without any KARMA, divine beings who bring about their own causeless existence

T

TAMAS: 1. Nature's quality of inertia 2. Inertia

TAMASIC: Lethargic, inert

TAMOGUNA: The negative polarity of the lower spiritual centres

TANU: To attenuate or reduce in force and amplitude

TAPAS or TAPAH: 1. To erase and cleanse the impurities of one's past 2. Physical-mental austerity or self-discipline 3. Penance

THALI: A copper plate

TIVRA: Supremely intense

TURIYA: The superconsciousness state, the transcendental state

TEJAS: Brilliant intelligence

U

UDARANAM: 1. Fully active 2. Illustrative

UDANA: Psychic expansion, activity of neurological systems

UDANA VAYU: Brainward-going PRANA

UDANAYA: Inward positive tendencies

UDITA: 1. Manifest 2. To be manifest

UPAYA PRATYAYA: A higher state characterised as being without distinction

UTTARESHAM: Consequence

V

VAIRAGYA: Automatic true dispassion or detachment from worldliness VASANAS: 1. Inbuilt habits and inclinations 2. Impressions of past life

VASHITVA: The power to subjugate anything and anyone

VEDAS: Ancient Hindu scriptures on religion, polity, medicine and science

VEDIC: Of the VEDAS

VEDANTA: Hindu philosophy, as described at the end of the VEDAS

VIBHUTI: Divine power, a side effect of YOGA VICHARA: 1. Inquiry 2. An instinctive thought VICHINNA: Hidden

VIDYA: Pure subjective knowledge

VIGYANA: Wisdom

VIKALPA: Doubt

VIPAKA: 1. Uncultured habits 2. Incorrect knowledge

VIRAMA PRATYAYA: A distinction in the Void, or the higher state

VISHUDDHA CHAKRA: The cervical centre

VITARKA: Inner discussion of investigation, understanding and conclusion

VRITTIS: Thought fluctuations of the mind or mental disturbances

VYANA: Circulation

VYUTTHANA SAMSKARA: Wandering thoughts in the CHITTA

Y

YAKSHA: A forest spirit

YAMA: 1. Restraint or a moral discipline 2. The sphere of death

YAMADOOT: A Messenger of Death

YOGI: A practitioner of yoga, a male ascetic, a seeker of spirituality

YOGINI: A female ascetic

YUGA: The Cycle of Creation